JOURNALISM, LITERATURE AND MODERNITY: FROM HAZLITT TO MODERNISM

Edited by Kate Campbell

Edinburgh University Press

© in this edition, Edinburgh University Press, 2000
Copyright in the individual contributions is retained by the author

This paperback edition 2004

Edinburgh University Press
22 George Square, Edinburgh

Typeset in 11pt Ehrhardt
by Hewer Text Ltd, Edinburgh, and
printed and bound in Great Britain by
Antony Rowe Ltd, Chippenham, Wilts

A CIP record for this book is
available from the British Library

ISBN 0 7486 2102 4 (paperback)

The right of the contributors
to be identified as authors of this work
has been asserted in accordance with
the Copyright, Designs and Patents Act 1988.

CONTENTS

CONTRIBUTORS

Laurel Brake is a senior lecturer at Birkbeck College, University of London; her many publications include *Subjugated Knowledges: Journalism, Gender and Literature in the Nineteenth Century* (Macmillan: 1994).

Leila Brosnan has taught at the Universities of Edinburgh and Salford, and is the author of *The Essays and Journalism of Virginia Woolf* (Edinburgh University Press: 1990), as well as articles and reviews on Woolf and novelists of the 1920s. She currently lives in London and works for the court service.

Kate Campbell teaches at the University of East Anglia and the University of Cambridge; her publications include *Critical Feminism: Argument in the Disciplines* (Open UP: 1992) and writing on early modernism.

Jon Cook is Dean of the School of English and American Studies, University of East Anglia; his publications include *Selected Writings: William Hazlitt* (OUP: 1991).

Geoffrey Hemstedt has recently retired from the School of English and American Studies at the University of Sussex.

Helen McNeil is the author of *Emily Dickinson* (Virago: 1986) and editor of the recent Everyman *Selected Poems* by Emily Dickinson (1997). Her essay for this collection forms part of a chapter in *Her Modern Body*, a forthcoming study of gender and cultural modernity.

Rachel Potter is a lecturer at Queen Mary and Westfield College, University of London. She recently completed her doctoral thesis, 'Unacknowledged Legislators: Women's Modernist Poetry' (Cambridge University: 1998).

Lyn Pykett is Professor and Head of English at University of Wales, Aberystwyth. She has written numerous books and articles on nineteenth- and twentieth-century writing, including *Engendering Fictions* (Edward Arnold: 1995). She has also edited two collections of essays: *Reading Fin de Siècle Fictions* (Longman: 1996) and *Wilkie Collins: Contemporary Critical Essays* (Macmillan New Casebook services: 1998).

Lorna Sage is a journalist and critic, and Professor of English Literature at the University of East Anglia. She has written for a wide range of publications including the *Observer*, *Times Literary Supplement*, *London Review of Books* and the *New York Times*, and is editor of *The Cambridge Guide to Women's Writing in English* (Cambridge UP: 1999).

Roger Sales teaches English at the University of East Anglia. His publications include *Jane Austen and Representations of Regency England* (Routledge: 1994).

Mark W. Turner is lecturer in English at Roehampton Institute, London. He is the author of *Trollope and the Magazines* (Macmillan: 1999) and co-editor of *From Author to Text: Re-reading George Eliot's* Romola (Scolar Press: 1998).   He is also co-editor of the new interdisciplinary journal *Media History*.

FOREWORD

Journalism's history is tied to print and paper money. With this new decoction of commentary, interpretation and opinion writing went off the gold standard, and became, in the course of the eighteenth century, openly a trade. One of the reasons why journalistic writing has had such a bad name from the start must be that it points up the ways in which modern literature has always been impure. It was written between the classical lines; but then so were modern neo-classical poetry and drama; and so was that other flourishing bastard form, the realist novel, written to the moment.

Journalism, chatty and informal as it sometimes sounds, in fact depends on a degree of distance, alienation even, of author from audience. It inserts itself between writer and reader, locates that gap and makes it wider. Reviewers, for instance, speak for the text but also read it for you. Flann O'Brien (Brian O'Nolan, Myles Na Gopaleen), who for years wrote a column in the *Irish Times* as well as two of the most bleak and original metafictions of the mid-twentieth century – *At Swim-Two-Birds* (1939) and *The Third Policeman* (1940, not published until 1967) – a great inheritor and mocker of the Jesuitical Joycean pretensions of literary modernism, once suggested (wearing his journalist's hat) an ingenious scheme for supporting indigent but proud men of letters who aspired to be hacks. They might be saved from poverty if they were hired by busy philistines to fondle and turn down the corners of the pages of their books and write suitably cultured notes in the margins. You could say that Grub Street was devoted to the retail dissemination of commonplaces – except that it is a condition of journalism that the discovery of cultural common ground is at once its project and an impossibility on which it thrives, so journalists are trimmers, they produce the continuities they pretend to assume, theirs is a proleptic existence, just one jump ahead.

But not exactly in the spirit of the avant-garde. A lot of the things poststructuralist thinkers celebrated thirty years ago about writing itself – that written words turn out to be illegitimate, promiscuous, vagrants in the world, excitingly in danger of becoming anybody's property – are deceptively close to what's been said for a lot longer about journalism. Poststructuralism policed the boundary between journalism and real writing still, however: journalism stayed outside the pale, because it was a jargon of the market place, and because it refused to kill off the author. Instead it made more authors, peddled personalities and claimed its own kind of surrogate authority. As so often, when journalistic mores seem to fit our models they turn out on closer inspection to be serving some rather different end.

The convention of anonymity is an apposite example of this. It was a widespread practice in newspapers and journals throughout the nineteenth century and a surprisingly long period of the twentieth century, and seems to have actually enhanced the sense that such writing had character and a position. The major periodicals spoke through their contributors in the weighty, collective style of the third person or the first-person plural, and so, more shrilly, did the smaller journals of various pressure groups. Informally, anonymity fed the clubbable culture of the men of letters, those in the know. It did create a certain licence, but not a free-for-all: it enabled writers to own and disown their words at the same time, and mystify the question of who was speaking for whom.

As a result, journalistic anonymity comes over as a performance, much more akin to multiplication of roles, avatars of the author and pseudonymous others than to the style of decentred subjectivity which we want of authentically literary texts written on the margins or on the front line. In 1938 Stevie Smith published an extraordinary novel about the shock-therapy of letting the coming war into one's consciousness, called *Over the Frontier*. It's a book about losing faith in daily words of wisdom, and – no accident – she gives her protagonist and alter-ego Pompey a sudden insight into the frightening cosiness of Fleet Street's 'free' market:

> 'I have broken the gentleman's agreement of all the shops, and especially of the Fleet Street shop that is so concerned with personalities, I have cried Stuff and Nonsense in the sacred places. I am an abomination and a desolation in the clear stream of slander, and what should I expect when next myself I presume upon the unwritten privilege of a free hearing . . .' In other words, literature and journalism find themselves battling for each other's territory.

There's a real challenge, then, in bringing journalism into fresh focus from the perspective of a specifically literary criticism. This book analyses diverse aspects and practitioners of print journalism during its heyday, from the 1820s to the 1930s, without assuming that we know how to frame the subject in advance. Nonetheless it's interesting and revealing that their writers return to certain themes that live long beyond the supposedly topical and disposable moment. Ego(t)ism is one, drawing together such odd couples as William Hazlitt and Dora Marsden: as though journalism had a kind of built-in code for its own mutations, linked with the fortunes of individualism. Are men or women more afflicted (or liberated) by egotism? Modern writing outside the realm of literature 'proper' – writing that comes from the shop that's concerned with personalities – opens up these questions in new ways.

The traffic between the book and the paper or magazine is fascinating, too. Journalism has turned out to be lasting, at least in the literal, physical sense: there are a lot of words preserved in archives and stacks that won't go away. And in any case, many essays that started out as journalism finished up being collected as books, some of them designed with that end in view from the start, like the serialised novels printed alongside them in Victorian periodicals. Again, the conventional distinctions between writing that's linear, consumable and disposable and the self-reflexive kind start to look promisingly provisional.

In this, journalism's past perhaps does mirror us to ourselves now. The present book is itself various and open enough in approach and style to suggest that the boundary between literature and journalism is not the only one in question – that academic criticism and journalism are entering into a new relation. The essay as a form – the book in which the argument is conducted in many different voices – devoted as much to finding the loose ends in our critical accounts as to tying them up, seems to point in that direction. I am bound to relish the prospect since, though journalism is not my subject, I have written as a journalist, or between the two worlds, throughout my academic life.

LORNA SAGE

ACKNOWLEDGEMENTS

Many thanks to the following individuals for variously assisting in the editing and production of this book: Rick Allen, Jon Cook, Duncan Double, John Fletcher, Lucie Green, Eric Homberger, Katie Law (Campbell), David Lawton, Tim Marshall, Ian Patterson, Rick Rylance, Lorna Sage, Vic Sage, Roger Sales, Lyndsey Stonebridge, William Weston; and all of the book's contributors who are not mentioned in this list.

Many thanks also to Nicola Pike, formerly of Keele University Press, for supporting this project in its initial stages; also to Nicola Carr, of Edinburgh University Press, for support, advice and invaluable patience. I am further grateful to the Supplementary Research Fund of the University of East Anglia for funding the translation of an article by Pierre Bourdieu in April 1998. I would also like to thank Pierre Bourdieu for having sent me the issue of *Actes de la Recherche en Sciences Sociales* (March 1994) on 'L'Emprise du journalisme' containing this eponymous article; and Beryl S. Fletcher for her prompt translation of it, now lodged in the University of East Anglia (UEA) library as 'The Power of Journalism'.

I am also grateful to the late Quentin Bell and the London Society of Authors on behalf of the Virginia Woolf estate for granting Leila Brosnan permission to quote archive and copyright material; and to Laura Riding's Board of Literary Management, Carcanet Press (Manchester) and Persea Books (New York), for granting Rachel Potter permission to quote from her works published by them.

I would further like to thank Barney Perkins of the National Art Library for finding the source of the Daumier lithograph reproduced in Elisabeth Luther Cary, *Honoré Daumier: A Collection of His Social and Political Caricatures* (G. P. Putnam's Sons: New York, 1907).

The cover illustration is from a lithograph reproduction by Honoré Daumier in *Charivari*, 31 January 1845 (F15, Newspaper Library, Colindale), captioned 'Abonnés reçevant leur journal et cherchant la manière de s'en servir'. It is reproduced by permission of the British Library.

INTRODUCTION: ON PERCEPTIONS OF JOURNALISM

KATE CAMPBELL

In exploring modernity this book does not separate literature from journalism. Late twentieth-century readers of English can see their connection in interviews, late-night talk shows, presidential parties, Tom Wolfe's prose, *Pravda* and 'eastern Europe', 'books pages', novel pages, literary biographies, the poet laureate writing in the Sunday papers. They also combine in liberal imaginations where journos, writers and thinkers meet and argue over ideas in smoky cafés and bars, as in some old Hollywood movie on the life of Marx, George Sand or Sartre. But such scenes are becoming less credible as challenge is muted through late twentieth-century employers' directives and secrecy clauses, opinion polls, short-term contracts, marketing priorities, poststructuralist complexities, social difficulties of smoking.

While 'the media' and undaunted popular imaginations thus tend to bring journalism and literature together, literary studies have mostly kept them apart, neglecting and disparaging journalism. The historical rationale of academic English maintained journalism's distinction from literature. An antagonistic relationship between the two was elaborated from the late nineteenth century, subsequently encapsulated in English teaching in F. R. Leavis's title *Mass Civilization and Minority Culture* (1930).[1] Few writers in the past were widely associated with both famously, Daniel Defoe, Jonathan Swift, Ernest Hemingway; writers of naturalism and reportage. Institutional connections were rarely noted.

If we are street-wise now in postmodern times, for approximately a century journalism tended to make up the devalued, diametrically opposing column on which literature's identity was based – roughly speaking, a factual, conventional, heavy-handed commercial practice, the antithesis of literature's integrity and creativity.[2] The more detailed grounds of literary hostility – the specific items in the devalued column – evidenced formidable and elastic powers of definition, encompassing for instance journalism's triviality, political interests, lack of integrity and autonomy, monologism.[3]

Its importance entailed the term's appropriation also within literature, however, to denote both objectionable and favoured writing; again its plasticity is striking. So for Baudelaire in the nineteenth century advancing a proto-modernist formalism and pronouncing 'Inspiration is definitely the sister of journalism', it was coded negatively as feminine, bourgeois writing nurturing an outmoded inner self and expressivism.[4] In Angela Carter's *Nights at the Circus* it also appears negatively, but contrarily by virtue of its hostility to an inner self. The journalist Waltzer demonstrates a scandalously un-bourgeois lack of interiority: 'subjectively, *himself* he never found'; 'sandpaper his outsides as experience might, his inwardness had been left untouched'; 'He was a kaleidoscope equipped with consciousness. That was why he was a good reporter'.[5] Such narrative observations urge an inner self capable of expression in writing; Waltzer's dereliction might make liberal humanists of robust poststructuralists.

Reversing the negative valuations put upon it, other writers and critics have used the term favourably. George Bernard Shaw and H. G. Wells upheld realistic, socially and politically engaged writing through celebrating journalism – the latter famously distancing himself from Henry James's formalism by declaring, 'I had rather be called a journalist than an artist, that is the essence of it'.[6] Apparently on similar grounds, crucially its non-elite associations, Stephen Spender related on 'Desert Island Discs' (2 April 1989) that the occupation on his passport was 'journalist'. Journalism's egalitarian tilt and modernity had earlier attracted the German cultural critic Walter Benjamin. Shifting to publicism in the *Frankfurter Zeitung* and other journals in the mid-1920s, Benjamin protested 'the pretentious, universal gesture of the book', approving rather 'leaflets, brochures, articles, and placards. Only this prompt language shows itself equal to the moment'.[7]

More often twentieth-century cultural analysts – Georg Lukacs, Theodore Adorno, Roland Barthes, Jürgen Habermas – have tended to arraign modern journalism and, as for many literary critics, it has widely been subsumed in critiques of mass culture. An American media critic, Joli Jensen, described the extent and intransigence of the condemnatory, monolithic stance at the start of the 1990s:

> Renowned scholars in history, literature, philosophy, and sociology seemed unable to shed their mistrust of, and disdain for, mass communication in any form. They returned over and over to a monolithic vision of the mass media as individual, social, and cultural corruption. I struggled to get past this vision . . .[8]

Jensen notes how leading American cultural critics (not unlike their transatlantic counterparts) have typically held the media responsible for redeeming the ills of modernity they also attribute to it. His study points to the oscillating exteriority and interiority of the media to modernity in such analyses – as if it is optional, somehow not constitutive of modern existence.

English Cultural and Media Studies have mostly moved on from the related ideological critiques of journalism that prevailed in the 1980s, and the 1990s have seen a great accession of literary interest in journalism.[9] But dismissive and monolithic criticisms, demonstrating extreme polarisation, still surface among cultural theorists and analysts – suggesting an ongoing rage of Caliban at reflections shattering Enlightenment ideals.[10] Looking shortly at a recent attack, an article by the French sociologist Pierre Bourdieu on 'The Power of Journalism', will suggest how 'the linguistic turn' indeed cashes out in contemporary discourse in journalism's continuing deprecation: a decentred, post-Saussurean sliding world sees (and doesn't see) derogatory references to journalism and the media succeeding references to capitalism.[11] In their talismanic charge there seems a sort of mason's handshake among intellectuals.

This book rejects the exclusive identification of journalism with newspaper writing and mass culture, and its consequent sequestration from literature – processes particularly associated with modernism, directly addressed in the chapters on Rebecca West and Virginia Woolf. It explores journalism's importance in modernity through examining a range of writing in journals, including writing by literary figures that has been relatively neglected or not seen as journalism. In this it employs the inclusive, formal understanding of 'journal-ism', as all writing in 'the public journals' (OED), that marked the word's introduction in England in the early 1830s. The range of production accommodated in the term is evident just prior to the word's appearance in the subject of the first chapter, William Hazlitt, whose writing in the early nineteenth century spanned the periodical and newspaper press.

On the word's importation from France the *Westminster Review* remarked how it 'was sadly wanted'. Acknowledging 'the intercommunication of opinion and intelligence', the neologism allowed for generic linkage between high cultural forms such as the periodical *Edinburgh* and *Westminster Reviews* and the mundane daily press.[12] The word's subsequent history is of attempts to curtail – otherwise, the often unbearable weight of – this cultural commonality: understanding of culture itself is vested in the term's reference. The linking of higher and lower forms, in distinction from the (then) book-encompassing term 'the press' and prevailing exclusive association of journalists with periodicals, was based on a shared temporality – frequent, serial, contingent, more or less quotidian.[13] It was also based on an expanding 'public' horizon, in both subject-matter and audience, seen in Dickens's, George Reynolds's and Mayhew's mid-century investigations of the London underworld. Here contemporary society was increasingly brought to account, as in realist fiction;[14] and criticism might be relatively free, released from a timeless metaphysical order of books as it seized the day – even 'journalistic' in the twentieth-century sense of stirring things up.[15] Criticism appeared in forthright, abrupt prose in the early nineteenth century in the *Edinburgh Review* under its first editor, Francis Jeffrey; was *not* tied to polite norms in fiercely partisan newspapers; was plainly subversive in the unstamped press.

Journals were thus widely seen as the discursive face of a democratising and modernising society in the early nineteenth century – vehicles of progress and freedom, as they surveyed the modern world.[16] Recognition of journals' role in the French Revolution, and their amenability to the 'off-hand expression of the mind', enhanced their claims to modernity on political as well as romantic and psychological grounds. So for the critic Frederick Oakeley, at mid-century,

> A book is a serious undertaking, and is generally kept by its author and revised, until much of its simplicity is refined away, its sentiment over-qualified, its style over-wrought. An article is written off at the flow of the intellectual tide.[17]

By the same tokens, many writers sought to dissociate themselves from journalism, in particular its subversive associations, cognitive dereliction and the generally unpolished and disruptive features shadowing Oakeley's endorsement – vehemence, simplification, triviality, emotion, disruption, desire.[18] Such traits had been identified in Alexis de Tocqueville's classic study *Democracy in America*. This momentously viewed newspapers as the literature of modern democracies even as it catalogued their menace for individual selfhood and departures from literature's normative attributes – 'Style will frequently be fantastic, incorrect, overburdened, and loose – almost always vehement and bold'. The French observer gives great space to journalism's difference from literature, even entertains its validation (here sounding like a populist journalist): the journalists 'indeed are not great writers, but they speak the language of their country and make themselves heard'.[19] Subsequent English perceptions of journalism were often filtered through de Tocqueville's widely read study, drawing on experience of a modern, cheap penny press in America.

The project of objective criticism in 'higher journalism' in the 1850s based in Oxbridge and the *Saturday Review* was an elite attempt to slough off the unacceptable associations of journalism by invoking two contrasting camps, at the start of a great expansion in both the periodical and newspaper press.[20] Similarly Matthew Arnold's 1887 identification of 'a new journalism' in W. T. Stead's editorship of the *Pall Mall Gazette* (1883–90) tacitly invoked the notion of a superior, objective, more reflective journalism affiliated to literature (a few years earlier he had specifically complained that the *Pall Mall* was 'fast ceasing to be literature').[21]

Yet Arnold's authoritative delineation of 'a new journalism' was a key moment in the negative identification of all journalism with newspapers (significantly, he has himself rarely been viewed as a journalist). His pronouncement responded to a build-up of innovations in contemporary newspapers involving presentation, 'human interest', campaigning journalism, a greater commercial emphasis, and the professionalisation of newspaper journalism: all these were instrumental in newspapers assuming their modern cultural centrality and in some respects displacing literature.[22] Echoing his earlier indictment of 'ordinary popular literature . . . working on the masses', trying to win 'inferior classes' 'with ready-made judgements and watchwords', and his highly specific criticism of contemporary papers, as well as widespread liberal dismay at the innovations in metropolitian papers after 1855, his attack proposed the identity of a 'feather-brained' 'new journalism' and 'the [new voters in the] democracy' in a new rule of desire over reason, gendered feminine as 'feather-brained'.[23] A vision of 'the democracy', passively 'being plied with fierce stimulants' and encouraged in instant gratification would likewise inform the criticisms of the Frankfurt school and F. R. Leavis and Richard Hoggart in England.

Yet Arnold's highly wrought prose, in the more popular periodicals of his day, was itself free with 'stimulants'. Like many condemnations of journalism, it was not so distinct from its target. Such condemnations were themselves a recurrent feature of periodical journalism, as the sanguine ex-*Pall Mall* editor and biographer of John Ruskin pointed out: 'during the time when Victorian writers were pouring scorn as men of letters upon journalism, the men of letters were busy at it'.[24] Just over a century later Pierre Bourdieu's analysis of 'The Power of Journalism' likewise – if inadvertently – impresses correspondences between supposedly distinct cultural fields that it seeks to keep separate.[25] As it is typical of a tradition of critique of journalism and its place in modernity that might have been presumed to be superseded, it is lastly worth moving to the present and focusing on the French sociologist's assessment of journalism's significance. This highlights the polarities characteristic of such critiques, and the role of a restricted understanding of journalism as newspaper writing in circumscribing characteristics that obtain elsewhere, thereby avoiding more tasking engagement with them. Hardly surprisingly, it caused a journalistic furore when it was published in book form in France.

Arguably the most curious feature of Bourdieu's self-refuting self-validating text is the knowledge it withholds, relating to its own appearance in an academic journal. This concerns correspondences between journalistic and academic fields – as for instance in the urgency now permeating the academy and a certain fetishisation of the new within it – and between different cultural orders and tastes. Bourdieu's own earlier work systematically expounded the latter, the commonality in different levels of culture – how 'taste' has been mystified, is not confined to dominant classes, no more innate (and in this sense 'pure') in dominant groupings than in lower cultural spheres: rather it appears a function of economic and cultural circumstances.[26] Here, though, in paragraphs of idiosyncratic diatribe echoing much other reprobation, if with a more sociological lexicon, the 'journalistic field' is shut down – in effect a mere paddock, defined catastrophically, terroristically:

> the journalistic field helps to buttress, within all fields, the 'commercial' at the expense of the 'pure', and those producers most susceptible to the blandishments of economic and political forces to the detriment of those producers keenest to defend the principles and values of the 'craft' . . . where it [the journalistic field] is concerned the 'commercial' carries far greater weight. (3–4)

The catalogue of seduction and deleterious effects includes 'uniformity of supply' in the media, and the fact that the

> very temporality of journalistic practice . . . *by making people live and think on a day-to-day basis and rate the value of information according to how up-to-date it is* (cf. the 'news freak' of TV programmes), favours a kind of permanent amnesia which is the negative in reverse of the worship of novelty as well as a proclivity to judge producers and products on how they stand in relation to 'the new' and 'the outdated'. (6; my italics)

Here, as so often in the past – as in Arnold's criticism – reflection on journalism minimises people's agency and tends to exclude, through its omissions, those involved with academic and intellectual journals from the tendencies it deplores. But as academics, is it valid to propose the incursion of the journalistic field's prioritisation of up-to-dateness into academic fields, disowning responsibility for such changes and their connection anyway to an economic order fewer and fewer people challenge? On a longer view, Bourdieu's concept of 'permanent amnesia' discounts the reflexivity that journalism has historically entailed. Unobtrusively its enabling of reflexivity has often worked to the world's denaturalisation, as readers read different versions of the contemporary and read the reading also, like Daumier's leisured figures from a *Charivari* of 1845 on the front cover of this book. These variously read a version of the world in *La Presse* and read another in the *Journal des Débats* (apparently), besides reading each other reading of course, in what seems as spiralling a reflexivity as any meta-fiction's.

Further, Bourdieu's emphasis on journalism's lack of purity overlooks literature's mixed historical brief, to teach and to delight, and the 'consumer'-oriented role of rhetoric in its production, as say in the designing medieval 'flowers' of Geoffrey of Vinsauf.[27] Nineteenth-century apprehensions of journalism as oratory, like twentieth-century approaches to it in terms of commerce and ideology, press the sense in which it represents the continuation of a rhetorical tradition in modern times. Yet the 'journalistic field' is, rather, aligned by Bourdieu alongside economic and political fields rather than 'scientific, artistic, literary or even legal fields', in distinctive subjection to the sanction of its 'consumers'. Virtually the sole positive function he articulates – the ability to jump the 'monopoly of the instruments of diffusion' of knowledge – is located outside the journalistic field, indeed in current society he identifies the journalistic field itself with the monopoly of knowledge distribution. Journalism has itself though historically exercised this broadcasting function repeatedly, taking philosophy and much else out of the closet.

Bourdieu's criticism has exemplary value when considering journalism's importance in modernity, as it has been discursively produced, in the 'Western world'. Much 'rings true', one hardly needs to be a scholar to hate journalistic distortions; his later commentary 'Journalism and Politics' exhibits a righteous indignation at journalism's levelling, depoliticising and dehistoricising devices.[28] But as in numerous analyses other conflicting perceptions and terms barely surface, leaving for instance 'purity' (of all grave things) unquestioned as a privileged value in the 1994 article. So Bourdieu's terms of trade are presented dichotomously, as between cultural and intellectual fastidiousness and political and economic journalistic interests – as if, say, newness isn't crucial in scientific paradigms of knowledge. Disproportionately, it seems, he aligns journalism with the political and economic. There is little sense of what would be lost without this 'field' that developed with modernity. Perhaps the genre of academic journal article invites a binary mindset that eclipses the journalistic field's own case against, say, artistic and literary fields? as if we must come to backing either one of 'journalism and literature' in modernity and there are not 'sound reasons for shifting between . . . two viewpoints, since neither can make any plausible claim to comprehensive validity'.[29]

This book opens up questions of journalism's importance in modernity through close studies running from the time in which its great power was first evident to the 1930s, when other media became important. Through

their different approaches and subjects the contributors challenge particular commonplaces about journalism and modernity. Understanding of
particular authors is contested, revised, supplemented. As writing is
discussed in new contexts it takes on a different character; longstanding
readings are challenged by closer attention to particular texts and
journals. In chapters on nineteenth-century journalism performance
and theatre and liberties are foregrounded; the first chapter proposes a
curious intimacy. The chapters relating to modernism contribute to its
continuing revision. They examine both the group of persons and the
writing practice from which it was traditionally distanced, women and
journalism. The modernism discussed here – using the term descriptively
rather than normatively, to denote writing dedicated to responding to 'the
modern' in contemporary society – is produced by women.

The variety of the chapters impresses journalism's claims for interdisciplinary and multidisciplinary study. Journalism facilitates these in its
crucible capacity, scheduling and rescheduling knowledge from diverse
fields for more common currency. The generality and facility that tend to
discredit it for purists seem a condition of interrelationship between
disciplines, and between the academy and what lies outside it. Yet its
interest and identity extend beyond the more obvious propositions and
knowledge content of particular journalism where it tends to be 'seen
through', with stylistic considerations effaced. For 'it' is a form of writing,
due attention in literature and creative writing departments.

The first two chapters of this book consider the journalism of established authors. In Jon Cook's chapter on William Hazlitt journalism and
philosophy meet: discussion of writing in a range of journals illuminates
tensions in a modern 'freedom of subjectivity' identified by Hegel. 'Twin
freedoms of expression and criticism' and desires of readers are shown to
have allowed Hazlitt varied authorial roles oscillating between theatrical
self-presentation and writing from the self. At stake in these is a political
vision of free exchange: an informal, familiar style challenges existing
hierarchical structures. Cook notes how, establishing a tension that will
prove pivotal in subsequent journalism, 'two expanding horizons both
indicative of progress' here intersect: an 'expansive communicability'
augured by the press, and increasing division of labour. In this account
new possibilities of political progress and intimacy are alike freighted in
the freedoms of Hazlitt's individual journalistic style, 'He brought a new
tense and tension into journalistic forms, one that we have learnt to call
Romanticism'.

Geoffrey Hemstedt's humane account of Charles Dickens's later
journalism traces how its ambivalences and contradictions correspond
to broad historical shifts; at its centre is always London asking to be read.

Increasingly the particularities of the city that Dickens presents appear within a controlling framework, as though under licence; here a reformist rhetoric is striking. The basis of Dickens's journalistic authority is examined. Attempts to record and understand and care are shown in tension with desires to reform and punish. Attention is drawn to the way particular reiterated themes can be tracked across the fictions and journalism – notably death by drowning in the Thames. The distinctive tension in the journalism appears to derive from the prior imaginative realisation of the scenes encountered and described; also from insecurities in a writer now seemingly controlling the gaze but haunted by a sense of being subject to it. The boundaries between factual and imaginative worlds could hardly be more fluid.

The identity of particular journalistic writing is rewritten in Roger Sales' study of newspaper journalism. Arguing its significance in terms of performance, this removes discussion of Mayhew's writing from the parameters of the factual and true that have traditionally dominated its discussion. Or more accurately, arguing opportunistic theatricalisation on the part of Mayhew's interviewees and Mayhew himself, it inserts facts of a different, more indeterminate order – facts of poor circumstances in conjunction with philanthropic responses, of abilities in performance and public entertainment, of psychic realities and perceived advancement or remuneration. Here the interviewed turn the occasions to their account by improvising roles that may benefit them, and otherwise using the opportunity to speak their 'hopes and dreams, fears and fantasies'; for Mayhew himself the role-playing encompasses both the respectable gentleman and the rebel. Far from persons being objectified in journalism, it becomes a scene of creativity and self-assertion.

Mark Turner and Laurel Brake examine some of the transactions and significance of particular Victorian journal publications. Mark Turner focuses on the *Fortnightly Review*, launched in May 1865. Here journalism comes to corporate life in his description of 1860s' journalistic culture. Turner addresses the 'progressive' *Fortnightly*'s seemingly anomalous neglect of women. He relates this to the Positivist beliefs of G. H. Lewes, its first editor, and the male-configuration controlling it. The exception to this neglect was serialised fiction produced by its star contributor Anthony Trollope, *The Belton Estate*: its discussion of property issues was highly charged for women. In characterising this journal operating like a 'Positivist men's club' Turner indirectly impresses the masculine gendering of other Victorian periodicals.

The freedoms and theatrical aspects of journalism recur in my chapter highlighting the journalistic form of Matthew Arnold's criticism. It sees this criticism as enacting tensions between liberal theory and political developments; and continuous with Arnold's earlier poetic activity. It pursues his dedication to publicity and contemporary responses to him in the 1860s: his criticism's conformity with publicity's centrality in Immanuel Kant's Enlightenment political theory and references to Arnold's philosophy alongside consumer society's publicity and a vulgar entertainer. This argues a more politically coherent thinker and more unruly writer than is usually seen – at a textual level a critic impatient of reason's authority and capacity to deliver the political modernity he subscribes to. His versatile, confessional persona and virtuoso prose dealing in 'human interest' align his writing with the 'new journalism' he condemned. Short-circuiting reason, it seems unidentified populist traits, as in *Culture and Anarchy*, have contributed to uptake of 'Arnoldian' tenets.

Laurel Brake's chapter on the significance of journal publication for Walter Pater details the considerations surrounding Pater's choice of publication for his Greek studies – *Macmillan's Magazine*, the *Fortnightly Review* and *Contemporary Review* and/or book form. It considers the general implications of serial publication for book production and argues the relative freedoms of journalistic publication for Pater's transgressive interests. Her broader argument is that, partly by virtue of escaping the attention of reviewers and the ring-fenced character of Greek studies, the permissiveness of periodicals enabled Pater to pursue 'a self-conscious and sustained project: the creation of a concerted opus which, drawing as it does on same sex traditions of masculinity within Western culture, I deem "gay".' Attention is here drawn to the respectable, family-oriented *Macmillan's* offering its readers incest and 'rapacious sexuality' in 'Hippolytus'.

Helen McNeil's chapter is the first of four chapters relating to modernism and gender. McNeil resists the dominance of the history of modernist texts, on historicist grounds – its eclipse of 'the mingled and immediate modernities of those who were primarily editors, journalists or activists'. She also, similarly, resists the dominance of suffragette feminism in accounts of Edwardian and pre-World War One feminism. Her revision turns on the idiosyncratic beliefs and writing of Dora Marsden, founder of the monthly *Freewoman*, which a few years later became the *Egoist*. Discussing Marsden's distinctive discourses of women, sexuality, the body, language, McNeil touches on other 'discourses of pre-war modernity'. A dense and 'mingled' history ensues, demonstrating journalism's indispensability in historicist and feminist analysis. Given the *Egoist*'s identity as one of modernism's most famous 'vehicles', the chapter's significance extends beyond these, however, to the 'history of modernist texts' itself – most notably, challenging long-standing narratives of women as not being themselves fully responsible for Ezra

Pound's involvement with the journal. McNeil elaborates the highly individualistic character of Marsden's feminism that embraced connection with this strand of modernism.

Absent from histories of journalism, absent from histories of literature: Lyn Pykett considers Rebecca West's neglect for decades. Again a different feminism and a different modernism are foregrounded. Pykett notes and demonstrates how West's critical articles mapped both modernity and modernism. Her early work spanned the *Daily News* and the *Freewoman*; following the First World War her writing appeared in an increasingly wide range of magazines, extending to *Woman's Journal*. Such activity placed her 'on the other side of that "great divide" which separates "mass culture [which] is somehow associated with women" from "real, authentic culture [which] remains the prerogative of men"'. For Pound she was 'a clever journalist, but not "of us"'. Rather than seeing West's prolific journalism as the apprenticeship of a novelist, Pykett sees it as the means by which she self-consciously constructed herself as a modern writer. She traces in her early journalism the development of a distinctively modern syndicalist feminism committed to democracy and social and political reform. Here journalism accommodates combative, irreverent, materialist and socialist criticism: it is 'passionately feminist, but it is suspicious of feminists and suffragists'.

Leila Brosnan's chapter alone in this book focuses directly on perceptions of journalism. At its centre are Virginia's Woolf's grotesque vilification of a journalist ('"pobbing and/ boobling, like a stew a-simmer"') and Julia Kristeva's reading of abjection. Brosnan underscores how an abusive private poem by Woolf prompted by a journalist's visit is broadly emblematic of the self-construction 'of the movement characterised as "modernism"'; and how critical neglect of Woolf's extensive journalistic production (1904–41) has perpetuated construction of a remote literary figure and movement. Her close reading of the poem's abusive terms links them to some of Woolf's more virulent literary criticism, also representations of her own journalism. Yet Woolf's poem demonstrates ambivalence that permits transgression of the journalism/ literature opposition and its usual gendering – appropriately, Brosnan argues, since Woolf so needs journalism that severing links with its world would be 'selfe murder'. Opposite but not entirely separate; antithetical but not entirely rejected: Brosnan proposes that, as for Woolf, many modernist writers' relationship to journalism is read in terms of 'the ambiguous both/and construction of abjection'. This accommodates journalism's higher profile within critical readings of the period.

Rachel Potter's chapter aptly concludes this book. It focuses closely on probably the least widely known writer in it, Laura Riding. But it is of broad interest in touching on fundamental issues in the conjunction 'journalism and modernity' – so, the nature of an ethical language in modern societies, the gendering of journalism's relationship with history, the claims of cognition and human connection. Potter relates the substantial shifts in Riding's attitudes to language and authority before and during her editorship of *Epilogue* (1935–38), spanning a broad range of responses towards journalism and different forms of it. Here we move from Riding's early sense of journalism's ethical dereliction and monetary fixation, and her championship of a criticism modelled on the law, to her increasingly gendered thinking and later project of ethical reassurance. Riding's gender analysis extends to proposing ' "a reform of newspaper technique by presenting news from the point of view of the woman reader" '. This account relates an unusually keen struggle between a sense of poetry's 'sacred apartness' and of an also-valued 'language of common meanings' lodged in journalism.

NOTES

1. Peter Keating, *The Haunted Study: A Social History of the English Novel 1875–1914* (Fontana: London, 1991), 285–329, describes the polarisation and proximity of journalism and fiction. Leavis's doctoral dissertation argued the importance of 'The Relationship of Journalism to Literature' (Cambridge University, PhD No. 66: 1924), but its broad, somewhat Arnoldian sense of journalism's importance never surfaced in comparison with his increasingly hostile pronouncements on it.

2. See Raymond Williams, *Keywords* (Fontana: London, 1988), 186–7, on the emergence of 'the modern complex of literature, art, aesthetic, creative and imaginative at the end of the nineteenth century'; journalism's restricted reference is an unremarked corollary of this.

3. On journalism as a monologistic writing form see Mikhail Bakhtin, *Problems of Dostoevsky's Poetics* (University of Minnesota Press: Minneapolis, 1984), 95.

4. Quoted in Peter Nicolls, *Modernisms* (Macmillan: Harmondsworth, 1995), 19.

5. Angela Carter, *Nights at the Circus* (Picador: London, 1984), 10.

6. George Bernard Shaw, *The Sanity of Art* (New Age Press: London, 1908); Leon Edel and Gordon N. Ray, *Henry James and H. G. Wells: A Record of Their Friendship* (Rupert Hart Davis: London, 1958), 264.

7. Walter Benjamin, *One Way Street and Other Writings* (NLB: London, 1978), 45.

8. Joli Jensen, *Redeeming Modernity: Contradictions in Media Criticism* (Sage: London, 1990), 9; see John Hartley, *Popular Reality: Journalism, Modernity, Popular Culture* (Arnold: London, 1996) for an important, invigorating corrective.

9. On changes in journalism criticism see Brian McNair, *News and Journalism in the UK* (Routledge: London, 1996). Laurel Brake and Jane Marcus in particular have contributed to exploration of the interconnection of journalism and literature (see Chapters 6 and 8 following).

10. On liberal expectations and disillusion with the press in the latter nineteenth century see A. J. Lee, *Origins of the Popular Press* (Croom Helm: London, 1976).

11. On the moment 'when everything became discourse' (journalism's 'moment' in cultural analysis, it seems), see Jacques Derrida, tr. Alan Bass, *Writing and Difference*, (Routledge & Kegan Paul: London, 1978), esp. 278–80.

12. [anon.], 'Du journalisme', *Westminster Review*, Jan. 1833, 195–208. On the lowly status of newspapers see ibid.; also David Roberts, 'Early Victorian Newspaper Editors', *Victorian Periodicals Newsletter*, Jan. 1972, 1–12.

13. The often-cited defence of the freedom of 'the press' in John Milton's *Areopagitica* refers in fact to books as much as other products of the printing press. In the early nineteenth century the term 'journalist' referred to writers in periodicals; by its end its customary reference was to writers on newspapers. Relatively recent studies distinguishing between the print culture of the book and journalism with respect to temporality include Benedict Anderson, *Imagined Communities* (Verso: London, 1983), 35–6; C. John Somerville, *The News Revolution in England* (Oxford UP: 1996).

14. Their joint recourse to photographic record prompts Louis Dudek to an isolated and untypical speculation, as to 'how far the entire realistic movement in literature is related to journalism' (*Literature and the Press* (Villiers Publications: Toronto, 1960), 118). Foucauldian studies of realism's significance have overlooked journalism – see especially Marc Seltzer, *Henry James and the Art of Power* (Cornell UP: Ithaca and London, 1984) viewing the journalist G. A. Sims solely as a writer of books.

15. The dominant sense of 'journalistic' which antedated 'journalism''s appearance in England in the nineteenth century was apparently to outreach (as in 'journalistic guides for the popular mind', *Theophrastus Such*, George Eliot: *OED*).

16. On the purposeful attempt to reach audiences traditional writing wouldn't reach see Terry Eagleton, *The Function of Criticism* (Verso: London, 1984); on newspapers' centrality to radical politics, Patricia Hollis, *The Pauper Press* (Oxford UP: 1970).

17. Frederick Oakeley, 'Periodical Literature', *Dublin Review*, June 1853, 545.

18. On alarm at the journalist as a subversive figure see Christopher Kent, 'Higher Journalism and the Mid-Victorian Clerisy', *Victorian Studies*, Dec. 1969, 181–98.

19. Alexis de Tocqueville, *Democracy in America*, 2 vols (Sever and Francis: London, 1863 [France, 1836]), Vol. 2, 66–7 and 71.

20. See Kent, 'Higher Journalism'.

21. Matthew Arnold, 'Up to Easter', *Nineteenth Century*, May 1887, 638–9; Joseph O. Baylen, 'Matthew Arnold and the Pall Mall Gazette: Some

Unpublished Letters, 1884–1887', *South Atlantic Quarterly*, Autumn 1969, 545. Stead's own antagonism to the literary (neglected here) seems to have been a catalyst of this polarisation.

22. Lucy Brown, *Victorian News and Newspapers* (Oxford UP: 1985), details changes within newspapers in this period that resulted in their recognisably modern identity (while interestingly discounting the phenomenon of 'new journalism' as such); Stephen Koss, *The Rise and Fall of the Political Press in Britain* (Fontana: London, 1990), focuses on political developments.

23. Matthew Arnold, *Culture and Anarchy*, ed. J. Dover Wilson, (Cambridge UP: 1988), 70; Arnold, 'Up to Easter', 638–9.

24. E. T. Cook, *More Literary Recreations* (Macmillan: London, 1919), 122.

25. Pierre Bourdieu, 'The Power of Journalism', tr. Beryl S. Fletcher (April 1998) from *Actes de la Recherche en Science Sociales* (March 1994); now lodged in University of East Anglia Library (references in text in brackets). A revised form of this article appears in Bourdieu, *On Television and Journalism*, tr. Priscilla Parkhurst Ferguson (Pluto: London, 1998). The journalistic dimensions of Bourdieu's article are underlined in *On Television*, 1–9 (France, 1966), and invite close study.

26. See Pierre Bourdieu, *Distinction: A Social Critique of the Judgement of Taste*, tr. Richard Nice (Routledge: London, 1994).

27. *The Poetria Nova of Geoffrey of Vinsauf*, tr. Margaret F. Nims (Pontifical Institute: Toronto, 1967), was apparently the most widely known medieval rhetorical treatise on the 'art of poetry'. It referred to figures of speech as 'colours' or 'flowers'.

28. Bourdieu, *On Television and Journalism*, 1–9.

29. John Dunn, *Western Political Theory in the Face of the Future* (Cambridge UP: 1993), 37–8. Dunn articulates the divergence and terms of trade between two sorts of liberalism that seem largely to underly opposition between journalism and literature.

1

HAZLITT, SPEECH
AND WRITING

JON COOK

The emergence of the newspaper and periodical press coincided historically with the affirmation of new kinds of freedom. One of these was a freedom of self-expression, the valuing of activities through which, as Charles Taylor has described it, 'each of us has to live up to our originality'.[1] In this view freedom of expression is connected to the discovery of a distinct and unique identity immanent in each person. In his remarkable study *The Sources of the Self*, Taylor argues that this kind of expressive self-hood is one of the key aspects of 'the modern identity'. In his book *The Philosophical Discourse of Modernity* Jürgen Habermas finds a similar emphasis in the work of Hegel. Writing in 1803 Hegel announced that 'the principle of the modern world is freedom of subjectivity', and Habermas emphasises that one of the implications of this for Hegel was '*individualism*: in the modern world, singularity particularised without limit can make good its pretensions'.[2] Hazlitt found a similar resonance in the works of Rousseau. In his *Conversations of Northcote* (1830) he hails him as a new Prometheus:

> Rousseau was the first who held the torch (lighted at the never-dying fire in his own bosom) to the hidden chambers of the mind of man - like another Prometheus, breathed into his nostrils the breath of a new and intellectual life, enraging the Gods of the earth, and made him feel what is due to himself and his fellows.[3]

Hazlitt's imagination of Rousseau identifies his self-sufficiency with a new freedom of criticism. Similarly, Hegel's 'freedom of subjectivity' includes '*the right to criticism*: the principle of the modern world requires that what anyone is to recognise shall reveal itself to him as something entitled to recognition'.[4] In the Preface to the first edition of *The Critique of Pure Reason* Kant provides a summary of this new critical ethos:

> Our age is, in especial degree, the age of criticism, and to criticism everything must submit. Religion through its sanctity and law giving through its majesty, may seek to exempt themselves from it. But they then awaken just suspicion, and cannot claim that sincere respect which reason accords only to that which has been able to sustain the test of free and open examination.[5]

In one of the moods of his writing Hazlitt had no doubt about the epochal role played by the press in realising the practice of 'free and open examination'. In his *Life of Napoleon* (1828), he claimed that the ' French Revolution might be described as the remote but inevitable result of the invention of the art of printing', and then puts this claim in the context of a brief history of communication:

> The gift of speech, or the communication of thought by words, is that which distinguishes men from other animals. But this faculty is limited and imperfect without the intervention of books, which render the knowledge possessed by everyone in the community accessible to all. There is no doubt that the press . . . is the great organ of intellectual improvement and civilization.[6]

The process is necessarily a critical one for Hazlitt. In the same passage he describes how 'the press opens the eyes of the community beyond the actual sphere in which each moves'. This awareness of a wider context is the basis for 'a body of opinion directly at variance with the selfish and servile code that before reigned paramount' (40). Opening the eyes of the community is double-edged: withdrawing respect from what had once required it, granting respect to what had previously been reviled.

In this passage from *The Life of Napoleon* Hazlitt can seem like a proto-McLuhanite. A communications technology is figured as extending human senses and capacities. Print perfects speech by transporting it beyond its immediate and evanescent contexts. It creates new solidarities and antagonisms based on a process that Hazlitt describes as a secular repetition of the original divine act of creation, 'a second breathing into the life of man' (38). The forms of communication enabled by print create a new and more extensive nervous system within the social body, and, hence, a new kind of society.

As will become clear later, this energetic optimism about printing and the press was only one aspect of Hazlitt's awareness of the culture which made his own style possible. At once a vivid incarnation of the twin freedoms of expression and criticism, his journalism also reflects upon the cultural and political consequences of a culture of the printed word. His thinking about these things is often guided by a range of comparisons between the spoken and the written or printed word. In what follows I want to explore some of the contexts out of which these comparisons emerge. This, in turn, should illuminate some of the tensions provoked by what Hegel called 'freedom of subjectivity'.

The nature of Hazlitt's authorship was crucially defined by writing for newspapers and journals. Like Dickens some twenty years later Hazlitt started work in 1812 as a reporter of parliamentary speeches for the politically liberal *Morning Chronicle*. The eighteenth century had seen a significant increase in the scale of the print industry and the shape of Hazlitt's career can be seen as one consequence of this growth. The cultural historian John Brewer gives some sense of the quantitative shift: 'In Charles II's reign fewer than 200 men were employed in the London printing trades. By the end of the eighteenth century over 3,000 employers, apprentices and journeymen operated more than 600 presses.'[7]

Hazlitt's first editor, John Perry, exemplifies the risks and rewards involved. When he died he left more than £100,000 in his will, money earnt as a result of a successful newspaper career. But, like another of Hazlitt's early colleagues, Peter Finnerty, Perry had encountered the force of the law. In 1793 he was charged with having 'printed and published a seditious libel' when the *Morning Chronicle* reported a meeting of the London Corresponding Society. In 1798 he was in Newgate Jail, imprisoned for breach of privilege. Both events indicate that the 'age of criticism' could be a risky affair. In 1813, when Hazlitt had moved on from being a parliamentary reporter to writing short essays and reviews for the *Morning Chronicle*, he visited John and Leigh Hunt in Surrey Gaol where they had been sentenced to two years' imprisonment for publishing a libel on the Prince of Wales in their weekly paper, the *Examiner*. In 1814 Hazlitt began a series of regular contributions to the *Examiner*, strengthening his connections to an oppositional press. Journalism could survive gaol, even be stimulated by it. What happened to Perry and the Hunts is clearly evidence of government repression. Then as now libel cases could be used to stifle criticism of government power. But the accusation of libel also points to a continuing and unresolvable problem about the boundary between legitimate criticism and illegitimate abuse, a problem that could set journalists against each other as much as against the government of the day. In 1818 Hazlitt countered the attacks made upon him by *Blackwood's Magazine* with a successful libel case. He lived in a culture where the main lines of the modern relation between press freedom and the law were becoming evident.

Hazlitt continued to make a living as a working journalist until his death in 1830. He wrote for a variety of newspapers, magazines and reviews. Apart from the daily *Morning Chronicle* and the weekly *Examiner*, he contributed to other newspapers such as the *Champion*; to the periodical press, including one of the most authoritative journals of the period, the *Edinburgh Review*; and, from 1820 onwards, to a new generation of politically liberal periodicals, including the *London Magazine*, the *Liberal*, and the *New Monthly Magazine*. A number of the books he published during the same period, such as *The Round Table* (1817), *Political Essays* (1819) and *The Plain Speaker* (1826), were collections in more or less revised form of work that had first appeared in journals or newspapers. The titles of two of these books, *The Round Table* and *The Plain Speaker*, were journalistic in origin, devices for linking together essays, otherwise published anonymously in different numbers of the same newspaper or journal or in different journals.

Hazlitt rarely wrote at leisure. He made his money by meeting frequent deadlines and by being continuously before his readership. One consequence of this was his concern with writing as a commodity. A letter of 1822 to Henry Colburn, publisher and editor of the *New Monthly Magazine*, is revealing. Although ostensibly discussing preparations for the second volume of one of his books, *Table Talk*, Hazlitt seems indifferent to the precise form of his work's publication:

> By the time you receive this, the New Volume will be done, and ready, if you desire it, to go to press with, or to send up lumps of 50 pages at time for the Magazine. It contains I hope better things than any I have done. I . . . have now done with essay writing forever. I do wish you would send me £30 by return of post . . .[8]

Printed language comes in 'lumps' (the OED gives no special meaning that would make the word a term of trade). It indicates Hazlitt's attitude to writing as a disposable and marketable commodity. It is part of a lexicon in his vocabulary which associated printed language with what is heavy, inert, indifferently formed. It seems the polar opposite to Hazlitt's epochal imaging of the printed word in *The Life of Napoleon* as 'a second breathing of understanding into the life of man'. The emphasis of the letter to Colburn is on a writing unredeemed by the breath of life or the power of speech. The free play of subjectivity is absorbed by an unremitting economic demand. Hazlitt wants his money 'by return of post'.

It is tempting to read this tense and impatient letter as evidence of Hazlitt's affinity with one of the great stereotypes of the journalist: the writer as hack. Hazlitt was hard up for much of his writing life and became adroit at trading – and recycling – his words for cash. But the letter to Colburn intimates something else as well, in the melodramatic, and, as it turned out, untrue flourish about giving up essay writing 'forever'. Hazlitt's fascination with drama as a form carried over into his capacity to treat writing as the occasion for theatrical forms of self-presentation. It was another consequence of his being continually before his public, like an actor performing nightly on a stage. He can announce, or intimate, different writerly identities: the popular tribune, the urbane critic, the wounded lover, the sociable conversationalist, the misanthrope, the stoical survivor. These arise, partly at least, as a response to the increasing curiosity about authors and their personalities which was evident in the literary culture of Hazlitt's time. They are Hazlitt's inventive responses to a readership's demand for distinctive and varied signatures of authorship at a time when the difference between those who wrote and those who read journals and newspapers was becoming marked. What informs each of these identities is an oscillation between playing an authorial role and writing from the self. Expression and performance are intricately combined.

Certainly one of the powers of Hazlitt's style can be in its direct and personal statement of belief, as in this example from 'On Consistency of Opinion' (1821): 'Many people boast of being masters in their own house. I pretend to be master of my own mind. I should be sorry to have an ejectment served upon me for any notions I may chuse to entertain there.'[9] This is Hazlitt in his role of plain-speaker. This version of the free self takes on its distinctiveness from implied opposition to the 'Many'. The prose style connotes a robust individualism, assertive about the right to freedom of thought and ironically alert, through the development of the analogy between house and mind, to the possibility of its denial.

In this kind of writing the self is declared through its independence and distinction from other selves. Its accompanying anxiety, at least in Hazlitt's case, is that one is alone and persecuted in a hostile world. But this is not the only modality of self-expression in Hazlitt's journalism. Other declarations can be softer, appealing to an intimate trust with the reader, as in this from 'My First Acquaintance with Poets' (1823):

> My soul has indeed remained in its original bondage, dark, obscure, with longings infinite and unsatisfied; my heart, shut up in the prison-house of this rude clay, has never found, nor will it ever find, a heart to speak to; but that my understanding also did not remain dumb and brutish, or at length found a language to express itself, I owe to Coleridge. But this is not to my purpose.[10]

The last sentence is both a self-reproach and a smoke screen. Hazlitt appears to upbraid himself for writing away from his main topic, his first acquaintance with Wordsworth and Coleridge, as though speaking out of turn or in a way that breaks some tacit understanding of just how much he can wear his heart on his sleeve when writing for *The Liberal*, the journal in which the essay was first published. It is a smoke screen because the passage anticipates a crucial theme of the essay, the release of confidence that is found in moments of recognition. These moments find one expression through a recollection in writing about a form of speaking. Coleridge's messianic and seductive power comes with the force of a revelation to the young Hazlitt when he hears Coleridge's sermon: 'a sound was in my ears as of a Siren's song' (107). Wordsworth is also described in terms of the powers of his voice, talking 'very naturally and freely, with a mixture of clear gushing accents in his voice, a deep guttural intonation, and a strong tincture of the northern *burr*, like the crust on wine' (118).

The evocation of these voices is part of a wider mood which is both idyllic and elegiac:

> In the afternoon, Coleridge took me over to All-Foxden, a romantic old family-mansion of the St Aubins, where Wordsworth lived. It was then in the possession of a friend of the poet's who gave him the free use of it. Somehow that period (the time just after the French Revolution) was not a time when *nothing was given for nothing*. The mind opened, and a softness might be perceived coming over the heart of individuals, beneath 'the scales that fence' our self-interest. (116)

Here, at least, seems an occasion when the conversation of the heart can and did occur. The mind's flourishing in free communication is presented by Hazlitt as the sign of a political hope. He invokes Wordsworth and Coleridge's belief in the 'One Life' and gives it his own inflection: freedoms of speech, of property and of politics flow together. The force of contrast plays a central part in developing the meaning. The sterile communication of the selfish and the guarded – 'when *nothing was given for nothing*' – throws into relief the generous, unfenced energies of the revolutionary idyll.

'My First Acquaintance with Poets' has a complex subject. Hazlitt's portrait of the young Wordsworth and Coleridge is presented as an episode in his own development, but the moment of their convergence in the 1790s is shadowed by their subsequent divergence and this gives the essay its political sub-text. It is a sustained comment on what happens to the power of imagination in a reactionary political culture. The expressive freedoms associated with modernity are marked by their evanescence. This is measured in a relation of writing to speaking. Writing is used to evoke free speech and to remind us of its loss. The sociability of the essay's tone, its relaxed geniality, is inflected by a mood which brings it close to an act of mourning.

Taken together, 'On Consistency of Opinion' and 'My First Acquaintance with Poets' indicate one of the patterns that the relation between writing and speaking can take in Hazlitt's journalism. The two are connected together in a chiasmic figure. On the one side is the enactment of those freedoms of expression and criticism described by Hegel and Kant. 'On Consistency of Opinion' confirms a freedom of speaking in a manner of writing. 'My First Acquaintance with Poets' reverses this relation. Writing becomes the nostalgic evocation of a power of speech which has been lost, or is threatened with loss, as a result of cultural and political change. In Hazlitt's case both evoke different identities for the author: one as an independent critical spirit asserting his free individuality; the other as the melancholy loner seeking out a companionship and recognition he is convinced he can no longer find.

These features of Hazlitt's style mark a junction point between the individual 'signature' of his writing and some of the freedoms associated with cultural modernity. They are also implicated in the style wars that characterised the journalistic culture of his time. An anonymous review in the *Literary Register* for 3 May 1823 described 'My First Acquaintance with Poets' as a 'disgusting' and 'prosaic piece of egotism', as nothing more than a 'display of personal conceit and vanity'.[11] This kind of accusation was nothing new. From 1817 onwards Hazlitt's writing was repeatedly accused of 'egotism'. A number of journals and periodicals, including *Blackwood's*, the *Quarterly Review*, and the *New Monthly Magazine*, seemed to have an agreed line in abuse. In addition to 'egotism', he was accused of 'gross indecency and profligate effrontery', 'blasphemous indecency', 'foppery, flippancy and affectation'; of being 'coarse and vulgar' and a 'slang whanger'.[12] What is at stake here has as much to do with politics as morality. Hazlitt's writing was attacked by the Tory press of his day because of his radical affiliations. The language of these attacks mixes together religious, sexual, stylistic and social transgressions. Hazlitt's writing is held to display something in public that should not be seen.

But the relation between politics and style goes further than what was known about Hazlitt's own political commitments. The attack on Hazlitt is not just personal. It is part of a wider and well-known assault on all those writers gathered together under the title of the 'Cockney School'. As with Keats and Leigh Hunt, the manner of Hazlitt's writing, as much as what he writes about, is the target for hostility. 'Egotism' is the negative name for a form of writing which, in explicitly drawing upon the self and its experiences, constitutes an unacceptable form of self-display. According to his enemies Hazlitt lacks impersonality, a proper distance between himself, his subjects and his readers. Lacking that, he appears also to lack a proper understanding of the cultural purposes of serious journalism.

A version of this seriousness can be found in the pages of one of Hazlitt's main antagonists, *Blackwood's Magazine*. An essay, 'On Truth', published in May 1818, gives a typical example of the *Blackwood's* manner:

> The purposes of life are so various, and its powers so limited, that the mind can scarcely reflect upon its state without discerning at once a vast inadequacy of the existence it carries on, to the requisitions under which that existence is held, and without feeling a nothingness in that present instant in which the form of its existence is brought, as in a concentrated image, before its inspection . . .[13]

In his book *The Making of the English Reading Audience, 1790–1832*
Jon Klancher, noting Hazlitt's hostility to this kind of writing, has
discovered a specific cultural and political project at work in the *Blackwood's* style. The 'mind' is a central character in a drama about its own
strengths and limitations:

> For underwriting *Blackwood's* adventure in non-fiction style is a full . . . blown
> ideology of the power of mind itself. At its most ambitious this discourse could
> explore an analogical space linking mental and social laws. If the individual reader
> experiences his own mental power in the act of reading such texts, they may also
> lead him to generalise such powers to those of the nation in which he participates as
> a reader – a member of a certain audience . . .[14]

Klancher's argument evokes the scale of *Blackwood's* ambition and its
fragility. The magazine contributes to a cultural politics of nation –
building by promoting a particular identity for the act of reading. The
elevation of its style and its impersonality are so many tokens of the high
seriousness of this mission. The 'mind' is a unified and unifying subject, a
collective and transformative mirror for a multiplicity of individual
masculine readers. Yet the process is also fragile and contingent. *Blackwood's* is one amongst a number of magazines competing for readers in a
cultural market place. The individual reader may engage in the kind of
reading which enacts *Blackwood's* claim to cultural leadership. Then again
he may not. Energetic abuse directed at the Cockney School helped secure
the attention of readers. It was like being let out into the playground after
listening to the headmaster's sermon.

Hazlitt had his own words for the kind of journalistic style represented
by the leading articles in *Blackwood's*. He called it 'pompous' or 'oratorical', characterised by 'words with the greatest number of syllables, or
Latin phrases with merely English terminations'.[15] The connection
between writing and speaking is at work again in the contrast he makes
between the oratorical manner and a prose style based upon the model of
conversation. In a series of essays and aphorisms written during the 1820s
Hazlitt tested the scope and the limits of this model. An essay, 'On
Familiar Style', first published in the 1822 edition of *Table Talk*, sets out
some of Hazlitt's basic assumptions before describing the 'pompous' or
'oratorical' style as quoted above:

> To write a genuine familiar or truly English style, is to write as anyone would speak
> in common conversation who had a thorough command and choice of words, or
> who could discourse with ease, force, and perspicuity, setting aside all pedantic and
> oratorical flourishes. (242)

Hazlitt is not unusual in seeking an idea of literary style in a manner of
speaking. In 1802 Francis Jeffrey had attacked the language of the Lake

Poets on the grounds that it deviated from a proper literary standard established by the language of 'good society'.[16] Jeffrey assumes that a good literary style models itself on the language of the socially elevated and powerful, that theirs is the most evolved, nuanced and discriminating idiom. Hazlitt wants to maintain the connection between talking, writing and style, but not anchor it to a version of social hierarchy. Jeffrey's account, his sense of what makes for a literary norm, provides a model for social condescension; he claims that 'just taste and refined sentiment are rarely to be met with amongst the uncultivated part of mankind', and, in a side-swipe at Wordsworth, asserts that 'poverty makes men ridiculous' (72). Hazlitt's apologia for conversational style is braced by the need to resist the temptations of this kind of urbane hauteur and so keep open the question of who is to be included in the community of good judgement.

The word used by his enemies to abuse him, 'egotism', is never far from Hazlitt's thinking about conversational style. In one of the entries in *Characteristics*, a collection of aphorisms first published in 1823, Hazlitt contrasts two kinds of talking:

> The best kind of conversation is that which may be called *thinking aloud*. I like very well to speak my mind on any subject (or to hear another do so) and to go into the question according to the degree of interest it naturally inspires, but not to have to get up a thesis on every topic. There are those, on the other hand, who seem always to be practising on their audience, as if they mistook them for a DEBATING SOCIETY, or to hold a general retainer, by which they are bound to explain every difficulty and answer every objection that can be started. This, in private society and among friends, is not desirable. You thus lose the two great ends of conversation which are to learn the sentiments of others, and see what they think of yours.[17]

Although appearing bluff and commonsensical, the passage sets out some delicate and precarious discriminations. 'Thinking aloud' blurs the distinction between private and public, inner and outer. It is linked to a freedom from constraint – 'I like very well to speak my mind' – and avoids the risks of an excessive self-absorption by a reflexive tact which is a part of the very process of conversation itself. If one side of 'the best kind of conversation' is 'thinking aloud', its other is an art of listening. The second style of talk, the manner of the debating society, is traced through with egotism as much in its refusal to listen as in its will to dominance and display.

In this passage from *Characteristics* Hazlitt is not concerned directly with the analogy between writing and conversation. But it can nonetheless be usefully referred to those occasions in his writing when the analogy is explicit. The essay 'On Familiar Style' finds the same force of egotism at work in writing which falls away from the standard modelled on common conversation. Hazlitt, labelled an egotist in the pages of *Blackwood's*, the *New Monthly Magazine* and the *Quarterly Review*, finds the same failure in his opponents. What the word mediates is a dispute about journalistic good manners, and, hence, the different versions of society modelled and rehearsed by different journalistic styles. According to *Blackwood's* Hazlitt's intimate style fails to address his readers as members of a properly constituted public, sharing standards of taste and judgement, bound together by collective civic and intellectual obligations. According to Hazlitt the 'pompous' or 'florid' styles, with their 'pedantic and oratorical flourishes', adopt a falsely public manner. They impose upon their audience by assuming conformities of taste and judgement which, in practice, are little more than exercises in snobbery and deception.

Hazlitt's essay, 'On Familiar Style', is engaged, then, with some fiercely controversial issues. The analogy between writing and talking helps define what is at stake: the question of what is to count as 'common' within common conversation; the related question of how the English can or should write and talk to each other; and, more particularly for Hazlitt, the question of how to write a conversational prose, which in his case means writing a prose that will listen as well as talk.

'On Familiar Style' is an essay in pursuit of what is to count as common. Hazlitt draws on some arguments that would be familiar to his readers. One of these is the assumption that a common or familiar style must be free from expressions 'which owe their signification and point to technical or professional allusions'; the same is true of his concern to avoid 'all provincial or bye-phrases'.[18] Both kinds of language were understandable only within the context of a particular profession, trade or region. As John Barrell and others have shown, these concerns have their precedents in eighteenth-century debate about prose style.[19] They recirculate in the early nineteenth century in the arguments of Jeffrey who recommends the language of 'good society' for the same reason and in Wordsworth who, in the Preface to *Lyrical Ballads*, claims that true poetry addresses the individual reader 'not as a lawyer, a physician, a mariner, an astronomer or a natural philosopher, but a man'.[20]

The journalistic writer, at least one as notably self-conscious as Hazlitt, encounters a dilemma characteristic of modernity. Two expanding horizons – both indicative of progress, both charged with the idea of a future different from the present – come into a confused and complicating relationship with each other. One is based upon an idea of an expansive communicability, exactly what Hazlitt writes about in the passage already quoted from *The Life of Napoleon* when he describes the press as the medium which renders 'the knowledge possessed by everyone in the community accessible to all'. But this encounters a countervailing tendency, one described by Adam Smith when he points out that the prosperity of modern, commercial nations depends upon an increasing economic productivity which is brought about by an increasing division and specialisation of labour. The social consequence of this is to fragment both knowledge and language in so far as either of these is shaped by economic activity.

The cross-cutting of these two tendencies – the ambition to disseminate knowledge in a context of its increasing fragmentation and specialisation – creates a fault-line which journalists and journalism endlessly negotiate. By the time Hazlitt was writing there was already an extensive body of commentary on the social and cultural consequences of the division of labour. Hazlitt shows a characteristically ironic awareness of the issue in another essay about the relation between speech and writing, 'On the Conversation of Authors', first published in the *London Magazine* in September 1820:

> An author is bound to write-well or ill, wisely or foolishly: it is his trade. But I do not see that he is bound to talk, any more than he is bound to dance, or ride, or fence better than other people. Reading, study, silence, thought, are a bad introduction to loquacity. It would sooner be learnt of chambermaids and tapsters. He understands the art and mystery of his own profession, which is book-making: what right has anyone to expect or require of him to do more – to make a bow gracefully on entering or leaving a room, to make love charmingly, or to make a fortune at all? In all things there is a division of labour.[21]

The essay as a whole is an extended and digressive reflection on the belief that the division of labour extends beyond economic life to 'all things'. It is also a good example of the conversational style at work in the way that it inhabits a perspective and then moves beyond it.

The opening movement of 'On the Conversation of Authors' consists of an ironic reflection on the way that authors are socially crippled by their trade. But the irony is not simply directed towards authors. The essay begins by appearing to answer a voice of unreasonable expectation, one that expects authors to be accomplished in all things, unscarred by the divisions of labour or leisure. They are if anything particularly its victims, an embarrassment to themselves and others, best dealt with by mocking laughter:

> Introduce him to a tea-party of milliners' girls and they are ready to split their sides with laughing at him: over his bottle he is dry: in the drawing room, rude or awkward: he is too refined for the vulgar, too clownish for the fashionable . . . You can scarcely get a word out of him for love or money. He knows nothing. (25)

There is enough biographical evidence to suggest that what Hazlitt is offering here is a self-portrait in the third person. But these traces of self-reference cannot be taken for granted. Hazlitt proposes the tongue-tied author as a contemporary social type. This illuminates one aspect of Hazlitt's conversational style: that it is likely to call upon its readers to draw implications rather than spelling everything out. But it also indicates that the intimacies Hazlitt's journalism offers are not always straightforward, that self-reference may be heavily disguised and defended.

Hazlitt's bluntly stated claim that authors know nothing, itself an ironic echo of Socrates, begins a counter-movement in the argument that takes two related directions: one placing authorship outside the division of labour; the other enquiring into the nature of the nothing or something that authors know. Hazlitt sets up a comic conversation between the writer and an impatient reader about what authors know. Its resolution appears bathetic. What authors know is based upon what they do. But this knowledge is of a distinctive kind:

> Book-knowledge in a word, then, is knowledge *communicable by books*: and it is general and liberal for this reason, that it is intelligible and interesting on the bare suggestion. That to which anyone feels a romantic attachment, merely from finding it in a book, must be interesting in itself: that which he constantly forms a lively and entire conception of, from seeing a few marks and scratches upon paper, must be taken from common nature: that which, the first time you meet with it, seizes upon the attention as a curious speculation, must exercise the general faculties of the human mind . . . (25–6)

By this stage in the essay Hazlitt wants to convert a comic tautology into a serious truth. What he means by book knowledge is not just the knowledge that books contain, but a special kind of knowledge that *only* books can contain. In its form it is close to a Platonic anamnesis, working by brief and powerful moments of remembrance and recognition. Book knowledge can dwell in the midst of specialisms, but moves beyond them. Hazlitt's concern with what can be taken from 'common nature' anticipates a similar preoccupation in the essay 'On Familiar Style' where he insists upon 'a stock of common sense and common feeling to furnish subjects for common conversation'. Literature is again invoked as proof: 'It is to this common stock of ideas, spread over the surface, or striking its roots into the very centre of society, that the popular writer appeals, and not in vain; for he finds readers' (26).

'On the Conversation of Authors' has an energetic restlessness about the validity of its own assertions. It puts the intimacy of literature with 'a common stock of ideas' to the test and discovers another source of social division, this time based upon literacy rather than trade or profession:

> Are we to be blamed . . . because the vulgar and illiterate do not always understand us? The fault is rather in them who are 'confined and cabin'd in' each in their own particular sphere and compartment of ideas, and have not the same refined medium

of communication or abstracted topics of discourse. Bring a number of literary, or of illiterate persons together, perfect strangers to each other, and see which party will make the best company. (26)

Hazlitt rapidly displaces this defence of the literary as a means of establishing a company among strangers. Within the energetic movement of the conversational style this judgement on the limitations of the 'vulgar and illiterate' is itself found wanting and, in the process, another dimension of commonness emerges:

> Books are a world in themselves, it is true; but they are not the only world. The world itself is a volume larger than all the libraries in it. Learning is a sacred deposit from the experience of ages; but it has not put all future experience on the shelf, or debarred the common herd of mankind from the use of their hands, tongues, eyes, ears, or understandings. Taste is a luxury for the privileged few: but it would be hard upon those who have not the same standard of refinement in their own minds that we suppose ourselves to have, if this should prevent them from having recourse, as usual, to their old frolics, coarse jokes, and horse-play, and getting through the wear and tear of the world, with such homely sayings and shrewd help as they may . . . In the field opposite the window where I write this, there is a country-girl picking stones: in the one next it, there are several poor women weeding the blue and red flowers from the corn: farther on, are two boys tending a flock of sheep. What do they know or care about what I am writing about them, or ever will? – or what would they be the better for it if they did? (27)

This shows a particularly intense working of the conversational style. What is to count as 'common' is once again put in question as Hazlitt moves the idea across a sequence of phrases: 'common feeling', 'common sense', 'common conversation', 'common herd of mankind'. The connotations of 'common' shift from the sense of what is shared to something like its opposite: the 'common' as the excluded and demeaned, those who are outside the communities of learning and taste. This refusal of settlement means that Hazlitt's conversational style checks its own tendency to assume the literary equivalent of a legislative authority. It does this through the equivalent of listening in prose. The bookish writer attends to a world beyond books and to conversations beyond the literary ideal of the common or conversational style. The mood of this thinking wavers between pathos and respect. It comes close to a sentimental defence of a popular culture that is regarded with condescension by the refined. But this in turn is checked by a dramatic shift in the tense structure of the passage from the generalised present of the conversational writer addressing his audience to the particular localised present of the writer at his desk, acknowledging the irrelevance of his work to a world of labour. The urbanity of Hazlitt's style gives way to an intensity created by this heightened moment of reflection. The writer presents himself in the moment of writing, not in relation to the audience that he assumes is present to him by way of print, but in relation to those whom he knows are not and cannot be his readers. This turn to the particular and the momentary does not provide Hazlitt with a sense of reassuring community. His landscape with a writer is haunted by indifference; each of its figures is absorbed in labour, either wrapped in a silence beyond the reach of 'common conversation' or engaged in conversations the writer cannot hear.

Hazlitt's attention to the shifting contexts of word use gives another feature of the conversational style. Within it the meanings of terms are repeatedly subject to revision, if not actively in dispute. The critic draws attention to the unresolved arguments that are carried by words. The writer's task is to negotiate the rapids, not hush the noise of a divided and controversial culture by pretending to an authority which works from on high to set out projects for the 'mind', or 'education', or the 'people'. For Hazlitt that work is best left to the egotists who run *Blackwood's*.

The twists and turns of an essay like 'On the Conversation of Authors' show Hazlitt combating the tendency in himself and his assumed readers to let beliefs settle into forms that satisfy a craving for dominion over others. In some forms this craving is evidently a manifestation of egotism and self-love. Hazlitt knows that language is the sensitive register of egotism and its opposite. It is used both to assert distinctions and to discover common ground. The problem is that one process can be used to disguise the other: lordly egotism can display itself as a desire for the common good. What will discriminate the one from the other is style, especially as this shows an ability to discriminate between talking to or at an audience.

The purpose of the conversational style is to be open to the contending forces at work in language. This is linked in Hazlitt's thinking to an account of truth which he states most explicitly in one of the aphorisms in *Characteristics*: 'Truth is not one, but many; and an observation may be true in itself that contradicts another equally true, according to the point-of-view from which we contemplate the subject.'[22] This provides a rationale for the aphoristic manner of *Characteristics*, a text which presents contradictory beliefs with equal conviction, although – and this is another aspect of aphoristic presentation – it does not set out to systematise these into a list of antinomies or a dialectical structure. This refusal of systematic form carries with it an echo of Hazlitt's advocacy of conversation as his preferred form of intellectual enquiry. If the conversational style is to remain conversational it has to be open to the unexpected and unanticipated voice which 'seizes upon the attention'. One part of Coleridge's significance for Hazlitt is that he had once been just such a voice; another is that he had ceased to be so.

Hazlitt's use of conversation as the basis of an analogy between writing and talking carries strong social and ethical implications. The society implied by the conversational style is clearly one of arguers, each with a claim to be heard. When the process works it is heuristic, learning 'the sentiments of others' and seeing 'what they think of yours', an equivalent to 'the test of free and open examination' quoted earlier which Kant saw as the basis for establishing valid beliefs in modern societies. It also summons expressive energies of a kind that informs Hazlitt's nostalgic ideal of British national identity, as in this 1816 review of Robert Owen's *New View of Society*:

> Does not Mr. Owen know that the same scheme, the same principles, the same philosophy of motives and actions, of causes and consequences, of knowledge and virtue, of virtue and happiness were rife in the year 1793, were noised abroad then, were spoken on the house-tops, were whispered in secret, were published in quarto and duodecimos, in political treatises, in plays, poems, songs and romances . . . [23]

Hazlitt mocks his opponent with a rhetorical question designed to show that his new view is not new at all, but had its origins in a continuous and collective movement of talking and writing, all of which has been turned into a monotonous system by Owen's work. This difference is itself the sign of another, between the democratic energies of 1793 and their loss in a period of post-Napoleonic reaction. The movement of Hazlitt's thinking is the same as in 'My First Acquaintance with Poets': energetic communication is remembered in the moment of its loss. Hazlitt's mockery of Owen underlines the fact that the analogy between writing and speaking can work to stress their differences as well as their similarities.

'On the Conversation of Authors' begins with the figure of the dumb-struck writer, constrained by the circumstances of his profession to a taciturn awkwardness in society. The author as social outcast is a recurring figure in Hazlitt's work. In a letter written to his son in 1822 Hazlitt elaborates on the dangers of the profession of authorship: 'Authors feel nothing spontaneously . . . Instead of yielding to the first natural and lively impulse of things, in which they would find sympathy, they screw themselves up to some far-fetched view of the subject in order to be unintelligible.'[24]

As the context makes clear, 'yielding to the first natural and lively impulse of things' is not simply something good in and for the self, a solipsistic pleasure, but a kind of communication with others which elicits sympathy. Although not directly a metaphor for conversation, 'the first natural and lively impulse of things' suggests the availability of a form of expression which the wilful alienations of authorship deny. Authors are creatures of artifice with their own brand of professionally induced egotism:

> They [authors] are intellectual dram-drinkers; and without their necessary stimu-
> lus, are torpid, dead, insensible to everything . . . They do not drift with the stream
> of company or of passing occurrences, but are straining at some hyperbole or
> striking out a bye-path of their own. Their minds are a sort of Herculaneum, full of
> old, petrified images; – are set in stereotype, and little fitted to the ordinary
> occasions of life. (234)

This presents authorship as a living death and one that is recognisably
brought about by the special circumstances of writing as a profession. As
in earlier eighteenth-century discussions about the effects of labour on the
body, the deformities of authors are highlighted by contrast with an ideal.
But the value of Hazlitt's ideal does not consist in its permanence or
harmony of form. The 'first natural and lively impulse of things' and 'the
stream of company or of passing occurrences' are valued for their
transience and energy. Authors' minds by contrast are full of old rubble
or set like pages of print, subdued to what they work in.

The rhetorical direction of Hazlitt's letter of advice to his son identifies
the character of authors with their deformity and alienation. It sets out
one side of a central ambivalence in Hazlitt's presentation of the relation
between the spoken and the printed word. Print can bring new life to the
powers of speech, as in the argument about the press and enlightenment
in *The Life of Napoleon*. But it can also mark the destruction of the vitality
of the spoken word and, with that, the possibility of authentic self-
expression. Instead of the individuating moment of Rousseau, freed by
authorship to express his individuality in all its distinctiveness, the culture
of the printed word produces an abstract conformity. Hazlitt comments
on this tendency on a number of occasions in his work in ways that
address both audiences and authors. In a survey of theatre written in 1820
he writes about the disproportion between general progress and individual experience:

> We participate in the general progress of intellect, and the large vicissitudes of
> human affairs; but the hugest private sorrow looks dwarfish and puerile . . . In a
> word, literature and civilization have abstracted man from himself so far; and the
> press has been the ruin of the stage, unless we are greatly deceived.[25]

The press is the agent of a new sense of historical scale. Readers
participate in epochal events, but outside the charmed circle of reading,
their experience decays, rendered trivial because it now appears as no
more than personal. What Hazlitt refers to as 'the circle of dramatic
character and natural passion' is replaced by an abstract conformity of
opinion.

A variation on this motif of abstraction occurs in a comment on modern
authorship in Hazlitt's *Lectures on the Age of Elizabeth* (1820):

Modern authorship is become a species of stenography: we continue even to read by proxy. We skim the cream of prose without any trouble; we get at the quintessence of poetry without loss of time. The staple commodity, the coarse, heavy, dirty unwieldy bullion of books is driven out of the market of learning, and the intercourse of the literary world is carried on, and the credit of the great capitalists sustained by the flimsy circulating medium of magazines.[26]

The relation between writing and speaking is signalled in the comparison between authorship and stenography. But the modern author, instead of taking dictation from the spoken word, takes it from the written. Another kind of excess emerges. Modern authors are subordinated to the printed words of others, caught up in a medium of circulation which sacrifices content to empty activities of communication. Modern readers no longer read books themselves but let modern authors in the form of reviewers do it for them. This process of abstraction is elaborated through the analogy between literature and money: magazines are paper money by comparison with the bullion of books. Enlightenment here has taken on the parodic form of making things light and therefore easy. The passage as a whole implies an attack on the progress of civilisation in so far as its main achievement is to produce a false refinement which fastidiously avoids the labour and dirt of primary experience. Modernity is understood as the erosion of capacity for experiences that we can call our own and communicate to others as our own.

But these comments on the abstracting power of the press do not assume a firm distinction between something called literature and something that would soon be called 'journalism'. Journalists are authors in Hazlitt's use of the term and can be presented as the exemplary form that authorship takes in the period of modernity. The continuity of Hazlitt's thinking about authors, and its tendency to turn towards paradox, is evident in his essay 'On the Periodical Press' (1823):

We will content ourselves with announcing a truism on the subject, which like many other truisms, is pregnant with deep thought, – *viz. That periodical criticism is favourable to periodical criticism* . . . It contributes to its own improvement – and its cultivation proves not only that it suits the spirit of the times, but advances it. It certainly never flourished more than at present . . . If literature in our day has taken this decided turn into a critical channel, is it not a presumptive proof that it ought to do so? We complain that this is a Critical age; and that no great works of genius appear, because so much is said and written about them; while we ought to reverse the argument, and say, that it is because so many works of genius *have appeared*, that they have left us little or nothing to do, but to think and talk about them . . . [27]

The dogged playfulness of tone here is an important part of the argument. Hazlitt appears to invite his readers to celebrate the fact that they live in a diminished culture and this points to a genuine tension in judgement at work in the passage. The argument can be taken straight: 'periodical criticism' is the characteristic literature of a modern age; this fact is proved by its own consolidation and flourishing which show that it is adapted to the needs of its readers; lamentations that this will stifle works of genius are misplaced; an abundance of criticism is indicative of an abundance of works of genius to criticise.

Yet Hazlitt's phrasing of the argument indicates a feeling of cultural belatedness. The stress on 'have appeared' begs a question about whether works of genius are still appearing, but the phrase may also be interpreted as an answer to the critic who claims that they no longer appear. Similarly 'they have left us little or nothing to do' implies diminished possibility. In the aftermath of works of genius there is conversation and thinking about them, but not significant new creation. Hazlitt appears to clash together the costs and the gains of modernity. The brightness of tone is so insistent that it reminds us of a darker possibility of loss, one that would accord with Hazlitt's own doctrine that the arts, unlike the sciences, were not progressive, that the greatest achievements in a particular form occurred at the moment of their first flourishing.

Hazlitt's thinking about the press is powerfully shaped by ambivalence but is not confined by it. His project of a familiar style, based upon an ideal of common conversation, has a tactical role in his fight against the Tory press. It arises from his attempt to resist a wider cultural tendency, the promotion of abstraction and egotism by the press. The losses Hazlitt mourns he also seeks to restore. If the press 'has been the ruin of the stage' then conversational style can perhaps renew 'the circle of dramatic character and natural passion' (305) which the culture of the printed word undermines. This possibility engages with another conception of authorship, one that Hazlitt defined in his account of Shakespeare:

> By an art like that of the ventriloquist, he throws his imagination out of himself and makes every word appear to proceed from the mouth of the person in whose name it is given. His plays alone are properly expressions of passion, not descriptions of them . . . Nothing is made out by formal inference and analogy, by climax and antithesis: all comes, or seems to come, immediately from nature . . .[28]

Shakespeare's example intimates an escape from the dilemmas of modern authorship. His art of ventriloquism avoids the distorting excess of the need for self-assertion – the 'straining at some hyperbole' which alienates authors from 'the first natural and lively impulse of things' – and the equal but opposite excess of 'stenography', the dictation of one kind of writing by another. Its ethical equivalent is what Hazlitt described in his essay 'On Consistency of Opinion' as disinterestedness, an awareness 'from the first suggestion of a subject, either by subtlety of tact, or close attention, of the full force of what others feel and think of it'.[29] The periodical essay as practised by Hazlitt becomes at once a means of self-expression but also the stage for other voices and performances. It registers the 'full force' of others in ways that can comfort, console, disarm or compete with the author's own assertions and explorations.

It is also a means of assuaging or controlling a kind of violence. Hazlitt's imagination is repeatedly drawn towards a Hobbesian world where rival egotists seek to vanquish each other. What disinterestedness anticipates is precisely a 'full force'. What Hazlitt picks out by this phrase is something different from the debating society manner which is 'bound to . . . answer every objection that can be started'. But Hazlitt's argument in 'On Consistency of Opinion' suggests something more:

> I think my sympathising *beforehand* with the different feelings that may be entertained on a subject, that prevents my retracting my judgement, and flinging myself into the contrary extreme afterwards. If you proscribe all opinion opposite to your own, and impertinently exclude all the evidence that does not make for you, it stares you in the face with double force when it breaks unexpectedly upon you . . . (23)

The emphasis on 'beforehand' suggests that disinterestedness is a capacity to anticipate what direction the blows will come from as much as a sympathetic investment in another's point of view. The suggestion is amplified by Hazlitt's account of what happens in the absence of this investment: excluded belief or opinion 'stares you in the face with double force'. The violence of the impact of other opinions is intensified and becomes disruptive. Disinterestedness is a training in poise, an intellectual equivalent of the skilled boxer's capacity to duck and weave.

But the ideal of poise first depends upon the well-founded assumption that the relation between different beliefs is essentially antagonistic, a matter of trading blows in words. The familiar or conversational style is poised between a dramatic flexibility, accommodating different points of view, and a combative stance where Hazlitt tries his strength against false or pernicious beliefs in a style braced by the energies of opposition. This in turn raises an important question about the gender of the conversational style. Within terms of one traditional stereotype of gender the conversational style assumes that the conversationalists are men. The 'thorough command', the 'ease, force, and perspicuity' Hazlitt associates with the conversational style are masculine virtues, ways of showing who is top dog. The writer displays his strength by acknowledging the existence of views antagonistic to his own and showing that they do not knock him off his stride. The implication of this is that the addressees of Hazlitt's writing are principally projected as men. To admit women into the conversation is to admit a disturbance, something which threatens 'ease, force and perspicuity'.

There is plenty of evidence in Hazlitt's writing to support this view. Women are presented in terms of their limitations and excesses. They are incapable of reason. They are 'pure egotists'; they can 'talk forever about nothing'; they are not 'philosophers or poets, patriots, moralists, or politicians – they are simply women'.[30] Hazlitt's thinking about the common included a distrust of 'common-places' or stereotypical formulae, yet his views on women seem governed by the standard prejudices of his time. But, here too, there is another movement of thought and feeling at work within Hazlitt's practice of the conversational style. Hazlitt's periodical essays are traced through with pathos as well as displays of 'ease, force and perspicuity'. They can show the need for another voice, and so another relation to others' voices, one which seeks out affection and commonality rather than antagonistic force. Need and curiosity are not punished in this other relation and, as recollected in 'My First Acquaintance with Poets', another kind of conversation is possible, one which admits the value of traditionally feminine virtues of sensitivity and soft-heartedness.

It may seem that the conversational style oscillates between equally traditional accounts of masculine and feminine virtue. However, the valuing of passivity goes further than this. The deformity of Hazlitt's masculine authors is linked to their denial of the 'first natural and lively impulse of things'. This cannot be captured by a masculine authority of style, whether in speaking or writing, but, according to Hazlitt, involves a willingness to 'drift' or be 'yielding'. This gives another aspect to the range of the conversational style, and to Hazlitt's understanding of disinterestedness. If there is an active and armoured version of disinterestedness there is another which is to do with the attempt to capture in writing the 'new' and the 'now'. Here disinterestedness comes close to a Keatsian 'negative capability'. The willingness to set aside determinate beliefs, to 'dwell in uncertainty', is the basis for an ecstatic participation in otherness.[31] The opening of Hazlitt's essay, 'The Indian Jugglers' (1821) is a case in point, structured by the alternation of a wrapped attention to the immediate power of a performance and a reflection on the way it challenges a collective *amour propre*:

> Coming forward and seating himself on the ground in his white dress and tightened turban, the chief of the Indian Jugglers begins with tossing up two brass balls, which is what any of us could do, and concludes with keeping up four, which is what none of us could do to save our lives, nor if we were to take our whole lives to do it in . . . To catch four balls in succession in less than a second of time and deliver them back so as to return with seeming consciousness to the hand again, to

make them revolve around him at certain intervals, like the planets in their spheres, to make them chase one another like sparkles of fire . . . there is something in all this which he who does not admire may be quite sure he never really admired anything in the whole course of his life.[32]

Hazlitt here multiplies analogies in his attempt to render the particular qualities of the Indian Juggler's performance. While each analogy gives an impression, their cumulative effect is not one of descriptive mastery but of a successive series of approximations. The presentation here is more than just an exercise in exotica. The Indian Juggler represents a power of composure and skill which becomes, for Hazlitt, a touchstone of our capacity for admiration and an overcoming of any will to mastery.

Across all the modulations of speech and writing in Hazlitt's work, there may be one thing that is constant, at least to a deconstructive critic. Whatever the detours and complications of Hazlitt's thinking it repeatedly gives priority to speech over writing. The ideal of conversational style serves to restore vitality and presence to the abstract anonymity of the written and the printed. The oscillation that Derrida finds in the texts of Rousseau can also be found in the works of Hazlitt: 'Rousseau condemns writing as destruction of presence and disease of speech. He rehabilitates it to the extent that it promises the reappropriation of that of which speech allowed itself to be dispossessed'.[33] Conversational style might be thought of as just such a rehabilitation, and also as the means of remedying speech's dispossession of the 'common' in the intricate divisions of a modern commercial society. What is written in the conversational style is what Derrida describes as a speech 'as it should be or rather as it *should have been*' (141). The repossession in writing of something lost in speaking is evident in another way, one that brings out another parallel between Hazlitt and Rousseau. Writing enables the tongue-tied author to speak. It restores an ease of expression which should have been there in a moment of speaking but could not be, whether through misunderstanding, social awkwardness or sexual embarrassment. Hence the author who is graceless and distorted in the eyes of society recovers himself in the act of writing. The conversational style emerges as much out of the absence as the presence of a speaking voice.

In Hazlitt's case the periodical essay was the medium for these recoveries of the self. He brought a new tense and tension into journalistic forms, one that we have learnt to call Romanticism. His work was certainly fostered by imagining different possible relations between writing and speaking. But the transition from the one to the other was not a seamless exercise in self-expression. Hazlitt uses his chosen medium to elaborate what Hegel described as 'freedom of subjectivity'. In the act of writing, however, expressing what is within can turn into something other: either inventing a self for the pleasure of others or registering the failure or untimeliness of expression. A further complication comes from Hazlitt's alertness to the dangers of solipsism and snobbery. One way out of these forms of self-confinement is by an ecstatic participation in otherness. Another is Hazlitt's engagement with the question of what is to count as common in a divided society. Knowing nothing like Socrates, Hazlitt's modern journalist is also a Socratic gadfly, finding what is common in the gaps and tensions rather than in the safe places of society.

NOTES

1. Charles Taylor, *The Sources of the Self* (Cambridge UP: 1989), 375.
2. Jurgen Habermas, *The Philosophial Discourse of Modernity*, tr. F. Lawrence (Polity Press: Cambridge, 1987), 16–17.
3. William Hazlitt, *Conversations of Northcote*, in P. P. Howe (ed.), *The Complete Works of William Hazlitt*, 21 vols (J. M. Dent: London, 1931–4), Vol. 11, 278. All subsequent references to Hazlitt's writings are, unless indicated otherwise, taken from the Howe edition. These references will take the form of 'Howe' followed by the volume number and page number. Page numbers only will be given in the text following the first full citation for a particular text.
4. Jürgen Habermas, *The Philosophical Discourse of Modernity*, 17.
5. Immanuel Kant, *Critique of Pure Reason*, tr. N. Kemp Smith (Macmillan: London, 1978 [1781]), 9.
6. Howe, Vol. 13, 38.
7. Originally from John Brewer, from a lecture delivered to a symposium, 'The French Revolution in Art', Clore Gallery, London, Dec. 1989.
8. H. M. Sikes, W. H. Bonner and G. Lahey (eds), *The Letters of William Hazlitt* (New York UP: 1978), 238.
9. Howe, Vol. 17, 22.
10. Howe, Vol. 17, 107.
11. Anon., 'The Liberal, no. 111', the *Literary Register*, 3 May 1823. For this and the following reference I am indebted to J. A. Houk, *William Hazlitt: A Reference Guide* (G. K. Hall & Co.: Boston, 1977), 44.
12. See variously the *Literary Gazette*, May and June 1817; *British Critic*, Dec. 1817; *Analectic Magazine*, Sept. 1818; *New Monthly Magazine*, Oct. 1818: cited in Houk, *William Hazlitt*, 13, 15, 19, 22.
13. Anon. 'On Truth', *Blackwood's Edinburgh Magazine*, May 1818, 123.
14. Jon Klancher, *The Making of the English Reading Audience, 1790–1832* (University of Wisconsin Press: Madison, 1987), 55.
15. Howe, Vol. 8, 243.
16. Francis Jeffrey, unsigned review, *Edinburgh Review*, Oct. 1802, collected in L. Madden (ed.), *Robert Southey, The Critical Heritage* (Routledge & Kegan Paul: London, 1972), 68–91, 72.

17. Howe, Vol. 9, 194.
18. Howe, Vol. 8, 243, 244.
19. See, for example, John Barrell, *English Literature in History: An Equal, Wide, Survey* (Hutchinson: London, 1983).
20. William Wordsworth, *Lyrical Ballads*, 1805 edn, ed. D. Roper (Collins: London, 1968), 33.
21. Howe, Vol. 12, 24.
22. Howe, Vol. 9, 225.
23. Howe, Vol. 7, 99.
24. Sikes, Bonner and Lahey, *The Letters of William Hazlitt*, 233.
25. Howe, Vol. 18, 305.
26. Howe, Vol. 6, 319.
27. Howe, Vol. 16, 212.
28. Howe, Vol. 5, 50.
29. Howe, Vol. 17, 23.
30. Howe, Vol. 9, 213.
31. For the text of Keats's famous letter on negative capability see Hyder E. Rollins (ed.), *The Letters of John Keats, 1814–21* 2 vols (Cambridge UP: 1958), Vol. 1, 191–4.
32. Howe, Vol. 8, 77–8.
33. Jacques Derrida, *Of Grammatology*, tr. G. Spivak (John Hopkins UP: Baltimore, 1976), 142.

2

DICKENS'S LATER JOURNALISM

GEOFFREY HEMSTEDT

Dickens worked as journalist for nearly forty years. He started out in the early 1830s as a shorthand writer, taking down parliamentary debates and, in the last days of stage-coaching, travelling throughout England to report political meetings. By his mid-twenties he had established a distinct voice, and a reputation as a knowledgeable commentator on London street life, through fifty-odd sketches and comic tales in such journals as *Bell's Life of London*. These pieces were collected as *Sketches by Boz*, (1836–7). In 1846 he was appointed as the first editor of the *Daily News*. He edited the weekly magazines *Household Words* in the 1850s and *All the Year Round* in the 1860s, and published articles and serial novels in both. His journalistic contributions to *Household Words*, which had originally appeared between 1850 and 1856, were first gathered together in 1868 as *Reprinted Pieces*, and various cumulative editions of the *All the Year Round* writings were published from 1860 as *The Uncommercial Traveller*. This chapter addresses these writings of the 1850s and 1860s in which Dickens may be seen to develop strategies of journalistic authority and to trace characteristically modern social phenomena as part of a changing national formation.

Sketches by Boz offers an exuberant and richly fanciful panorama of London as a city of improvised identities and social performance. Its 'perpetual stream of life and bustle' is rendered in rolling inventories of the commodities citizens use, and of the detritus they use again. At the same time, through motifs of self-invention and concealment, criminality, the prison-house, shame and display, the river and the crowd, and by beginning to frame a complex and interlocking urban demography, the young writer prefigures his life's work as a novelist. To read the later journalism as an extension of *Sketches by Boz* is to encounter continuities and contrasts. The territory Dickens knows most intimately is always London. Although by the 1850s Newgate no longer displays 'the gibbet with all its dreadful apparatus' outside its walls (*Boz*), Dickens is still moved 'touching its rough stone to think of the prisoners in their sleep'

(1860, 'Night Walks': *UC*, 130).[1] He still wanders the streets at night, or when the fashionable districts have been vacated out of season. Contemplating the empty city, he asks, 'Where are all the people who on busy working-days pervade these scenes?' (1863, 'The City of the Absent': *UC*, 239), or imagines that if 'the enormous hosts of dead . . . were raised while the living slept, there would not be the space of a pin's point in all the streets and ways for the living to come out into' ('Night Walks': 133). Increasingly, however, he is saved from such fancies. The modern city will yield its secrets not only to a writer who sounds like the last man alive waiting for an apocalypse, but also to the detective police who, now that the tyro Boz has become Mr Dickens the distinguished public man, are happy to have him accompany them on their night patrols.

Given that his name was worth money it is surprising to recall that Dickens's contributions to *Household Words* were originally published anonymously. However, he was distinctly proclaimed as the author of his articles in *All the Year Round* to boost circulation, and for the same reason he developed *Great Expectations* (from what he had initially conceived as a much shorter piece) for serial publication in the magazine. The device of presenting himself additionally in the persona of the Uncommercial Traveller allowed him to lay claim to an open journalistic agenda. As a traveller in 'Human Interest' he was by implication otherwise disinterested. 'I never get any commission' (1860: *UC*, 1).

Considered together his journalism of the 1850s and 1860s exhibits the kind of topical inventiveness and whimsicality that makes such a claim plausible. He has 'a large connection in the fancy goods way' and his contributions include what we would now think of as travel features, from home and abroad, impressionistic and full of detail at the same time – facetious anecdotes about meals and hotels, or what it is like travelling on the Calais night-mail, appealing to readers as fellow-strugglers in the pursuit of value for money, and the reasonable treatment to which the bourgeois consumer has a right; mini-fictions, strung together thematically; birthdays, odd things that happen in barristers' chambers, stories about dogs, or donkeys, or parrots. Recollections, reveries, peregrinations. This is recognisably make-weight writing, column-filling, but beyond this, in the majority of the pieces, there emerges a more purposeful celebration of the resources of 'this great country' England. In this project the conditions under which commerce flourishes furnish the stock-in-trade of the self-proclaimed 'Uncommercial', who proceeds to order its elements in a controlled reformist rhetoric.

He sets up a typical platform for national renewal in an article on the schools of the Stepney Pauper Union (1863, 'The Short-Timers': *UC*). The streets of London display 'shameful instances of neglect of children' who should be part of 'England's strength, not its weakness' (*UC*, 209). As a corrective, in the Half-Time Schools military and naval drill is carried out with 'perfect uniformity, and yet an individual spirit and emulation' (*UC*, 212). Children drawn from the 'criminal population' are seen to delight in performing those feats of mental arithmetic with which Murdstone and Pumblechook persecute David Copperfield and Pip, and in passing the test of a truly national curriculum.

> Tell me something about Great Britain, tell me something about its principal productions, tell me something about its ports, tell me something about its seas and rivers, tell me something about coal, iron, copper, tin and turpentine. The hollow square bristles with extended arms. (215)

He quotes letters of commendation from mercantile employers ('Give us drilled boys, for they are prompt, obedient and punctual') and notes approvingly that 'the girls make excellent domestic servants' (*UC*, 218). Order and method, then, provide the foundations of acceptable working-class citizenship, legitimated by fitness for employment, focused on domestic service to answer the needs of the bourgeoisie, and mercantile and military service which together guarantee national power and wealth. Dickens's early journalism, *Boz*, drew its energy from recording the seemingly boundless diversity of identities caught in a volatile process of self-invention. He observed the crowd in the streets and markets, in drinking places, on excursions, or forced to rub shoulders in the omnibus, for ever coming together and dispersing, reconstituting itself, always multifarious. As we will see, something of this survives in the later journalism, together with the record of the idiosyncratic ways of getting a living, the shifts and improvisations which characterised for Boz an earlier social dynamic, but 'The Short-Timers' declares a contrasting principle by which a text might be ordered; the systematic obliteration of difference, rather than the celebration of it.

Modernity, as Dickens presents it in the journalism of the 1850s and 1860s, is registered in the emergence of structures and institutions which enable the people to function coherently as a mass, but he apprehends the contending values of sameness and diversity in contradictory ways. Consider the drumming rhythm of the Short-Timers' catechism, 'tell me something, tell me something', on and on. In another context, that of *Hard Times* ('Now, what I want is, Facts') Dickens describes this kind of reiterative emphasis as 'inflexible, dry, and dictatorial'. In *Hard Times* again, Coketown exhibits the repetitive deadness of modernity:

> The jail might have been the infirmary, the infirmary might have been the jail, the town hall might have been either, or both, or anything else, for anything that appeared to the contrary in the graces of their construction.[2]

When the Uncommercial visits the Britannia Theatre in Hoxton, however, he admires a ventilation system 'ingeniously combining the experience of hospitals and railway stations' (1860, 'Two Views of a Cheap Theatre': *UC*, 31). This is ingenuity applied on a grand scale, a new building raised in five months with one man's capital investment of £25,000, and designed to accommodate an audience of thousands. Comparably, whereas in *Boz* food is typically distributed through the shifting enterprise of small traders ('little fivepenny dabs of dingy bacon', a screw of tea, the kidney-pie man 'with his warehouse on his arm'),[3] the Uncommercial describes a newly established mass-catering project in Whitechapel as a model of how working people can 'avail themselves of the advantages derivable from system, and from the combination of numbers, in the purchase and cooking of their food' (1863, 'The Boiled Beef of New England': *UC*, 253).

Dickens recognises that there is a plot in these oppositions. 'Bound for the Great Salt Lake' (1863: *UC*), in which he describes the preparations for departure of a group of Mormon emigrants from the Port of London, combines his early and late journalistic styles. The first movement, developed around the refrain 'Down by the Docks', assembles the gear and clutter of a colourful local economy; vegetables 'crossed with fish and seaweed', polonies and saveloys, hornpipe shows and penny waxworks, pawnshops, parrots, Malays and Chinamen, cheap undertakers, 'bare tattooed arms, Britannia's daughters, malice, mud, maundering and madness' (221). This impressionism is overtaken by a steadier reportage, reflecting the principle of order aboard the emigrant ship:

> They came from various parts of England in small parties that had never seen one another before. Yet they had not been a couple of hours on board, when they established their own police, made their own regulations, and set their own watches at all the hatchways. Before nine o'clock, the ship was as orderly and quiet as a man-of-war. (223)

For Dickens the dockside is both a centre and a margin; a centre because the energies of national production and international exchange are to be found drawn together there, and marginal because this London locality bears the traces of exotic cosmopolitanism. It is a haven and a base of preparation, the starting point of many journeys, and by the same token a kind of frontier, between Britannia and the rest of the world. It is also the source of many potential narratives, which can be exploited allusively rather than systematically, and from which Dickens the journalist can develop a mode of writing which persuades by its vivid particularity, but which stops short of sustained analysis. From *Boz* onwards he is thus a masterly 'local colour' writer, but in the later writing he also falls into the habit of pontificating digressively. Dickens was temperamentally cut out to relish the journalist's right to have opinions, and to claim authority simply by uttering them, preferably in terms the reader is ready to hear. Thus he writes of the people of the Pacific islands, 'The noble savage is a wearisome impostor wherever he is'; of Welsh emigrants, 'The intelligence here was unquestionably of a low order, and the heads were of a poor type' (1863, 'Bound for the Great Salt Lake': *UC*, 230).

These successive rhetorics are complementary, and systematically balanced. These are not the opium-ridden riverside warrens where Jasper will lose himself in *The Mystery of Edwin Drood*, or Dorian Gray engage in unspeakable dissipations. We may savour the picturesque commotion of the docks, and not be apprehensive about their darker disorder, because it is subordinated in the larger frame of discipline and purpose by which the project of emigration is validated, with the writer assuming authority as legitimator. The Uncommercial formalises this authority by setting out much of his account in transcribed interviews, as he interrogates the Mormon agent or one of the emigrants, a Wiltshire agricultural labourer. This device both anticipates the forms of modern broadcast journalism, and confers on the journalist something of the authority of an accredited investigator, with a right to take evidence as it would be taken in an official court of enquiry. Indeed, when the piece was reissued Dickens added a note recording that its first publication had prompted discussion and correspondence with Lord Houghton, who had undertaken 'philosophical and literary research concerning these Latter-Day Saints', and he quoted a Parliamentary Select Committee on Emigrant Ships as confirming his judgement of the sound administration of Mormon voyages.

Thus the credentials of 'investigative' journalism are established. It should be emphasised that Dickens created his own version of this role at a time when the institutional identity of the journalist, his place in the orders of public authority, was uncertain. It may be argued that this has always been the case, and continues to be, but Dickens took exceptional pains to use his high profile as a famous author to establish a quasi-professional status for writers. Again and again he gains a privileged right of access, to a workhouse, a hospital, the Royal Naval Dockyard, to a school, a lead-works, to accompany the police, to inspect business ledgers and so forth, partly in his role as journalist but also, as he implies in noting the forms by which he is addressed, simply by virtue of his class status. The Uncommercial represents himself as gentleman, journalist and professional man. He retains something of Boz's irregular point of view, as an invisible observer of street life (down by the docks), but as the national scene is subjected to regulation his rhetoric acquires a more respectable register. At the same time, what legitimates his observations about the people of the South Seas or the Welsh is anybody's guess. The first is a throw-away line introduced by slack nonsense about 'lovely islands, where the savage girls plait flowers' but the second ('the heads were of a poor type') suggests that the Uncommercial is trading in official theory of some kind. But then as reporter, feature writer, columnist and sketch writer by turns he is in any of these functions answerable to no other editor than himself, and can say pretty much whatever he wants, and assume that most of his readers will believe he knows what he is talking about.

More purposefully, in his journalistic persona he projects that independence on which the press has traditionally based its claim to be considered as a Fourth Estate. In *Heroes and Hero-Worship* (1840) Carlyle, whom Dickens revered, credited Burke with having originated the term; Burke had declared that in the reporters' gallery of Parliament there sat a Fourth Estate more important than all the others assembled in the building. We are reminded that Dickens began his writing career in that same gallery. He may seek respectability, and respect, for the journalist, but he is at pains to avoid identification with the Establishment. The political posture he adopts as a result is complex, and can best be traced in a comparative reading of a number of pieces.

In 'The Great Tasmania's Cargo' (1860: *UC*) he reports on a visit to the Liverpool workhouse, where he has seen a regiment of soldiers lately returned from service in India, starved and diseased at the end of their voyage. At first he draws on the satirical languages he has established in *Little Dorrit*, speaking of 'Circumlocutional embellishments of the soldier's condition' emanating from 'the Pagoda Department of that great Circumlocution Office on which the sun never sets', and personifies government agents he has interviewed as 'my official friend Pangloss' (72–3). However, this facetiousness soon gives way to a harsher and more particular language: 'They were so horribly reduced, that they were awful to look upon. Racked with dysentery and blackened with scurvy . . .'; the food with which the men have been supplied is inedible, the biscuit 'a honey-combed heap of maggots, and the excrement of maggots' (75). As an investigative reporter Dickens reviews depositions given at inquest, interviews the soldiers themselves, and refutes official accusations that they have sold their rations for drink. He brings before his readers evidence of a national scandal involving official incompetence and neglect of duty. He closes in editorial high-style:

> No punishment that our inefficient laws provide, is worthy of the name when set against the guilt of this transaction. But, if the memory of it die out unavenged, and if it do not result in the inexorable dismissal and disgrace of those who are responsible for it, their escape will be infamous to the Government (of whatever

party), that so neglects its duty, and infamous to the nation that tamely suffers such intolerable wrong to be done in its name. (82)

The essay is loud with indignation, but in the end curiously indirect and diffused in its effect. Some officers, it seems, have been 'condemned' by the coroner's jury, but none is named. Similarly, for all its satiric origin, the collective soubriquet 'Pangloss' functions to protect the writer's sources as effectively as 'Deep Throat'. The spectacle of emaciated soldiers in their workhouse beds has been so shameful, says the Uncommercial, 'that as an Englishman I blush to remember it'. So he calls for justice. But our laws are 'inefficient' and when when we look again at that last paragraph we see not the certain prospect of 'punishment', but rather the suspicion that 'dismissal and disgrace' are not after all inexorable. The Uncommercial gains a singular credit in this exercise. He has taken up the soldiers' cause. He condemns not the government in office for what has happened ('the guilt of this transaction' lies with its unnamed functionaries), but 'Government (no matter of what party)' – no definite article here – who might let such functionaries retain their posts. Although such an outcome will be infamous to the nation, as it will to that abstraction 'Government', the Uncommercial has somehow avoided the collective infamy by declaring his personal shame. He blushes as he writes. He proclaims himself to be a true Englishman and, as a fearless representative of the Fourth Estate, a guarantor of the moral health of the nation, fit to stand shoulder to shoulder with the suffering soldiers whose cause he champions: 'Who doubts that if we all did our duty as faithfully as the soldier does his, this world would be a better place?' (73).

There is something familiar about these strategic self-positionings, stock-in-trade of the British journalist. Dickens is independent, 'Uncommercial', but he acknowledges that he has a place in a national freemasonry that is at once democratic and paternalist. This is most evident in his writings about the London police. He was particularly well qualified to be a police correspondent. He had worked as a court reporter and, more importantly, throughout his writing life he found his deepest inspiration in the secret places of the city. The rapid development after the 1840s of police methods of institutional organisation, surveillance, detection, regulation and record was in many of its aspects both foreshadowed and directly represented in Dickens's writings. From the very beginning (from *Sketches by Boz*) he had been street-wise, a night-walker, haunting the river and the warrens of St Giles. Observing people on the streets and in places of entertainment, or itemising the gear and clutter of their lives piled up in pawnshops or in the second-hand clothes markets in Monmouth Street, he could unfold their hidden histories. As a boy, with his father held in the debtors' prison, making his way to his work at

Warren's Blacking in the Strand, he had had to make shift in those same streets. He wrote down what he had heard, like an interpreter, helping his readers find their way in unfamiliar places. Sam Weller interprets for Pickwick in his turn, as the Artful Dodger does for Oliver.

Thus when in 1851 Dickens goes 'On Duty with Inspector Field' (*RP*) and the rendezvous is made 'in the shadow of St Giles's steeple' before they cross to the Borough, he is revisiting a long-familiar beat, and Field's sergeant casts the beam of his bull's eye lantern on things the writer has seen before and already shown to his readers. His admiration for the police officers is reflexive. They too know many languages, the cant of the gonophs and Rat's Castle, voices from Ireland and the West Indies and, this being the year of the Great Exhibition, Detective Sergeant is 'weary of speaking French all day to foreigners' (513). They too are establishing the credentials of their profession; if we remark that Inspector Bucket of *Bleak House* is a founding model of the literary detective, then we note too that Inspector Field (on whom Bucket was partly modelled) was having to invent his own role.

For this night's meeting Field has come from patrolling the deserted galleries of the British Museum,

> from the ores and metals of the deep mines of the earth, and from the Parrot Gods of the South Sea Islands, and from the birds and beetles of the tropics, and from the Arts of Greece and Rome, and from the Sculptures of Nineveh, and from the traces of an elder world, when these were not. (514)

In *Sketches by Boz* Dickens had noted in a pawnbroker's shop 'cards of rings and brooches, fastened and labelled separately, like the insects in the British Museum' (*Boz*, 189). Part of the enterprise of those sketches was to set before the reader the heterogeneous commodities and phenomena of city life, in inventoried clusters; inventories as a provisional kind of record, because the clutter of the city was so confused and so quickly reconstituted that it could rarely be ordered into categories as in this pawnbroking example. Here, in 1851, by moving from the galleries of the Museum, with their epical but taxonomically ordered displays, into the darkness of the uncharted slums, Field shares with Dickens the challenge to map out the conditions of urban crisis and to understand its impacted complexity, to render it subject to record and reform.

Dickens reports Field's tour of duty in the present tense, a running commentary on a sequence of word-pictures intercut with a flow of dialogue in which interrogation and surveillance blend with the social reformer's portrayal of human misery.

> Saint Giles's church clock, striking eleven, hums through our hand from the dilapidated door of a dark outhouse as we open it, and are stricken back by the

pestilent breath that issues from within. Rogers to the front with the light and let us
look!

   Ten, twenty, thirty – who can count them! Men, women and children, for the
most part naked, heaped upon the floor like maggots in a cheese! Ho! In that dark
corner yonder! Does anybody lie there? Me sir, Irish me, a widder, with six
children . . . Wheresoever Mr Rogers turns his flaming eye, there is a spectral
figure rising, unshrouded, from a grave of rags. (517)

This recalls *Bleak House*, which Dickens was writing concurrently, and in
which St Giles is Tom-all-Alone's.

   As, on the ruined human wretch, vermin parasites appear, so these ruined shelters
   have bred a crowd of foul existence that crawls in and out of gaps in walls and
   boards: and coils itself to sleep, in maggot numbers, where the rain drips in,
   fetching and carrying fever . . .[4]

Here the figurative language is extended, becoming part of a larger symbolic
design tracing poverty's revenge through pestilence. Government, of
course, can do nothing to shield citizens from this contagion, because it
lacks the machinery and (in the writer's angry arraignment) the will to deal
with the conditions in which disease is generated. The writer and the police
inspector, with their complementary expertise, can be guides to a fuller
knowledge. As novelist and reporter, here again Dickens positions himself
independently of Government as an authoritative witness, this time with a
prophetic insight into the horrors of modern urban life.

   Can we perhaps detect a further, unconscious, source of this authority?
At a lodging-house at the Old Mint in the Borough, the party is guided by
its keeper, Deputy. (The name came back to Dickens in the last months of
his life, when he used it in *Edwin Drood* for the night-wandering, lurking
boy who stones the drunken Durdles to his bed, and knows secrets.) As
the bull's eye lantern is closed, this Borough Deputy lights the way with a
'flaring candle stuck in a blacking bottle'. At this cue the running
commentary is thrown into the first person, and when the police lantern
is unshuttered the 'I' of the narrative is suddenly the object of its beam,
not a director of it.

   Some wake up with an execration and a threat. – What! who spoke? O! If it's the
   accursed glaring eye that fixes me, go where I will, I am helpless. Here! I sit up to
   be looked at. Is it me you want? Not you, lie down again! and I lie down, with a
   woful growl. (520)

Does Dickens know these places so well because in his imagination and
his own secret history he has dreamed of finding himself there? Well,
maybe. The journalist declines to reveal his sources.

   Instead, he can be indignantly insistent on his own respectability, and is
quick to speak on behalf of an affronted bourgeoisie. Ironically, another
figure whose command of language and modes of utterance, like that of the

police, rivals his own is 'The Begging-Letter Writer' (1850: *RP*). 'He writes in a variety of styles: sometimes in low spirits; sometimes quite jocosely' (381). If he is then a kind of mirror-image, Dickens represses the recognition, and instead has him taken up by the Mendicity Society: 'I presented myself at a London Police-Office with my testimony against him' (383). There is something of Micawber behind this figure, as there is something of Dickens's father in Micawber, and his uneasy and slightly hysterical reaction may be prompted by the changes of status his fame has brought about. It is as if the great writer is importuned by the ghost of his own father. In 'The Ruffian' (1868: *UC*) he rails against insubordination on the streets. He would have the Ruffian's back 'scarified often and deep' (302). He objects to 'the blaring use of the very worst language possible, in our public thoroughfares' (305), and is pleased to find that the newest Police Act has made such talk a punishable offence. Armed with this knowledge he pursues a young Irish woman (prudently 'on the opposite side of the way') for a mile until he can find a police officer and give her in charge: 'I asked the constable did he know my name? Yes, he did' (306). The following day he attends the Magistrate's Court, and insists that she be fined and sent down.

His professional delight in the language of the streets clearly has its limits, but he still claims credit for his sharp ear for demotic languages. In 'Two Views of a Cheap Theatre' (1860) he objects to a preacher's implausible impersonation of an artisan, 'represented by a suggestion of a dialect that I certainly never heard in my uncommercial travels, and with a coarse swing of voice and manner . . . as far away from the fact as a Chinese Tartar' (35). Watching a pantomime at the same theatre he admires the realism of representations of shopkeepers and 'the passengers in the thoroughfares', remarking that the audience will swallow anything 'concerning Knights and Ladies, Fairies, Angels, or such like, but they are not to be done as to anything in the streets' (33). Even so, there is a suspicion that the writer himself transcribes or invents language-uses differentially, as indices of either social deviance or conformity. He uses conventions of spelling to suggest unruly Gorblimeyism. For example, the Wapping Workhouse (1860: *UC*) is populated by 'Refractories'.

> 'A pretty Ouse this is, matron, ain't it?' said Refractory Two, 'where a pleeseman's called in, if a gal says a word.'
>
> 'And wen you're sent to prison for nothink or less!' said the Chief, tugging at her oakum as if it were the matron's hair. 'But any place is better than this; that's one thing and be thankful.' (24)

Compare this with 'A Poor Man's Tale of a Patent' (1850: *RP*), in which Dickens sets out a case for the modernisation of the patent laws by having a decently humble artisan tell his own story.

> I am not a Chartist, and I never was. I don't mean to say but what I see a good
> many public points to complain of, still I don't think that's the way to set them
> right . . . I read the paper, and hear discussion at what we call 'a parlour,' in
> Birmingham, and I know many good men and workmen who are Chartists. Note.
> Not physical force. (462)

This is characteristic of Dickens's indirect assembly of the terms in which
a reformist programme might be framed. The English workman asks only
for a reasonable legislative provision so that his skill may contribute to the
wealth of the nation. This resourceful artisan is no revolutionary. There
are Refractories, however, and public spaces must be cleared of roughs
and foul language. Dickens complains (1869, 'On an Amateur Beat': *UC*)
that there are in London 'much-puffed streets and courts which no man
durst go down . . . in the days of steam and gas and photographs of
thieves and electric telegraphs' (346). The Chief Commissioner of Police
must use these systems of record and communication to make the city
safe. Scrooge had famously asked, 'Are there no prisons? Are there no
workhouses?' At the end of his career, the Uncommercial too, it seems,
can still find a use for them.

At the same time he shows how a knowledge of the circumstances of the
poor can be used to ease their want and suffering. 'A Small Star in the
East' (1868: *UC*) describes a visit to the East London Children's Hospital,
on the borders of Ratliff and Stepney, by the 'impure river'. In this piece
the docks are not figured as exotic borderlands.

> A squalid maze of streets, courts and alleys of miserable houses let out in single
> rooms. A wilderness of dirt, rags, and hunger. A mud-desert, chiefly inhabited by a
> tribe from whom employment has departed, or to whom it comes but fitfully and
> rarely. They are not skilled mechanics in any wise. They are but labourers, – dock-
> labourers, water-side labourers, coal-porters, ballast-heavers, such-like hewers of
> wood and drawers of water. But they have come into existence, and they propagate
> their wretched race. (319)

Dickens enters these lodgings, and interviews the unemployed men; there
is no boiler-making work to be had, no coal-portering. He finds women
engaged in slop-work, one earning tenpence halfpenny for a pea-jacket
which takes her two days to make. He remarks on her 'cheery help-
fulness', but the detail of her payment may remind us that Mayhew
showed how thousands of slop-workers had recourse to prostitution to
make up a living wage. Dickens reports that the women can get eighteen
pence a day in the lead works, but an Irish woman tells him that many of
them suffer from lead-poisoning. She shows him a young woman lying
sick; 'and her brain is coming out at her ear, and it hurts her dreadful'
(321). When he returns to the subject of the lead factories the following

year (1869, 'On an Amateur Beat': *UC*) he has, it seems, been nobbled by the employers, and acknowledges that it must be remembered that many of the workers are 'very capricious and irregular in their attendance' (352). Here, however, he sustains a detailed account of a failing system of production and a corresponding failure of social provision – 'These people had a mortal dread of entering the workhouse, and received no out-of-door relief.' In a case where, the father being in hospital, the Union does make provision for a family, the mother and five children receive four shillings and five loaves a week. Contemplating the suffering of the children in these crowded slums he is 'quite unmanned' (326).

All of this sets up his account of the new Children's Hospital, established by a house-surgeon from another London hospital and his wife, whose knowledge and systematic record of the lives of their patients align them with the writer and the detective police:

> Both the lady and the gentleman are well acquainted, not only with the histories of the patients and their families, but with the characters and circumstances of a great number of their neighbours: of these they keep a register. It is their common experience, that people, sinking by inches into deeper and deeper poverty, will conceal it, even from them, if possible, until the very last extremity. (329)

A number of meanings are enfolded here. Dickens implies that these are the deserving poor, who are too proud to show that they are in need of help, but this concealment may also owe something to their suspicion of authority, and an inability to distinguish between surveillance and charitable provision. Thus the contradictions evident in the writer's own treatment of the poor, as he alternately calls for them to be cared for or policed, reflect the uneven development of the reformist project he espouses.

Such ambivalences pervade Dickens's journalistic writings. *Sketches by Boz* described London as a changing city, of new social roles and commercial ventures mixed in with traditional enterprises, plate-glass shop fronts and gaslit gin palaces alongside small proprietors and street sellers whose way of life reached back to Hogarth, or earlier. At its best the later journalism recalls Dickens's fascination with these juxtapositions, and reminds us that London presented itself to its citizens like a living text; nowhere more vividly than in his account of 'Bill-Sticking' (1851: *RP*). If we were taken back to mid-nineteenth-century London we would find many of its surfaces smothered in bills and posters. The practice of fly-posting as Dickens records it is evidence of speculative, opportunistic, improvised economic activity, in an arena of competition. A bill had a life for only as many hours or days as it was not covered by another, or ripped down by a commercial rival. At the same time advertisers sought more respectable and securer means of addressing their public, and the monthly episodes of Dickens's own novels were bound between dozens of advertisements, for other publications, entertainments, furniture, patent medicines, clothing, in fact for almost anything people could be persuaded to pay for. This was an apt form of publication for one who from his first sketches had read in the city's signs of dress and commodities the meanings of its panoramic social display. The bills offer another text to the literate citizen, though the King of the Bill-Stickers remembers an earlier time when 'there were more caricature wood-block engravings for posting bills than there are at the present time' (419) and acknowledges that there are yet some bill-stickers who cannot read. 'But they know which is the right side up'ards of their work' (422). So does Dickens, as he describes

> an old warehouse which rotting paste and rotting paper had brought down to the condition of old cheese. It would have been impossible to say, on the most conscientious survey, how much of its front was brick and mortar, and how much decayed and decaying plaster . . . The building was shored up to prevent it tumbling into the street; and very beams erected against it were less wood than paste and paper, they had been so continually posted and reposted. The forlorn dregs of old posters so encumbered this wreck, that there was no hold for new posters, and the stickers had abandoned the place in despair, except one enterprising man who had hoisted the last masquerade to a clear spot near the level of the stack of chimneys, where it waved and drooped like a shattered flag. Here and there, some of the thick rind of the house had peeled off in strips, and fluttered heavily down, littering the street; but still, below these rents and gashes, layers of decomposing posters showed themselves, as if they were interminable. (414)

'Knowing all the posters that were yet legible, intimately', he is able to decipher the fragments of this heaving palimpsest, and to register the inventory of commodities and entertainments they proclaim. We read of such rotting and beam-shored buildings in *Oliver Twist* and *Bleak House*, and 'Bill-Sticking' has the distinctly Dickensian city texture, of decay and newness compacted. The King of the Bill-Stickers, fearing the agents of the state who pick their way among the ruins where modern commerce lets rip, thinks the journalist is a tax-collector, and shies at being interviewed. He must keep pace with new trade practices, which demand both the increasingly centralised organisation of his craft and the arcane street knowledge of its freebooting operatives. Like the police detectives, and like Dickens himself, he must map out new orders in London's secret territories.

In such a project, as so often in these writings, we recognise a natural extension of the design and the rhetorics we find in Dickens the novelist. London is his inspiration, his beat, at once the object of detailed observation and analysis, and the source of fantasy. When he was approaching the serial publication of a novel he might steal a march of three or four months of copy, but at some stage in the run the printer's deadline would catch up, and he would be writing nearly twenty thousand words a month for immediate publication, with the printer's runner at the door. When the pressure eased, still he wrote compulsively, and in the articles for *Household Words* and *All the Year Round* the nature of that compulsion may be read in reiterated themes as a kind of psychic signature.

One such theme, the Thames 'as a common place for suicide', keeps coming to Mr Dickens rather as King Charles the First keeps straying into Mr Dick's memorial in *David Copperfield*. In 'Night Walks' (1860: *UC*), choosing to wander by Bethlehem Hospital, he speculates that when they dream the sane are indistinguishable from the insane. 'Do we not nightly jumble events and personages and times and places, as these do daily?' (132). In *Bleak House* (1852–3) he had written of London as 'a desert region blasted by volcanic fires', and now he contemplates 'the real desert region of the night', as in a waking dream. Again in *Bleak House*, Esther Summerson describes the Thames on the night of her mother's death.

> The river had a fearful look, so overcast and secret, creeping away so fast between the low flat lines of shore: so heavy with indistinct and awful shapes, both of substance and shadow: so deathlike and mysterious. I have seen it many times since then, by sunlight and by moonlight, but never free from the impressions of that journey. In my memory, the lights upon the bridge are always burning dim; the cutting wind is eddying round the homeless woman whom we pass; the monotonous wheels are whirling on; and the light of the carriage-lamps reflected back, looks palely in upon me – a face, rising out of the dreaded water. (*BH*, 771)

Now, seven years later, the night-walking journalist is still not 'free from the impressions of that journey'.

> But the river had an awful look, the buildings on the banks were muffled in black shrouds, and the reflected lights seemed to originate deep in the water, as if the spectres of suicides were holding them to show where they went down. (129)

The railway terminus, with the morning mails coming in, affords him an interlude of bustling activity and 'remunerative company' (a promising topic for feature writing), but even there he envisions 'the locomotive post-offices, with their great nets – as if they had been dragging the country for bodies' (135).

This motif has a complicated history in Dickens's writing. Most familiarly it affords a conventional presentation of the fallen woman and the river; Nancy in *Oliver Twist* ('I shall come to that at last'), or Martha, rescued at the river's edge in *David Copperfield*. At the culmination of the sequence just quoted, Esther comes upon Lady Dedlock on the steps of the graveyard as if upon a woman drowned; 'I lifted the heavy head, put the long dank hair aside, and turned the face. And it was my mother cold and dead' (*BH*, 812). Dickens opened his last completed novel, *Our Mutual Friend* (1864–5), with a set piece of trawling the Thames for corpses, and developed much of the plot from it. In the journalism, too, there are many such figurations. 'The Shipwreck' (1860: *UC*) is an account of the loss, off Angelsey, of the Royal Charter, bound for Australia, but more particularly of the business of the recovery and identification of the drowned. Much of 'Down with the Tide' (1853: *RP*), describing the work of the Thames River Police, is taken up with details about suicides. Waterloo Bridge is the favourite jumping-off point. Dickens presses the question. Yes, but which *side* of the bridge do they prefer? (The Surrey side, it turns out.) There are references to the Paris Morgue, which he visited on many occasions. In 'Lying Awake' (1852: *RP*) the effect is hallucinatory.

> I wish the Morgue in Paris would not come here as I lie awake, with its ghastly beds, and the swollen saturated clothes hanging up, and the water dripping, dripping all day long, upon that other swollen, saturated something in the corner, like a heap of crushed, over-ripe figs that I have seen in Italy. (436)

In 'Wapping Warehouse' (1860: *UC*) he describes an encounter by the river with 'a figure all dirty and shiny and slimy' who may be 'the drowned man about whom there was a placard on the granite post', and who gives a facetious account of the drowning habits of despairing women: 'Ketches off their bonnets or shorls, takes a run, and headers down there, they does' (19–20).

'Some Recollections of Mortality' (1863: *UC*) combines a sustained account of the Paris Morgue with a memory of being present 'in the hard winter of 1861' at the recovery of a corpse from the Regent's Park canal:

> . . . looking over the bridge parapet . . . I saw, lying on the towing path with her face turned up towards us, a woman, dead a day or two, and under thirty, as I guessed, poorly dressed in black. The feet were lightly crossed at the ankles, and the dark hair, all pushed back from the face, as though that had been the last action of her desperate hands, streamed over the ground. Dabbled all about her, was the water and the broken ice that had dropped from her dress, and had splashed as she was got out. The policeman who had just got her out, and the passing costermonger who had helped him, were standing near the body; the latter with that stare at it which I have likened to being at a waxwork exhibition without a catalogue; the former, looking over his stock, with professional stiffness and coolness, in the direction in which the bearers he had sent for were expected. So dreadfully forlorn, so dreadfully sad, so dreadfully mysterious, this spectacle of our dear sister here departed. (193–4)

The convention which shadows Nancy and Martha and Lady Dedlock is here realised as fact, a set-piece fulfilled, and ready to be set down, the exact observation of the reporter combining with the well-tried rhetoric of the novelist. It is apt, in the context of this whole body of journalism, that the scene should incorporate 'the professional stiffness and coolness' of the policeman, the representative of order and reform. Even so, the reader may recognise that what Dickens here sees in the fading light of a winter afternoon he has imagined many times, in many forms, and this is what lends his journalism its visionary tension. In *Bleak House*, *Little Dorrit* and *Our Mutual Friend* he develops epical symbolic registers of the life of the modern city. In the grandeur of this design the themes he chooses, pollution, disease, the burial of the dead, the prison, the generation of waste, are overwhelmingly at odds with the more deliberate reformist postures and the localised topics he adopts in this journalism. But we may still find traces of dreams in these reports, reluctant revelations, a barely controlled unconscious energy. Dickens may perform the part of the journalist as public man, but another remembered self is startled in the beam of the policeman's lantern. 'Here! I sit up to be looked at. Is it me you want?'

NOTES

1. All quotations, unless otherwise indicated, are taken from *The Uncommercial Traveller and Reprinted Pieces etc.*, The New Oxford Illustrated Dickens (Oxford UP: London, 1958); sources are distinguished in text through *UC* and *RP*.

2. *Hard Times*, The New Oxford Illustrated Dickens (Oxford UP: London, 1955), 23.

3. *Sketches by Boz*, The New Oxford Illustrated Dickens (Oxford UP: London, 1957), 55 (abbreviated to *Boz*).

4. *Bleak House*, The New Oxford Illustrated Dickens (Oxford UP: London, 1948), 220 (abbreviated to *BH*).

PLATFORM, PERFORMANCE AND PAYMENT IN HENRY MAYHEW'S *LONDON LABOUR AND THE LONDON POOR*

ROGER SALES

SWELLING THE ORANGE

An elderly party who hawks cutlery in the streets is performing his poverty in front of Henry Mayhew. He has grafted all his life and yet has fallen on very hard times after a bout of rheumatic fever. He claims that he and his wife have been 'nearly starving' for some time, adding that this is 'as true as you have got the pen in your very hand.' The cupboard is bare:

> Sunday after Sunday we have been without a bit of dinner, and I have laid a-bed all day because we have had no coal, and then been obliged to go out on Monday morning without a bit of victuals between my lips. I've been so faint I couldn't hardly walk.

Walking is also a problem for him because he has worn out his shoes. He holds up his foot so that Mayhew can, if he wants to, see for himself: 'look at these shoes, the soles is all loose, you see, and let water'.[1] Addressed here and elsewhere as 'sir', Mayhew as well as his readers are being pressed by this artful cadger for the money to buy a pair of new shoes and perhaps just a bit of coal and food too, governor.

The discussion of Mayhew's work has tended to revolve around the question of whether or not he, with the pen in his very hand, provided a factually accurate account of the London poor. Radical historians such as E. P. Thompson and Eileen Yeo argue that his articles from 1849 to 1850 as Metropolitan Correspondent for the *Morning Chronicle* established the foundations for later systematic empirical social surveys of poverty.[2] David Englander shows that Charles Booth's notebooks contain interviews that were similar to the ones that Mayhew conducted.[3] Revisionists such as Gertrude Himmelfarb draw attention to Mayhew's faulty statistics, as well as to the way in which he merely reproduced many of the existing ways of categorising poverty. More particularly, Himmelfarb insists that he should be seen as just a journalist rather than as one of the respected founders of social and cultural history.[4] According to her version, journalists can never be completely trusted to get their facts right since they have to rush to meet deadlines and are always tempted towards the kind of colourful exaggerations that sell papers.

Although it is probably right to see Mayhew as being primarily a journalist rather than an early social scientist, this does not mean having to subscribe to Himmelfarb's negative and clichéd view of journalism. The question of how new the 'new journalism' of the 1880s really was is too big to be addressed in any detail here. It is nevertheless possible to suggest in passing that Mayhew pioneered almost all of the techniques that have become associated with later journalists such as W. T. Stead: illustrations, cross-headings, the orchestration of campaigns around particular stories and, above all else, the use of interviews. At a more general level, Mayhew, like Stead, showed how journalists could become theatrical performers in their own texts.[5]

Mayhew's interviews, or street-biographies, will be the main focus of attention here. It will be suggested that the way in which many historians debate the factual accuracy of these interviews misses the point that they were essentially theatrical occasions during which, as has already been seen, poverty was performed in either overstated or understated ways. Another point that can get overlooked by those preoccupied with the question of Mayhew's accuracy is that many of the performers expected some kind of payment for their trouble. If they did not want cash itself, then they still wanted to take advantage of the opportunities that Mayhew provided for them to advertise themselves and their wares. It will also be argued, in conclusion, that attempts to claim that Mayhew was either a radical or else a supporter of established views fail to notice that what is crucial about his writings is the continual tension between these two positions. This is recognised by Anne Humpherys, who suggests that Mayhew the rebel and Mayhew the gentleman are in constant dialogue with each other.[6] She thus identifies, without quite putting it in these terms, another of the essentially theatrical performances that takes place throughout *London Labour and the London Poor*.

The way in which the kind of questions posed by many historians about Mayhew's accuracy miss what seems to me to be the distinctive feature of his writing can be seen from the discussion of an interview that he did with a returned convict in a lodging-house. A historian, F. B. Smith, played the detective and searched the Australian archives to see how truthful this convict was in his interview with Mayhew.

The archives revealed that this old lag, one David Evans, exaggerated and heightened certain details about his life and also told downright lies about other ones. They revealed, more generally, that he was self-consciously staging a performance.[7] To take just one example, Evans spends the last part of an interview (in which the underworld cant often has to be translated by Mayhew) describing how he was tough enough to take and survive a series of brutal floggings:

> In all I had 875 lashes at my different punishments. I used to boast of it at last. I would say, 'I don't care, I can take it till they see my backbone'. After a flogging, I've rubbed my back against a wall, just to show my bravery like, and squeezed the congealed blood out of it. (3, 388)

Smith can show that Evans probably took no more than three hundred lashes during his whole time as a convict.

A costermonger told Mayhew how he placed small oranges in boiling water so that they would swell to a more attractive size. The street-biographies, rather than being judged simply in terms of their factual accuracy, need to be seen as being produced by the equivalent of boiling water. Evans himself at one point claims to have been a member of the swell-mob, dressing himself up as a gentleman so that he can pass off forged banknotes at respectable shops. This was known as doing 'a little soft' (3, 386). He uses the interview, manipulating it as much as Mayhew may be manipulating him, to swell his bravery and to boast about his 'I can take it' contempt for authority. He has backbone. Perhaps Mayhew the gentleman becomes Mayhew the rebel in recording this particular story.

Mayhew himself must of course take some of the blame for the way in which some historians continue to debate the accuracy of his work in such literal terms. He claims at the very beginning of his investigations that his survey of the London poor will provide 'a literal description of their labour, their earnings, their trials, and their sufferings, in their own "unvarnished" language' (1, xv). He vouches for the accuracy and authenticity of his work both in this general preamble to it, as well as in many of the conclusions to the individual interviews themselves, including his comments on Evans. It is as true as the fact that he had a pen in his very hand, and true because this pen allegedly allows him to make literal transcriptions of the voices of the people. Yet Smith's research, fascinating as it is, is not so much the revelation that it purports to be but merely the confirmation of what readers or spectators can hear for themselves from the dramatic script. It is reasonably clear from the text itself, without any archival context, that this old bird, famous for five minutes, is using the platform provided by Mayhew to stage himself as he wants to appear to be. He is not alone in this: other male contenders for the mantle of working-class hero include the sewer-hunters and the character who tells Mayhew how he went into the rat-pit for a lark and killed eight rats with his own bare teeth – or perhaps it was really with his bare cheek.[8] Mayhew, at times knowingly, records fancy as well as fact. He allows the poor to tell him their hopes and dreams, fears and fantasies.

Mayhew was not in a position to go to Australia to check a single story and, more generally, was frequently presented with local stories that were impossible to verify. Some historians have taken what is often a rhetoric about documentary accuracy much too literally. Mayhew interviewed cab-drivers just before he listened to David Evans's tall stories. He meets an old hackney-coachman who had apparently heard the chimes at, and indeed well after, midnight. The Prince of Wales, no less, took over his cab one night forcing him to be a passenger. He also just happened to be the cabbie who

> used to drive Lord Barrymore on his rounds to the brothels – twice or thrice a-week sometimes. He always used to take his own wine with him. After waiting till near daylight, or till daylight, I've carried my lord, girls and all – fine dressed-up madams – to Billingsgate, and there I've left them to breakfast at some queer place, or to slang with the fishwives. (3, 350)

Perhaps Mayhew really did stumble across a character who had this intimate knowledge of the rambles and sprees of the Regency rakes through the underworld.[9] Alternatively, he may just have interviewed an obscure old party who nostalgically, and perhaps rather sadly, appropriated to himself all the stories that circulated amongst this fraternity as a whole. If so, then this interview was yet another platform on which interviewees were allowed to act out their fantasies. Mayhew the rebel recorded such fancies, even though Mayhew the professional gentleman was of course only interested in hard facts that could be verified. A large number of his interviewees claimed to have seen better days, although some were very reluctant indeed to be cross-questioned any further about them.

Mayhew's street-biographies were assembled in a number of different ways. They were, occasionally, based on unsolicited letters that he received. In the main, however, they were based on face-to-face indivi-dual interviews, although group interviews were also employed. These were sometimes impromptu, such as the times when he discovered roomfuls of coal-whippers and ballast-heavers, and quickly started to take statements. Yet most of his meetings such as those with street-sellers, thieves and swell-mobsmen were advertised in advance and followed a planned dramatic script. At some point during the proceedings indivi-duals were invited up on to the platform to give improvised performances, as happened at the meeting of the ticket-of-leave men that was held at the National Hall in Holborn.

Mayhew himself gave a long, introductory speech in which he detailed some of the ways in which such characters were harassed by the police. After 'loud and prolonged applause' (3, 433), individuals were then invited up to the platform or stage to testify. The first to perform was 'Peter' who, like David Evans, told the story of his transportation. After detailing the way in which he had been prevented from educating himself while he was a convict, he turned to the related problems of trying to go straight on his return. He may, or may not, have been telling the truth about his life of crime. It seems that he was mainly concerned to stage a convincing theatrical performance for his audience. He dramatises, in Jack-the-lad style, his arrival at Southampton:

> On my release I received £6. I came to Southampton with one of the officers of the establishment, who was kind enough to ask me to take a drop of brandy. Not having had any spirits for four years previous, this little got into my head, and having drank another glass or two I was intoxicated, and I spent all my money that night – yes, and got locked up into the bargain. (Laughter). (3, 434)

The speech is obviously designed not just to win Mayhew's approval, but also to provoke applause and laughter amongst the spectators in the hall. 'Peter' is another character who prides himself on being able to take 'it', if not his liquor. Six other ticket-of-leave men then performed their stories, most of which continued to blame the police and magistrates for victimising them. Henry Vizetelly, who later accompanied Mayhew during his investigations of the prison system, recalled how attendance at such meetings was secured 'with the promise of a supper, or its equivalent'.[10]

Mayhew often edited the street-biographies in such a way that they appeared to be relatively private meetings between the journalist with the pen in his hand and the interviewee. This gives the impression that they had very little in common with the platform performances that were such an integral part of the group meetings. It seems likely, however, that Evans was self-consciously playing to a gallery consisting of some of the other inmates of the lodging-house when he told Mayhew his tall stories. The presence of an audience needs to be assumed, even when the text itself suppresses information about it. Although part of Mayhew's own performance was to cultivate the image of himself as a lone traveller and explorer in a strange country, he was in fact quite often accompanied by guides, informants and stenographers. H. Sutherland Edwards claimed that when Mayhew was at the height of his popularity working for the *Morning Chronicle* he 'had an army of assistant writers, stenographers, and hansom cabmen constantly at his call'.[11] Although this high level of support was not available to him after he had left this paper, apparently as a result of his criticisms of Political Economy, it would still be a mistake to accept without question his self-image as a lone traveller or explorer. He was not, however, as dependent as were women social explorers such as Flora Tristan on the services of guides.[12]

Mayhew's interviews in the workplace sometimes took place in front of other employees. Many of his home visits involved him in interviewing an individual in the presence of his or her family. His arrival in certain areas of London often caused a crowd to gather: 'As I dived into the court, a crowd followed me to see whither I was going' (1, 153). There were probably many occasions when such a crowd stayed together to watch the show. It was, perhaps, only when Mayhew was cruising the streets and casually encountered particular individuals that the interview was on something approaching a one-to-one basis. This is not to imply that such interviews, conducted 'on the blob' in street-slang, were devoid of theatricality and performance (John D. Rosenberg rightly suggests that all the street-biographies need to be seen as being dramatic monologues in prose: 1, vii). It is, rather, to indicate that it is more accurate to see Mayhew's interviews as being public performances rather than more private confessionals.

It appears at first that Mayhew is the only person present when a young pickpocket is interviewed. It is only after the interview has been concluded that the audience for it make an appearance on the stage. Mayhew invites the pickpocket to 'flare', or steal, a handkerchief from his own pocket. The boy is then given more opportunities to perform his skills:

> To see him pick the pockets, as he did, of some of the gentlemen present on the occasion, was a curious sight. He crept behind much like a cat with his claws out, and while in the act held his breath with suspense; but immediately the handkerchief was safe in his hand, the change in the expression of his countenance was most marked. (1, 412)

The pickpocket is clearly self-consciously staging a performance for an audience of gentlemen here, and perhaps getting paid for it. Yet, although the evidence is initially suppressed, this is what he has been doing from the start of the interview.

A SHILLING MAN

Just as Mayhew the gentleman is often reticent about the presence of spectators at both curious and ordinary sights, so he is sometimes very coy about how much individual interviewees were paid to perform on the platforms that he provided for them. He is more open about financial transactions and rates of exchange in relation to the group meetings. He concludes the meeting with the ticket-of-leave men with an offer of financial help:

> In the meantime, if I can assist any of you with the loan of a few shillings – but, mind you, come to me gently, and not thick and fast – I will do what I can to help you. (Hear, hear.) I am a person who work [sic] myself for all I get, and remember I call myself a "shilling man", and not one of your 'sovereign people.' (Laughter). (3, 439)

As there were fifty ticket-of-leave men at this meeting, Mayhew probably had to spend some time dispensing loans. Perhaps those who had actually performed on the platform felt that they were entitled to more money than those who had not. At the end of the meeting of thieves, Mayhew offers to pay for a night's lodging for those who were unable to afford it.

Although Mayhew often represses information about how he exchanged cash and commodities for performances, there are still enough often chance and seemingly marginal remarks left in the street-biographies for this process of exchange and mart to be reconstructed. It seems very likely that many of his interviews with the costermongers, particularly those 'on the blob', were preceded by a purchase or the promise of a purchase. He buys some walnuts from a barrow-boy who tells him about street-slang. He is asked, at the end of this short interview, whether he wants to buy any more. Other interviewees offer to let him taste the food they are either preparing, such as soup, or else selling, such as muffins. He offers to provide a hot dinner for a watercress girl, which she refuses because she eats meat on Sundays only. This dinner is remarked upon only because it was refused, suggesting the existence of ones that were accepted but left unrecorded. The dinner that was provided prior to a group interview for all the residents of a lodging-house, together with some hangers-on who had got wind of it, is recorded. A hawker of spoons eventually persuades Mayhew the gentleman to buy him a small glass of rum to wet his whistle before the interview begins.

A number of interviewees are ever so anxious to provide services for Mayhew. A street-sweeper offers to run errands for him. Another sweeper, who had formerly been a servant, insists on brushing his clothes during the course of the interview:

> Once or twice whilst I was listening to his statement he insisted upon removing some dirt from my shoulder, and, on leaving, he by force seized my hat and brushed it – all which habits of attention he had contracted whilst in service. (2, 475)

This sweeper was obviously expecting Mayhew, like his other customers, to tip him. When this does not happen, he drops a very heavy hint by ostentatiously performing yet another service for this apparent gentleman who is not behaving like one. Many of the other interviews contain hints to Mayhew that some form of payment was expected. A seller of periodicals just happens by complete coincidence to remember a gentleman who never bought anything, but always gave him a penny for his trouble. A street-orderly with a deadpan sense of humour recalls that he very occasionally got 'the price of a pint of beer given to me by gentlemen making inquiries' (2, 263). A woman crossing-sweeper did not have to work nearly so hard to get paid for her performance. Mayhew, the shilling man, gives her 'a small piece of silver for her trouble' (2, 480). Women often played up their deference, whereas some men felt the need to exaggerate their heroism. An unemployed fire-eater let it be known that he would be happy to be interviewed by Mayhew 'for a consideration' (3, 113). He claims that he has not eaten – food, that is – for two days which was probably more truthful than his boast that he too had been in the rat-pit and killed twenty of them for a wager.

One of the reasons why Mayhew is often silent about how he purchases performances is because he himself is playing the part of an eminently respectable gentleman. As has been seen, he offers the ticket-of-leave men loans rather than cash-in-hand so that nobody could accuse him of corrupting and debauching the poor with easy, sleazy money. His loans were usually not interest-free, although his 5 per cent rate was considerably lower than that charged by professional money-lenders. His interviews for the *Morning Chronicle* had provoked readers to send in donations for what were seen as being deserving cases. The fund at one time stood at over eight hundred and fifty pounds. *London Labour and the London Poor* was not nearly so successful in flaring the pockets of its readers. The fund only reached thirty pounds which was spent as follows: '£4.10s of which have been dispensed as gifts, and £24.10s advanced as loans to 19 people, to be repaid, with interest, at the rate of 5 per cent per annum'.[13]

Those who were interviewed by Mayhew had the chance not just of telling tall stories or dramatising their deference, but also of improving their financial position. A standing patterer, who claimed to be the son of a clergyman and cried throughout his interview, was loaned the money to start up in the cloth-cap trade. A seller of cotton and tape was provided with money to replenish her stock, and had her husband's funeral paid for by Mayhew's readers or spectators. A blind harp-player, who claimed that his life was made a misery by naughty street-urchins, also received money.

The platform provided by the interview was often used for detailed and specific requests for assistance, which may have been premeditated ones. A bird's nest seller knew exactly what he wanted to get out of Mayhew and his readers: 'I could get a goodish rigout in the lane for a few shillings.

A pair of boots would cost me 2s, and a coat I could get for 2s 6d'. The 'lane' is Petticoat Lane. Mayhew the respectable gentleman did not acquiesce immediately to this demand. He tested the boy's character by getting him a job running errands for a week. If he was artful and dodgy, then he would steal some of the goods that were entrusted to him. Although merely a 'shilling man', Mayhew's theatrical party-trick was to give convicted thieves a sovereign to change for him to see if they did a runner with it. According to him, they never did. After the bird's nest seller had proved that he could take it and not steal it, Mayhew bought him 'a suit of clothes' and loaned him 'sufficient money to start him in some of the better kind of street-trades' (2, 77). A mudlark did even better out of his encounter with Mayhew. He came to Mayhew's house wearing neither a shirt nor shoes and was given two shillings 'for his trouble'. He and his sister immediately put this money to good use, buying sprats with it to sell in the streets. A friend of Mayhew's found the boy a job at an 'eminent printer's'. He graduated from here to earn nine shillings a week 'at one of the daily newspaper offices' (2, 158).[14] An interview with Henry Mayhew held out the promise of long-term, as well as short-term, material gains for those members of the deserving poor who also had the right theatrical patter.

Interviewees usually knowingly and cleverly made their pitch towards the end of the interview, after they had provided Mayhew with the information that he wanted. The wife of a chickweed-seller shows him the pawnbroker's tickets and claims that 'warm clothing would be the greatest blessing I could ask': the pitch had to be modest and yet it also had to hover on the verge of assertiveness. Mayhew's readers provided the money for this family to move to 'a more comfortable home' and to redeem their clothes from pawn (1, 155). A nutmeg-seller is one of the many characters who uses the interview not just to make out a general case for membership of the deserving poor, but also to put a particular and probably premeditated proposition to Mayhew at the end of the interview:

> With a couple of pounds I could, I think, manage to shift very well for myself. I'd get a stock, and go into the country with a barrow, and buy old metal, and exchange tin ware for old clothes, and, with that, I'm almost sure I could get a decent living. I'm accounted a very good dealer. (1, 332)

Mayhew assures his audience that this man has good character references.

Despite Mayhew's own reticence on the subject, it is reasonably clear that many of his interviewees were very canny wheelers and dealers who regarded their information as a commodity which had to be purchased either directly through cash-in-hand, or else through some of the more indirect methods already described. They had the knowledge and Mayhew wanted it. Some interviewees did not want Mayhew's money so much as his seal of approval. A blind street-seller of needles ended his interview with a request for Mayhew to write him a reference:

> If I could only get some friend to give me a letter of recommendation to Mr Day's Charity for the Blind, I should be happy for the rest of my days. I could give the best of references to any one who would take pity on me in my affliction. (1, 344)

One of the most frequent requests made to Mayhew was to sponsor particular individuals for emigration. If interviewees did not want his shiny shilling, they were usually after something else.

THE SHOP-WINDOW

Mayhew only actually names his subjects when they are already street-celebrities such as Jack Black, the rat-catcher, and Edward Albert, 'the negro crossing-sweeper, who had lost both his legs' (2, 490). Yet his physical descriptions of his interviewees, together with the often very precise information about where they might be found trading, probably made it relatively easy for readers or spectators to identify them. The street-biographies often begin by pinpointing a location or pitch: 'I now give an account of the street-trade, the feelings, and the life of a poor blind woman, who may be seen nearly every fine day, selling what is technically termed "small-ware", in Leatherlane, Holborn' (1, 393). Those interviewees who were selected to have engravings done of them must have been particularly easy to spot.[15] A rhubarb and spice-seller, who had his portrait included, was furnished with a glowing testimonial by Mayhew: 'The old man appears to sell excellent articles, and to be a very truthful, fair-dealing man' (1, 455). The street-traders had a number of grievances: they were continually being moved-on, and moved off the pavements into the streets by the police and so did not have the same opportunities for advertising themselves and their wares as did the shopkeepers. An interview with Henry Mayhew could become their shop-window.

Such exposure was welcomed by honest traders and, although no evidence exists, it is not inconceivable to imagine that some of them might have tried to pay Mayhew in cash or goods to include them in what is, at one level, an important trade gazette. Exposure was not so welcome for some of those who worked on the shady side of the street. A cough-drop seller and a seller of supposedly indecent literature were both reluctant to answer too many of Mayhew's questions because they were obviously very shifty rip-off merchants. The character whose dodge was to collect old tea-leaves, so that they could be treated and sold again as new, insisted that the interview contained nothing that could be used to identify him and thus used in evidence against him. Goose Gander, one of the leaders of the tumbling boys, refused to declare how much he earned a week. Like some other interviewees, he knowingly underestimates his income in the hope of attracting a gift, but also perhaps so that he does not get his grubby collar felt too many times by policemen who might have been reading Mayhew's work.

Although there were certainly some individuals who did not want their activities spotlighted by Mayhew, others were more than happy enough to boast about how they were 'fly to a dodge' in much the same manner as David Evans boasted about his floggings. Many of the tricks that were described were, however, old-fashioned ones that did not work, or 'friz', anymore, because too many people were 'wide-awake' to them. Mayhew finds out, amongst other things, how Scotch haddock and Irish linen are got up from inferior articles. He sometimes shows not just what is on the barrow, but also the sleights of hand that are used to create it behind the scenes.

A coster girl whose picture had already been engraved refused to do an interview with Mayhew 'some dozen times' because, according to him, 'she was afraid to give the slightest information about the habits of her companions, lest they should recognise her by the engraving and per- secute her for the revelations she might make' (1, 45). If true, this indicates that the eighteen-page instalments of *London Labour and the London Poor*, priced at two pence, had a readership among the classes surveyed as well as amongst those who were surveying them. Other evidence supports such a conclusion.[16] This means amongst other things that even those traders who operated at the lower end of the market might stand to benefit from the advertisements provided by Mayhew.

Some of Mayhew's interviewees used the exposure given to them not so much to sell their particular wares or services, as to establish their good character. They self-consciously employ Mayhew to write an open reference, or testimonial, for them. The insufferable 'Billy', a cross- ing-sweeper who works in an aristocratic neighbourhood, dictates a long list of the gifts that he has received from his patrons: 'I should like you to mention Lady Mildmay in Grosvenor-square, sir. Whenever I goes to see her . . . I am safe for 5s and at Christmas I have my regular salary, a guinea' (2, 469). Mayhew's detractors sometimes question the accuracy and authenticity of his interviews by drawing attention to his use of leading questions and other strategies that reveal his superiority. Another way of reading the street-biographies is to emphasise how Mayhew himself is often manipulated by characters, who clearly have an eye to the main chance. It is not just the standing patterers, who see Mayhew as a fellow writer, who are actually capable of dictating very precisely what he should include in the published interview.

ANSWERING A GOOD MANY QUESTIONS

Mayhew's stage, like the streets, is crowded with hundreds of characters jostling for space and a hearing. Some performers, often women, were certainly very subdued and ever so humble. The coster girl whom Mayhew gets as a last-minute replacement curtseyed 'to every question that was put to her' (1, 45), as did a girl crossing-sweeper. This was how female members of the serving classes were expected to behave towards a gentleman, although there is still a sense that such deference might have been overplayed in these meetings. One of the 'catch-'em-alive' sellers (who sold fly-papers) is described as being 'as nervous as if in a witness-box' (3, 30) just before his interview. Other interviewees, however, were by turns garrulous, dogged, bad-tempered and forthright. Mayhew has to change his line of questioning to prevent a regular scavenger from losing his temper. A fruit-seller, who was initially reluctant to be interviewed, simply ignores Mayhew's questions. She has a pitch to make and makes it.

Mayhew, the professional gentleman, suggests that the street-folk are a wandering tribe of primitives and outcasts who are untouched by society. Yet the interviews themselves often tell a very different story. Many of Mayhew's characters are not the untouchables who have been totally ignored by society but, rather, professional interviewees. As suggested, they are often very sharp, or 'fly', when it comes to knowing when to make their pitch. The two orphaned flower-girls insist on demonstrating that they can read, knowing that this will enhance their charitable status. Himmelfarb is wrong to claim that Mayhew's poor had already been extensively surveyed by royal and select committees.[17] These inquiries tended to concentrate on the moral risks in industrialised workplaces for those such as women and children, who were deemed to require protection because of their alleged diminished responsibility. Yet Mayhew's poor were nevertheless interviewed from cradle to grave, not so much by such government committees, but rather by policemen, magistrates, poor-law guardians, mendicity officers, missionaries and the like. A whelk-seller recalls having to explain to a passing 'missionary cove' (1, 164) that it was not murder to boil whelks while they were still alive. On the streets your business is everybody else's business. Mayhew himself played or performed the part of the 'missionary cove' at times, and yet he also provided the theatrical space for such a performance to be questioned.

When conducting interviews at the Asylum for the Houseless Poor, he notices a certain glibness in the answers he receives. This was probably because some of his questions were hardly new to those who were continually called upon to explain their lives to Victorian petty official-dom.

Mayhew's poor, perhaps swelling the orange, often boast about how they come out on top during their frequent encounters with officialdom. A shorthand card-seller upstages the prison chaplain during one of the weekly interviewing sessions. A cake and tart-seller plays the wide-boy, doing all the voices, in front of the Lord Mayor. There was apparently absolutely no nervousness at all in the witness-box on this particular occasion:

> The first time I was up before the Lord Mayor – it's a few years back – I thought he talked like an old wife. 'You mustn't stand that way', he says, 'and you mustn't do this and mustn't do that'. 'Well, my lord', says I, 'then I mustn't live honestly. But if you'll give me 9s a week, I'll promise not to stand here, and not to stand there; and neither to do this, nor that, nor anything at all, if that pleases you better'. They was shocked, they said, at my impudence – so young a fellow, too!' (1, 199)

The charges were apparently dropped. Impudence was one dodge, abjection or subjection was another one. Performing well during an interview or interrogation could, quite literally, be the difference between life and death on the London streets. A street-seller of dogs' collars, who had previously been a sailor, tells Mayhew how he was interviewed at Somerset House by an admiral in order to get his safe berth at Greenwich Hospital:

> and arter telling the admiral my service, and answering a good many questions as he put to me, the admiral says, says he, 'The order will be made; you shall go into the house'. I think the admiral knowed me or something about me, you see. (1, 360)

He cried during his interview with Mayhew and perhaps did the same at Somerset House.

THE RESPECTABLE REBEL

Mayhew provided a platform on which individuals, many of whom had considerable experience of being interviewed, exaggerated their lives, made out cases as to why they deserved to be given money and often shamelessly advertised themselves and their wares. They were not, however, the only performers on this platform. Mayhew developed a detached, scientific rhetoric to distance himself from his subjects and yet he shared their delight in performance and theatricality. Perhaps the anthropologist who explored darkest England was just another of the parts that he played. He enquires early on in his investigations about the possibility of attending one of the costermongers' raffles:

> 'If you was to go to the raffle to-night, sir', said one of them to me, many months ago, before I became known to the class, 'they'd say to one another directly you come in, "Who's this here swell? What's he want?" And they'd think you were a "cad", or else a spy, come from the police. But they'd treat you civilly, I'm sure. Some very likely would fancy you was a fast kind of gentleman, come there for a lark. But you need have no fear, though the pint pots *does* fly about sometimes.' (1, 58)

Mayhew, like other underworld journalists, was indeed later mistaken for a police spy, when trying to conduct interviews at a lodging-house.[18] He was also mistaken for other figures of authority such as a ragged school teacher, a collector of dog-tax and the landlord of a derelict building. This is not surprising as he was usually dressed (or 'square-rigged', in street slang) like a gentleman. His costume included a frock-coat, waistcoat and wing-collar. Yet, as Jonathan Raban points out, Mayhew's gentlemanly appearance was 'an artfully stage-managed posture'.[19] He may have had street credibility as a gentleman because he dressed like one (almost to the point of caricature) and also went to some places where gentlemen were seldom seen. The costume nevertheless disguised the fact that he too was usually chronically short of money and was himself a street-trader of sorts. He found stories, sometimes having to pay for them, and then sold them. He had been bankrupt like many of his subjects and, despite the scientific rhetoric and all the impressive-looking statistics, he too was a wanderer of the city streets, a buyer and seller of the stories to be found there.

Mayhew wanted to be taken for a professional gentleman, and so would have been shocked to be seen as just another swell or 'fast kind of gentleman, come there for a lark'. Yet the fast gentleman was another of the parts that he was able to play on the stage provided by *London Labour and the London Poor*. He clearly enjoyed it when interviewees flattered him by recognising that he too was 'fly', wide-awake to every move on the board. He may have fulminated about the immorality of the penny gaffs, but he still visited one and what is more provided his readers with detailed instructions about how to get there. His interest in the sleeping arrangements at common lodging-houses bordered on the obsessive. He also went to the rat-pit, although he had to content himself with watching dogs rather than men doing the killing. The fast gentleman felt attracted towards parts of the underworld that the professional gentleman had to find repulsive.

It has been argued that, instead of getting trapped into debates about the factual accuracy of Mayhew's journalistic street-biographies, they should be seen as performances. These performances were usually first staged in front of an audience, before they were staged again in front of Mayhew's readers. Some interviewees told complete lies, some exaggerated or swelled the orange, whereas others told the truth. Some were paid either directly or indirectly for their performances, others were not. Mayhew himself performs the part of the professional gentleman and, more furtively, that of the fast gentleman or swell. The rebel is another part in his repertoire. To make such points is not to devalue, or be cynical, about *London Labour and the London Poor*. It is, rather, to recognise what is both distinctive and exciting about it: namely that it is primarily a dramatic or theatrical text.

Mayhew and his work faded surprisingly quickly into the very obscurity from which he had rescued many of his interviewees. Although later underworld writers such as George R. Sims were clearly aware of *London Labour and the London Poor*, Mayhew's own decline and fall appears to have been something of an embarrassment to them.[20] It is difficult therefore to make a strong case that Mayhew was a major influence on the 'new journalists' of the 1880s, especially given the fact that they looked to America as well as to Britain for their inspiration, particularly in the campaigns against specific institutions. What can be said, however, is that thirty years earlier he anticipated and pioneered most of their so-called innovations. He may not have invented the journalistic interview, but he was the first person to use it on such a scale. Although it is certainly possible to suggest such connections, it might still be better to see *London Labour and the London Poor* as representing a turning point about which journalism did not turn. This is partly because of the sheer size of the project, which ultimately defeated even Mayhew. *London Labour and the London Poor* may also stand alone in its commitment to the ordinary and everyday. Mayhew did not conduct celebrity interviews, which were a feature of both American and British 'new journalism', and made relatively little use of expert witnesses in his later work. He was a fast gentleman who was no stranger to the criminal and sexual underworlds that were later to attract as well as to repel W. T. Stead. Yet his real strength lay in his ability to provide a platform on which those who led quite mundane lives, often far removed from the dangerous delights of the underworld, could also perform.

This might seem a perverse conclusion to reach about a text which talks about its characters as if they were a race apart, indulging in strange customs and unspeakable rites. More specifically, Mayhew's poor can appear to be either objects in a cabinet of grotesque curiosities, or else exhibits who have escaped from a freakish peep-show at a circus. Yet his overarching scientific theories about different races are often called into question as character after character comes up on to the stage to perform an everyday story about trying to make ends meet. This basic story is often in danger of becoming mundane and thus losing its journalistic appeal. What usually prevents this from happening is that poverty is not just related in a matter-of-fact way, it is performed. The basic facts may be similar and yet, in performance, they become individualised. *London Labour and the London Poor*, initially published as indicated in instalments, is an open-ended Victorian soap-opera. It creates the illusion of gritty, and at times very dirty, documentary realism and yet is primarily a highly theatrical text.

Mayhew, himself a performer, had the ability to draw out performances from others. He may have huffed and puffed about how all the facts that were given to him were scrupulously verified, even though what he really relished was the theatricality of many of his interviewees. David Evans probably only received three hundred lashes, so at one level Mayhew's accuracy is called into question. He is accurate, however, at a much more important and profound level because he reveals, and revels in, the heightened theatricality of the stage-play world of Victorian metropolitan life.

NOTES

1. Henry Mayhew, *London Labour and the London Poor*, ed. John D. Rosenberg, 4 vols (Dover Publications: New York, 1968), Vol. 1, 340. All subsequent in-text references – volume number followed by page references – are from this edition, a reprint of the 1861–2 edition (itself drawing on an earlier edition of 1851–2). Mayhew acknowledges two collaborators, and probably also received help from one brother: I follow others in attributing authorship to Mayhew throughout – a very convenient fiction. I take no examples from the fourth volume, however, because none of the interviews here were conducted by Mayhew himself. The full text runs to just under two thousand densely packed pages. The easiest way to overcome the very real problems caused by length would have been to have followed some other commentators and looked in detail at only two or three of the street-biographies. My argument concentrates, however, on the centrality of apparently marginal details about performance and payment, and so gives more of a sense of the range of Mayhew's work. My examples privilege mostly Mayhew's male characters. For a feminist reading see Carolyn Steedman, 'The Watercress Seller', in her *Past Tenses: Essays on Writing, Autobiography and History* (Rivers Oram Press: London, 1992), 193–202. I acknowledge my debt to conversations about Mayhew with Kate Campbell, Patricia Hollis, Emma Padfield, Lorna Sage and Geoffrey Searle.

2. See their introductions to E. P. Thompson and Eileen Yeo (eds), *The Unknown Mayhew: Selections from the* Morning Chronicle *1849–50* (Pen-

guin: Harmondsworth, 1973), 9–55 and 56–109. See Volume 3 of *London Labour and the London Poor* for material from the *Morning Chronicle* investigations.

3. David Englander, 'Comparisons and Contrasts: Henry Mayhew and Charles Booth as Social Investigators', in David Englander and Rosemary O'Day (eds), *Retrieved Riches: Social Investigation in Britain 1840–1914* (Scolar Press: Aldershot, 1995), 105–42. This chapter summarises the historiographical debate about Mayhew, 105–7.

4. Gertrude Himmelfarb, *The Idea of Poverty: England in the Early Industrial Age* (Faber & Faber: London, 1985), 313, on Mayhew as journalist (in part repeating earlier criticisms of Mayhew's work: see, for example, 'Distressed Populations: A Warning and a Doubt', the *Economist*, 16 Nov. 1850, 1264–5). For a much more positive view see George Woodcock, 'Henry Mayhew and the Undiscovered Country of the Poor', *Sewanee Review*, 92 (1984), 556–73.

5. Three essays in Joel H. Wiener (ed.), *Papers for the Millions: The New Journalism in Britain, 1850s to 1914* (Greenwood Press: New York, 1988) address the origins of 'new journalism'. For Stead as an underworld journalist see Judith R. Walkowitz, *City of Dreadful Delight: Narratives of Sexual Danger in Late-Victorian London* (Virago: London, 1992), chapters 3 and 4. For underworld writings more generally see Peter Keating's *Into Unknown England 1866–1913: Selections from the Social Explorers* (Fontana: London, 1976).

6. Anne Humpherys, *Travels into the Poor Man's Country: The Work of Henry Mayhew* (Caliban Books: Firle (Sussex) 1977), 11. This remains the best study of Mayhew; see also Humpherys's shorter *Henry Mayhew* (Twayne Publishers: Boston, 1984) and studies of Mayhew's contemporaries in 'G. W. M. Reynolds: Popular Literature and Popular Politics', Joel H. Wiener (ed), *Innovators and Preachers: The Role of the Editor in Victorian England* (Greenwood Press: London, 1985), 1–21, and 'Popular Narrative and Political Discourse in Reynolds's Weekly Newspaper'; Laurel Brake, Aled Jones, Lionel Madden (eds), *Investigating Victorian Journalism* (Macmillan: Basingstoke, 1990), 33–47.

7. F. B. Smith, 'Mayhew's Convict', *Victorian Studies*, 22 (1979), 431–48.

8. For Mayhew's treatment of rats and rat-catchers see Christopher Herbert, 'Rat Worship and Taboo in Mayhew's London', *Representations*, 23 (1988), 1–24. On Mayhew's obsessions with dirt see Peter Stallybrass and Allon White, *The Politics and Poetics of Transgression* (Methuen: London, 1986), 128–33.

9. On the Regency underworld see my 'Pierce Egan and the Representation of London', in Philip W. Martin and Robin Jarvis (eds), *Reviewing Romanticism* (Macmillan: Basingstoke, 1992), 154–69. Mayhew shows that the fast gentlemen were still larking about in the 1850s: *London Labour*, Vol. I, 170, 178, 181 and 417. See also Donald A. Low, *Thieves' Kitchen: The Regency Underworld* (Allan Sutton: Gloucester, 1987).

10. Henry Vizetelly, *Glances back through Seventy Years*, 2 vols (Kegan Paul et al.: London, 1893), Vol. 1, 406–7.

11. H. Sutherland Edwards, *Personal Recollections* (Cassell & Co: London, 1900), 60.

12. See Flora Tristan, *The London Journal of Flora Tristan 1842*, tr. Jean Hawkes (Virago: London, 1982), 47–8, 59, 83–5, 142 and 156. On Tristan see chapter 4 of Deborah Epstein Nord, *Walking the Victorian Streets: Women, Representation and the City* (Cornell UP: Ithaca, 1995).

13. As quoted in Humpherys, *Travels*, 69.

14. Mayhew states here that he gave the mudlark two shillings. Earlier on, however, he remembers it as being only one shilling (1, 70).

15. It was not just the portrait itself that may have changed interviewees' lives. At least one of them, Old Sarah, the blind hurdy-gurdy player, rode in a cab for the first time on the way to have her engraving done (3, 159).

16. Some street-biographies that came to Mayhew in the form of letters were prompted by the reading of *London Labour and the London Poor*. A gingerbread-seller was familiar with Mayhew's earlier work on street cries (1, 200). A street-poet claimed Mayhew's revelations were hotly debated amongst this fraternity (1, 273). Mayhew sometimes read out a previous interview, perhaps as a way of relaxing his current interviewee. The inmates of the lodging-house where he laid on the dinner were apparently delighted at finding themselves in print when he read out an earlier interview with them.

17. Himmelfarb, *The Idea of Poverty*, 356.

18. Mayhew reveals that the police often adopted theatrical disguises: a street-seller tells him, 'if the police detectives is after anythink, they go as hawkers, or barrowmen, or somethink that way' (2, 105).

19. Jonathan Raban, 'The Invisible Mayhew: London Secrecies', *Encounter*, 41 (Aug. 1973), 64–70, 64; also, his *Soft City* (Hamish Hamilton: London, 1974), 124–5 and 87–91. Mayhew rejected his professional, upper middle-class family background for the hand-to-mouth existence of a bohemian journalist and writer.

20. For more details see George R. Sims, *My Life: Sixty Years' Recollections of Bohemian London* (Everleigh Nash: London, 1917), 33–4.

4

HYBRID JOURNALISM: WOMEN AND THE PROGRESSIVE *FORTNIGHTLY*

MARK W. TURNER

The 1860s was a decade of far-reaching change for middle-class periodical culture and for journalism generally in Britain. The last of the taxes on knowledge was repealed in 1861 and the number of daily and weekly newspapers and weekly and monthly periodicals was increasing dramatically. The shilling monthlies, proliferating in the early 1860s on the crest of the *Cornhill*'s success, sought to develop a new market providing serial fiction, poetry, miscellaneous articles, and wood-block illustrations suitable for the middle-class drawing room. New methods of marketing were being devised to take advantage of the expanding print culture, as a full-page advertisement (designed to look like newspaper copy) for *Good Words* in 1863 in *The Times* indicates. The advertisement was expensive at £130, and it was noted by the *Publishers' Circular* to be 'a new feature in the advertising of our popular periodical literature'.[1] Authors and literary personalities, partly due to Dickens's huge popularity, were beginning to be promoted widely as anonymity was undercut in numerous ways – through advertisements, literary gossip columns, trade journals and so on. Here we see what would develop into a recognisably modern journalism over the following two decades.

The *Fortnightly Review* was in the vanguard of change in the 1860s.[2] Avowed as an experiment, it attempted to create yet another middle-class reading market, one that would accept serious articles on politics alongside serial, circulating-library fiction. It was an attempt to combine the higher journalism of the quarterly reviews with the popular appeal of the new shilling monthlies; the *Fortnightly*, however, cost twice as much and came out twice as often as a magazine like the *Cornhill*. In this chapter, I want to explore the cultural formation of the *Fortnightly Review* and consider the innovation and radicalism of the periodical under its first editor, G. H. Lewes. For a progressive periodical launched at a moment of increasing calls for extending women's rights, there is a remarkable absence of women in the periodical, which I link in part to the Positivist social configuration associated with it. In a magazine claiming a radical stance, the non-fiction almost never addresses women or women's reform issues directly: the inaugural serial novel by Anthony Trollope, *The Belton Estate*, seems to be the most significant and sustained bid for women readers. Under Lewes's editorship (May 1865–November 1866), we can see not only the difficulties in forging a hybrid journalism in an increasingly competitive market, but also the importance of gender in understanding both the magazine's identity and marketability.

RADICAL JOURNALISM?

In May 1865 Trollope's *Belton Estate* launched the experimental *Fortnightly Review*. Founded by a collective of proprietors including Trollope, the periodical signalled its progressivism formally and politically through frequency, signature and non-partisanship. Modelled on the French *Revue des Deux Mondes*, the *Fortnightly* broke with tradition in English periodical culture. The experimental elements, however, were only variously successful. Twenty months after the *Fortnightly* began, it changed its format to the more conventional monthly. Either consumers would not alter their reading habits or distributors would not accommodate the unusual fortnightly pattern.[3]

The policy of signature was discussed in the prospectus:

> we propose to remove all those restrictions of party and of editorial 'consistency' which in other journals hamper the full and free expression of opinion; and we shall ask each writer to express his own views and sentiments with all the force of sincerity. He will never be required to express the views of an Editor or of a Party. He will not be asked to repress opinions or sentiments because they are distasteful to an Editor, or inconsistent with what may have formerly appeared in the Review. He will be asked to say what he really thinks and really feels; to say it on his own responsibility, and to leave its appreciation to the public.[4]

Discussion concerning anonymous journalism was not new. In the 1830s Edward Lytton Bulwer argued for signed journalism in *England and the English* whilst the *New and Monthly Magazine and Literary Journal* asserted that the mysteriousness of anonymity was 'the charm of our periodical literature'.[5] By the 1890s, signature had become widespread, although anonymous articles still appeared. The *Fortnightly*'s decision to include signature was just one moment, however significant, in a century of debate about the question of anonymous journalism.[6] What makes the *Fortnightly*'s decision to sign most interesting is that in the years just before the second Reform Bill, anonymity was linked to debates over the secret ballot, so that the signature policy took on a political dimension advancing the cause of Liberalism.[7]

In addition to the innovations of signature and fortnightly distribution, the magazine's prospectus promised 'the Review will be liberal, and its liberalism so thorough as to include great diversity of individual opinion within its catholic unity of purpose'. Unlike the great quarterlies or even weeklies such as the *Saturday Review*, the *Fortnightly* espoused a move away from party politics, 'to further the cause of Progress by illumination from many minds'. But while the editor G. H. Lewes did wish 'to seek its public amid all parties',[8] one suspects that the much used word 'liberal' in the prospectus ought really to be spelled with a capital 'L'. The experiment of a non-partisan open forum style was never realized in full, as Trollope wryly observed:

> Liberalism, free-thinking, and open inquiry will never object to appear in company with their opposites, because they have the conceit to think that they can quell those opposites; but the opposites will not appear in conjunction with liberalism, free-thinking, and open inquiry. As a natural consequence, our new publication became an organ of liberalism, free-thinking, and open inquiry.[9]

Trollope moved away from the *Fortnightly* and its progressive position after November 1866, when Lewes resigned owing to poor health. The journalistic novelty, then, was limited, if we consider that the fortnightly frequency changed, the open forum was really more of a closed shop, and the signature policy had precedents. What is most innovative about the periodical is its hybridity in combining elements from the traditional quarterlies with the new fiction-led magazines.

THE MALE CONFIGURATION

Trollope, James Cotter Morison, Frederic and Edward Chapman, Frederic Harrison and E. S. Beesly were among the original all-male company of nine who invested £9,000 in founding the *Fortnightly* with G. H. Lewes as editor. The connections between the men are interesting. The Chapmans were cousins and Frederic had recently taken over Chapman and Hall after Edward's retirement. Chapman and Hall had already published seven Trollope novels. Morison was a member of the Positivist Society, well known as a *Saturday Review* contributor, and a friend of fellow Positivists and writers including George Meredith (who also became a *Fortnightly* writer). G. H. Lewes, too, was a Positivist and a well-known journalist who had been friends with Trollope at the *Cornhill*. Frederic Harrison and E. S. Beesly were both committed Positivists. Such connections impress the fact that middle-class publishing was an intricately networked and cosy business, and for the most part a male domain.[10]

The social configurations around a range of magazines in the mid-nineteenth century show similarities in the male circles that ran the publications. For example, the weekly *Punch* dinners initiated in 1841 were well known and immortalised by Thackeray in his playful rhyme, 'Mahogany Tree', so named for the table around which the *Punch* diners sat:

> Here let us sport,
> Boys, as we sit;
> Laughter and wit
> Flashing so free.
> Life is but short –
> When we are gone,
> Let them sing on,
> Round the old tree.[11]

Describing the *Punch* club, one of the original founders of the magazine recalled that 'its object was to form a little society amongst ourselves to talk over and settle upon subjects for the paper of the coming week'.[12] *Macmillan's* (founded in 1859) originated in Thursday evening gatherings at the firm's Covent Garden branch. Established writers such as Tennyson, Huxley and Kingsley gathered with up-and-coming men such as Edward Dicey and Alfred Ainger to smoke, to drink, and to talk at what came to be called the 'Tobacco Parliament',[13] a name which resonates class, leisure and politics. The *Cornhill* began a month after *Macmillan's* and was the brainchild of publisher George Smith and his author Thackeray. At its centre were a half-dozen male contributors who formed the core of the magazine's non-fiction and who gathered with other contributors at Smith's jovial monthly dinners.

Many firms involved in publishing periodicals were located at Paternoster Row or more generally in the area running from Fleet Street to Bank, and until the 1980s, the area remained the centre of the newspaper industry in London. The press industry had grown up in an environment of court, church and crown, especially dominated by male professions around the fields of law and commerce. Publishing offices were places where men might drop in, talk business, drink some tea and perhaps meet others in passing. The area was a focus for men. *Punch*, *Cornhill*, *Macmillan's* and, as we shall see, the *Fortnightly*, all share a similar social formation: it was in the spirit of men's clubs that many periodicals were conceived.

The founding proprietors of the *Fortnightly* present us with a familiar pattern. A group of well-off men most of whom were friends with social and business connections – at the very least acquaintances – decided to found a periodical. They had a few meetings and chose an experienced journalist friend to edit, who in turn rounded up an impressive list of friends and acquaintances as contributors to make an impact with the first issue: Walter Bagehot, George Eliot and Frederic Harrison. The first issue came off smoothly and the periodical was generally well received, its eminent contributors duly remarked. Untypical in this periodical's roots is the absence of a publishing house: there is no Smith, no Bentley, no Macmillan, no Blackwood and subsequently no obvious house style.

COMTE, POSITIVISM AND THE *FORTNIGHTLY*

By the time Lewes left, the *Fortnightly* was already known as partisan and Liberal, and Lewes's successor John Morley extended the radical base. Lewes had been editor at the *Leader* in the early 1850s where he earned his reputation as a liberal and even a radical. In those pages he heralded the virtues of Auguste Comte's Positivism, to which he had been enthusiastically attached since the 1840s. Although there seems to have been some fall-off in this attachment,[14] in public discourse Lewes was unequivocally linked to Positivism, as an 1868 *Edinburgh Review* article on the philosophy suggests:

> Than Mr. Lewes Positivism has no more earnest, intrepid, or persevering advocate in England. Some are more fanatical in their devotion, and have resigned their reason and judgment more entirely to the thoughts of the great master; others, like Mr. John S. Mill, less affiliated to the system, have expounded it, in our view, with a higher, or at least a more discriminating success; but there is no one who has been more faithful to it in his whole mode of thought, or who has more frequently recurred to its characteristic ideas, and explained them with more clearness, comprehension, and force. It has been Mr. Lewes's mission to develope [sic] and spread these ideas in opposition to the old modes of thought, as the destined means of regenerating human knowledge and society.[15]

The anonymous writer of the article was John Tulloch, a High Anglican Scotsman who would have been opposed to Lewes's devotion to science. Lewes was not the missionary zealot Tulloch suggests, but he had advocated early Comtism in the *Fortnightly*. Lewes's connection to Comte's early Positivist philosophy is important to establish here, in that it suggests one reason for the scarcity of women contributors and women's issues in the *Fortnightly* in its first eighteen months.

Lewes became familiar with Comtism in the original French and did not need the assistance of later English translations before becoming a follower. He was an acquaintance of Comte and visited him in Paris. A letter from Comte to Lewes in October 1848 acknowledges the Englishman's appreciation of Comte's Positivism: 'Je suis charmé que mon récent *Discours* vous ait tant satisfait. C'est d'un bon augure pour le succès moral et social du positivisme qui, dans votre pays, est encore loin de corre-spondre à son succès intellectuel.'[16] Lewes had written a letter to Comte in which he declared how highly he thought of the *Discours*, especially the 'chapter on women'.[17] This chapter was translated by J. H. Bridges in 1865 as 'The Influence of Positivism on Women'. In Comte's social reorganisation, philosophers, women and the working classes were an important triumvirate who would unite to regenerate society. He advo-cates the chivalric spirit of medievalism, when women were properly honoured, and finds a model for the treatment of women in the cult of the Virgin. The role of woman is to modify the actions of men through affection and superior morality:

> Morally, therefore, and apart from all material considerations, she merits always our living veneration, as the purest and simplest impersonation of Humanity, who can never be adequately represented in any masculine form. But these qualities do not involve the possession of political power, which some visionaries have claimed for women, though without their own consent. In that which is the great object of human life, they are superior to him; but in the various means of attaining that object they are undoubtedly inferior. In all kinds of force, whether physical, intellectual, or practical, it is certain that Man surpasses Woman, in accordance with a general law which prevails throughout the animal kingdom . . . Hence we find it the case in every phase of human society that women's life is essentially domestic, public life being confined to men.[18]

Women, whose dedication to the cause is essential to Positivism, are responsible for the early education of children, and their influence on public life is exerted through the institution of the salon. Apart from the salon, the family remains the 'distinctive sphere of work' for women.[19] Theology will be replaced, in a practical way, by the worship of women. Men will kneel down and pray to Woman rather than to God (as Comte himself did in worshipping his dead beloved, Clotilde de Vaux), and the object of Positivist prayer will be Humanity.[20] These are the points from the chapter on women which Lewes said he found especially rewarding in his reading of Comte in the late 1840s.

There was more to Comte than his views on women, and the reliance of Positivism on science and rationalism as a principle for faith seems to have been the primary appeal to Lewes. He did not always champion Comte's cause uncritically, and in the late 1850s, his position on Comte was far less enthusiastic than when he wrote for the *Leader*. Lewes broke with Comte for reasons that are uncertain, but in his 1857 edition of the *Biographical History of Philosophy*, he asserts that 'in the *Cours de [la] Philosophie Positive*, we have the grandest, because on the whole the truest system which Philosophy has yet produced'.[21] To a greater or lesser degree Lewes respected and adhered to Comte's early articulation of Positivist principles, which can be distinguished from Comtism in its later, more religious, formulation. By the mid-1860s, Comte was again on the public agenda, partly because of Bridges' translation and partly because of J. S. Mill's critique of Comte, also published in 1865. These and other books about Positivism were taken up by most periodicals of higher journalism, and Lewes responded with two articles in the *Fortnightly*. In 'Comte and Mill', he criticises the dogma of later Comte while maintaining a deep respect for his earlier ideas (much like Mill), and he is careful not to detract from the general notion of Comte as a great mind.[22]

Lewes as the first editor had a great deal to do with the progressive tendency the *Fortnightly* projected and it seems to me that his liberalism was informed by acceptance of Positivism. The cultural formation of the *Fortnightly* focused around the male-dominated Positivist circle. Richard Congreve, recording a history of Positivists in a private notebook, remembers how he first came upon Positivist thinking:

> By the publication of Mill's Logic attention had been called to [Comte's] high importance as a thinker, and I can remember in the society in which I then mixed at Oxford [and?] Rugby, that from time to time discussion arose as to the value of his thought. My more intimate personal friends had many of them read parts of his writings, and consequently we talked over his conclusions.[23]

Congreve and his friends discussed the intellectual possibilities of Positivism, apparently in the same way that the Apostles at Cambridge gathered earlier in the nineteenth century. Richard Dellamora has considered the gender construction of the Cambridge intellectual group of Apostles and how the homosexual desires shared between the men can be seen in, for example, Tennyson's *In Memoriam*.[24] Similarly, the works of English Positivists seem to have been affected by their roots in an all-male intellectual forum, albeit one less formalised than the Apostles or than a later group such as the Metaphysical Society which dominated the discourse of the *Nineteenth Century*.

I would argue that the configuration of these male intellectual discussion groups is analogous to that of the men's clubs – venues where men of like minds meet to talk and to (homo)socialise. Christopher Kent maintains convincingly that the professional network of men who were Positivists (Oxford graduates, often with independent means) strengthened a unified, club mentality. 'Even the profession to which so many of the Comtists belonged', Kent observes, 'was organized like a club: one became a barrister, after all, by eating dinners at one of the Inns of Court.'[25] Of course, many of the Positivists were also club members;

Beesly, for example, wrote several letters to Congreve from the Reform Club where many *Fortnightly* contributors were also members.[26] This is not to say, however, that because the intellectual milieu of the Positivists functioned as an all-male club that their thinking was necessarily linked to the Establishment. Quite the contrary, the political mission of Positivism was distinctly anti-Establishment.

The political aspect of Positivism, within the Religion of Humanity's broader mission to reorganise society, was an important part of the project. In his annual lecture-sermon to the Church of Humanity in 1859, Congreve concentrates on China, Italy and the relation of the labourer to the capitalist. He admits that such political issues are not usually discussed from the pulpit, but the nature of Positivism was to stand 'in lively contrast to' Christian tradition.[27] In 1866, a collection of foreign relations essays, *International Policy*, was published by Chapman and Hall (reviewed in the *Fortnightly*, 15 July 1866). The title-page epigraph is from Comte ('The fundamental doctrine of modern social life is the subordination of Politics to Morals') and the Preface states that 'certain principles are adopted equally by all the contributors, and they are adopted from the *political* and social system known as Positivism'.[28] Contributors included Congreve, Harrison, Beesly and Bridges. At the time of the Franco-Prussian War, Congreve, Beesly and Bridges published the pamphlet *Religion of Humanity, Republic of the West*,[29] which declared the Positivists' anti-war stance (although they supported France) and called for a united, perhaps federal, Republic comprised of France, Italy, Spain, Germany and England. In the days of Empire, this call for a European Community was indeed radical. The Positivists, then, had a significant anti-Establishment political dimension to their project. But to a large extent, the group that functioned like other all-male intellectual forums replicated their structures in the *Fortnightly*.

GENDER AND HYBRID JOURNALISM

The cultural and social formation of many of the contributors – the closeness, shared beliefs and sense of mission – surrounding the *Fortnightly* may go some way in explaining the absence of women in the periodical in 1865–6. Of 131 different contributors under Lewes, only four are identified by the *Wellesley Index* as women. These four women wrote seven contributions in total. Two were critical notices, and five were full-length articles. One article and one notice were by George Eliot and appeared signed in the first number, to lend prominence to the journal. Catherine Helen Spence helped write an article but was not actually given credit in the magazine, so her contribution is, in effect,

silenced which leaves just three articles after the first number.[30] Two on
music were written by Leonora Schmitz and one on housing for the poor
was by Octavia Hill. The articles signed by women (if we include Eliot's)
account for 1.6 per cent of all the articles written under Lewes's editorship;[31] by comparison, the conservative *Edinburgh Review* in 1865–66 had
three women reviewers accounting for 3.8 per cent of the articles. As
would be expected, more miscellaneous magazines published a greater
number of articles by and about women. During 1865–6, *Macmillan's*
carried serial fiction by Margaret Oliphant, Charlotte Yonge and Caroline
Norton and a range of non-fiction by Frances Power Cobbe, Frances
Verney, Lucy Duff-Gordon and others. In *Blackwood's* Margaret Oliphant, Anne Mozley and Elizabeth J. Hassell wrote more than a dozen
articles between them, many addressing women's issues directly. By
comparison, the *Fortnightly's* experimentalism did not extend to redres-
sing the gender imbalance in non-fiction.

In the first two years of John Morley's editorship (1867–8) of the
Fortnightly, articles by and about women were more numerous than
under Lewes. Frances Power Cobbe wrote on progress, Millicent Fawcett
on women's education and R. M. Pankhurst on women's right to vote.
There were a couple of critical notices by women as well. With Morley we
see a shift in policy, though the absence of women and women's issues
under Lewes may not have been entirely on intellectual grounds but
partly self-interested. For considering his unconventional 'marriage' to
George Eliot and the precarious position in which the relationship put
them, he perhaps shied away from advocating women's issues in order not
to attract attention to his own position and add to their difficulties. The
absence of both women and any official declaration on women's issues can
be registered, perhaps, then, as an outcome of Comtist attitudes alongside
more personal considerations.[32]

While during Lewes's tenure no full-length articles address women or
women's issues directly, other non-fiction occasionally glanced towards
them. For example, John Dennis's review of John Malcolm Ludlow's
Woman's Work in the Church asserts that

> it is the mere reiteration of a truism to affirm that a woman's best place is home,
> that her highest duties are those of a wife and mother, granting, however, that there
> are numerous single women to whom 'official duties' could be assigned.[33]

While we might consider this merely an individual opinion in a journal
of free thought, what needs to be emphasised is that there is no counter-
discourse advocating a more liberal position on women's roles. Certainly
the political climate in 1865–6, in the run-up to the Reform Bill debates
in 1867, provided ample opportunity to discuss women's issues. Apart

from *Blackwood's*, mentioned previously, other periodicals, particularly progressive women's periodicals such as the *Englishwoman's Review of Social and Industrial Questions* and *Victoria Magazine*, kept women's issues in the public domain, and private groups like Emily Davies's Kensington Society discussed such questions as women's franchise.[34] Both were part of the discourse of a burgeoning middle-class feminism and were responding to the absence of women's discussion of political issues within the clubland formation of the popular periodical press. In June 1866, J. S. Mill presented a petition to Parliament for women's suffrage which went unmentioned both in the 'Public Affairs' and 'Causeries' sections.[35] A whole range of women's issues was being discussed elsewhere in public and in private which Lewes's *Fortnightly* non-fiction largely neglects.

The gendering of the *Fortnightly* is related to its attempt to be both a review and a magazine. The title signals hybridity – a *Review* that appears fortnightly rather than quarterly – and the combination of forms can be seen in the contents. The 'Public Affairs' section provides news summaries similar to weeklies like the *Saturday Review* and the fortnightly frequency creates a sense of topicality and news-value which the quarterlies clearly did not wish to project. A number of articles in the *Fortnightly* were based on recent book publications and so were review-like, but the books were not foregrounded at the beginning of the article as they were in the quarterlies. Furthermore, a single book was often reviewed rather than a clutch of books on a single topic, as in the traditional quarterlies. Alongside these review articles were pieces on socio-political topics (especially about reform and the franchise) and also articles more closely resembling magazine articles, for example personal reminiscences. Lewes's 'Causerie' section opened up a space for the editor to address readers informally within a serious journal, and it is possible that the Causeries were intended to include women readers. Such hybridity, blending elements of the quarterly, monthly and weekly periodicals, was part of the *Fortnightly*'s attempt to create a new market, distinct from the market of the other progressive magazine of higher journalism, the *Westminster Review*. The magazines shared a number of contributors and covered similar topics, although the *Westminster* dealt with more home politics and the *Fortnightly* projects internationalism. The *Fortnightly*, at one level, had to differentiate its radicalism from that of the *Westminster*, which was closely identified with Mill's feminism: there was presumably economic and symbolic capital in Lewes's divergence from Mill on women's issues.

The *Fortnightly*'s hybridity can also be seen as part of its Positivist philosophical position. In his article on 'Comte and Mill', the editor notes that one primary tenet of Comte's early formulation of Positivism was its emphasis on the relations between phenomena:

> In the *Philosophie Positive* . . . [Comte] laid down the rule that no function could be studied except in relation to its organ or its acts; he pointed out the error of separating psychological phenomena from their connections with other phenomena, and declared that the anatomical point of view ought to predominate.[36]

Here, Lewes is discussing the debate about Subjective and Objective Method which Comte's philosophy addresses. But what is noticeable in Lewes's reading of Comte is that fusion is at the centre of Positivism – an attempt to merge the discourses of philosophy with science and religion. This is what Lewes calls Comte's 'gigantic scheme',[37] and this totalising hybrid scheme – embracing a range of intellectual discourses – is equally at the centre of the *Fortnightly*'s modern project. The periodical's Positivism and hybrid form make it distinctly modern, and the one can be seen as an intellectual basis for the other. Generic distinctions between periodicals would have been significant for readers who consumed shilling monthly magazines, for example, as family entertainment with something for everyone. Reviews, however, were weighty, serious, party political to a large degree and book-like. The *Fortnightly* – by blending the discourses of 'high' and 'low' culture, by placing a philosophical review article alongside an instalment of a serial novel – would have sent conflicting signals to the periodical-reading public: two shillings fortnightly instead of one shilling monthly; fiction alongside serious review-like articles. Where was the *Fortnightly* to be read: in the club, the drawing room, or the study? The proprietors, aiming to create a new reading market with a new type of journal, blending elements of the popular with high seriousness, were indeed innovative.

THE BELTON ESTATE:
SERIALISING WOMEN'S ISSUES

The serial fiction was one regular feature friendly to women readers. However the decision to include fiction was not unanimously welcomed by the proprietors. In his *Autobiography*, Trollope records his doubts about including fiction in the *Fortnightly*:

> It had been decided by the Board of Management, somewhat in opposition to my own ideas on the subject, that the *Fortnightly Review* should always contain a novel. It was of course natural that I should write the first novel, and I wrote *The Belton Estate*.[38]

Trollope's opposition probably stems from the belief that the inclusion of fiction implies a particular type of magazine and would detract from the

journal's more intellectual *Review* status. Responding to Lewes's suggestion that *The Belton Estate* ought to be the first entry in an issue, Trollope
advises:

> As to putting Belton E. first in No. 3, do just as you please. I have a strong opinion
> against putting the novel always first as it indicates an idea that it is our staple; –
> which indicates the further idea that the remainder is padding. Were I Editor I
> think I should always give the novel a distinctive place just before the Chronique.
> But that is a matter of small, or no, moment.[39]

The inclusion of fiction was apt to be perceived as financially desirable in
the competitive middle-class periodicals market in the mid-1860s.

Lewes's 'Criticism in Relation to Novels' in the *Fortnightly* appears to
argue against the very sort of fiction his magazine was publishing:

> Instead of compensating for the inevitable evils of periodical criticism by doing our
> utmost to keep the standard of public taste, too many of us help to debase it by
> taking a standard from the Circulating Library, and by a half-contemptuous, half-
> languid patronage of what we do not seriously admire.[40]

His article contends that higher standards ought to be maintained by
reviewers because 'the critic demands a closer adherence to truth and
experience' than popular novels often contain.[41] He has in mind sensation
novels which can be strong in plot but weak in realism. Ironically,
however, in attacking circulating libraries, Lewes attacks Trollope,
circulating-library author extraordinaire. While Trollope's fiction is
mostly unsensational and true to Lewes's realist principles, it was largely
consumed by the kind of readers Lewes dismisses. Trollope apparently
felt the sting of Lewes's attack on domestic realism, articulated in the
second article of the 'Principles of Success in Literature' series, in which
Lewes deplores 'coat-and-waistcoat realism, a creeping timidity of invention, moving almost exclusively amid scenes of drawing-room existence, with all the reticences and pettinesses of drawing-room
conventions'.[42] About the article, Trollope wrote to Lewes 'It is beautiful,
but, oh, so cruel'.[43] Reading an instalment of *The Belton Estate* in the
same issue as Lewes's criticisms of circulating libraries or of drawing-
room realism accentuates the fissures in the hybrid *Fortnightly*. Despite
his attacks on some forms of realism, Lewes's 'Principles of Success in
Literature' series generally admits the importance of the novel as a
contemporary form; furthermore, the presence of fiction in a serious-
minded review was a significant part of the *Fortnightly*'s progressive
hybridity.

Of course, new shilling monthlies were repeatedly being founded since
the success of the *Cornhill* and its imitators, and the power of the
quarterlies was on the wane. It could be argued that combining fiction,

and circulating-library fiction at that, with serious review articles was a way of attracting readers, especially women in an expanding market. In making such an attempt in Britain, the *Fortnightly* was indeed innovatory, but the proprietors were following the lead of the *Revue des Deux Mondes*. The *Fortnightly* closely resembles its French model in a number of ways: fortnightly publication; an outward-looking, international emphasis; the promotion of the author; the absence of women's voices; the presence of fiction and poetry.[44] At the time the *Fortnightly* was launched with *The Belton Estate*, the *Revue des Deux Mondes* was serialising George Meredith's *Ordeal of Richard Feverel*; Meredith's *Vittoria* followed Trollope in the British periodical. A successful foreign model was not enough to ensure financial success in England and the *Fortnightly*'s circulation never reached above 1,500 by the time the proprietors sold to Chapman and Hall. The hybrid periodical did have its own followers, but the *Contemporary Review*, founded in 1866 and modelled to an extent on the *Fortnightly*'s open forum, noticeably does not include fiction.

The *Fortnightly*'s inaugural novel covers familiar territory for those acquainted with Trollope's fiction. As the *London Review* puts it in their review of the novel, 'it is time . . . that Mr. Trollope should forbear from leading us through the same familiar scenes'.[45] Such scenes depict a spirited, often fortune-less heroine who experiences complicated relations with a lover or two. Trollope concurred with some reviewers when he estimated a decade later that 'it has no particular merits, and will add nothing to my reputation as a novelist', and 'I seem to remember almost less of it than of any book that I have written'.[46] The novel did not bring in the intended readers, and the *Athenaeum* endorsed its own view by asserting that 'the verdict of periodical readers was, we believe, unfavourable'.[47]

What is interesting about Trollope's novel is its relation to the rest of a periodical which is otherwise so strikingly silent about women's issues. The heroine Clara Amedroz, without a fortune because of her brother's reckless gambling, is stoically serious in her approach to life. Left with a helpless and self-pitying father after her brother's suicide (all of which is revealed in the opening chapter), Clara perceives:

> It was her duty to repress both the feeling of shame and the sorrow, as far as they were capable of repression. Her brother had been weak, and in his weakness had sought a coward's escape from the ills of the work around him. She must not also be a coward! Bad as life might be to her henceforth, she must endure it with such fortitude as she could muster.[48]

This strong-willed woman compensating for the weaknesses of men around her was not new to Trollope readers or fiction readers generally, and it is perhaps worth noting that such a passage showing the moral superiority of women fits comfortably within the ideal Positivist construction of society. Clara is less endearing when she says, 'I think it would be well if all single women were strangled by the time they are thirty' (ch. 8, I, 415). She is alluding to the predicament of an increasing number of unmarried women, a key issue in the 'woman question'. 'Having neither father, mother, nor brother; without a home, without a shilling that she could call her own – with no hope as to her future life' (ch. 21, II, 513), Clara struggles to accept her attraction to her lovers while resenting her *need* for a husband to maintain her position.

Clara tries repeatedly to preserve a sense of self-worth by rejecting attempts by her cousin and lover Will to give her the Belton Estate which has fallen to him after her brother's suicide: by rejecting property specifically, she rejects the system upon which male wealth is based. Trollope continually writes of the 'Beltons of Belton' and of the pleasures of ownership to establish the inexorability of the patrilineal inheritance. At one point Clara calls Will's plan to give up Belton 'a romantic notion' (ch. 24, II, 665) because it flies in the face of respectable behaviour. But Will links the property with Clara whom he loves – if he cannot have her, he does not want the estate:

> he did not wish, in his present mood, to be recognized as the heir. He did not want the property. He would have preferred to rid himself altogether of any of the obligations which the ownership of the estate entailed upon him. It was not permitted to him to have the custody of the old squire's daughter, and therefore he was unwilling to meddle with any of the old squire's concerns. (ch. 20, II, 415)

Clara is part of the property, and Will wants all of it or nothing: the discourse cuts both ways, critical of the system, yet barely able to figure relationships outside appropriation. It is not an accident that chapter 31 in which Clara finally agrees to marry Will is called 'Taking Possession'.

The discourses circulating around women in the novel are in fact related to discourses on property and law current in the *Fortnightly* and elsewhere during the serialisation. Reviewing Mill on political economy in June 1865, Frederic Harrison writes,

> But there is a question which underlies the whole problem [of the cultivation of land], which is the social ground of property and the appropriation of land. No one does, no one can treat this fundamental political principle as a purely economic question. The first thing a rational philosophy has to do is to establish the basis of property; the rights, the duties, the relations of proprietors; the political, social, and moral functions which ownership in land implies.[49]

For Harrison, population and property are the two great elements of all economic systems. Property was one subject treated in exchanges about

Positivism generally,[50] and such discussions of political economy as Harrison's coincided with the debates which led to the 1867 Reform Act. Also in the *Fortnightly*, Richard Ellerton proposed universal (male) suffrage a month later, and Thomas Hare put forward his suggestions for electoral reform in October. Significantly, the whole of the second Reform Bill debates centred on questions of land since property was the basis of one's right to vote. Property equalled political power. Discussions about land, population and suffrage intersect with discourses in the novel and in the broader periodical culture which make more explicit the links between women's rights and property. Accordingly, an anonymous writer reviewing Bessie Rayner Parkes, Anna Swanwick and F. P. Cobbe in the *Westminster Review* in October 1865 asserts that,

> when the United Kingdom has perhaps 200,000 more women than men, what a stupid as well as unmanly insult it is, to tell women that they must not seek to maintain themselves, but must set their caps to get husbands who will maintain them![51]

In the context of the woman question, the statement affirms the need for women's employment and self-determination. Clara enters this discourse in her proud response to her aunt's plan to provide for her through Captain Aylmer:

> How can I help it that I am not a man and able to work for my bread? But I am not above being a housemaid, and so Captain Aylmer shall find. I'd sooner be a housemaid, with nothing but my wages than take the money which you say he is to give me. (ch. 8, I, 415)

A *Westminster* article in 1864 about marriage laws is worth citing lastly, since it conveys the contemporary awareness of the interrelationship of marriage and property so keenly: 'The contract of matrimony gives rise to legal consequences so important (especially with regard to the possession and transmission of property), that it is but right that society should establish certain constituted methods of entering into it.'[52] I've suggested how the discourse in *The Belton Estate* addresses precisely the connections between land, marriage and women's independence. Such legal and political economy issues, then, were an element of both fiction and non-fiction, and in this serial novel by Trollope it seems we may be glimpsing discussions among the *Fortnightly*'s contributors that fed into the creative work.

It is vital in the novel that Clara challenges assumptions about marriage, property and inheritance, even if she is not so challenging that she refuses marriage altogether. 'I'm not prepared to alter the ways of the world,' Clara maintains, 'but I feel myself entitled to grumble at them sometimes' (ch. 7, I, 408). Like Trollope's heroine, many women in the

1860s were questioning a whole range of legal issues. In 1865, for example, a group of Manchester feminists were organising campaigns for property reform and for a mother's custody rights,[53] and as mentioned earlier, women were combining to petition Parliament for suffrage in 1866. The petition's argument was carefully focused upon a single woman's right to own property. If the vote depended on ownership of land, and if women could legally own land, why, then, could they not vote?[54] The petition's reasoning shows how property was a contested site of meaning in the late 1860s. Will's insistence that he not accept his inheritance and that he offer Clara the Belton Estate indicates how both men and women could challenge legal precedent and social convention.[55] *The Belton Estate* addresses contemporary reform movements which concurrent *Fortnightly* non-fiction almost never confronts directly, and the discourse of property and marriage which surrounds Clara, Will and Captain Aylmer highlights the fragility of the gendered issues of political economy and law.

The serial raises women's issues in other ways, for example through the discourse of the sexual woman. It is worth considering here Clara's relationship with her friend and neighbour on the Belton Estate, Mrs Askerton, who is a fallen woman. The relationship between the two women is especially significant because it shows them supporting one another despite society's discomfort. In the middle of the 1860s, with the popularity of sensation novels causing controversy in numerous periodicals, Trollope's sympathetic portrayal of a fallen woman exploits interest in the figure while challenging the convention in novels that fallen women must either die (as in Gaskell's *Ruth*) or be mad (as in Braddon's *Lady Audley's Secret*).

My account of the early volumes of the *Fortnightly* under Lewes has suggested the complexity of the cultural formations of periodicals in the mid-nineteenth century and the need to consider gender when looking closely at periodical literature. The *Fortnightly*'s political and formal progressivism – based on open politics, fortnightly frequency and a policy of signature – was not sustained. Its politics became known as Liberal and Positivist and it did not survive as a fortnightly for very long. Its most immediate legacy to a distinctly modern journalism was the policy of signature, which was taken up by other periodicals of the higher journalism shortly after the *Fortnightly*'s founding; but this development would have happened around then anyway. In the *Fortnightly*'s hybridity, we see an attempt to yoke the readers of the higher journalism with those of more popular fiction-led magazines; its championing of hybridity and totalising ambitions alike were indicative of the periodical's resolute modernity and Positivist roots. The *Fortnightly* under Lewes functioned like a Positivists' men's club, and its non-fiction tended to discount women contributors, women's issues as such, and many women readers. Only the serial fiction, inaugurated by Trollope's *Belton Estate*, carried explicit discussion of a range of women's issues – employment, property, marriage and sex. The creative hybridity of the periodical was not enough to bring in substantial numbers of readers each fortnight, and the collective which founded the magazine was forced to sell. Lewes's successor John Morley managed to extend the Positivist base whilst simultaneously giving room to women – a lasting change.

NOTES

1. *Publishers' Circular*, 26 (2 Feb. 1863), 56.
2. See E. M. Everett, *The Party of Humanity: The* Fortnightly Review *and Its Contributors, 1865–74* (University of North Carolina Press: Chapel Hill, NC, 1939).
3. See Anthony Trollope, *An Autobiography* (Oxford UP: 1989 [1883]), 190.
4. Prospectus, *Fortnightly Review*, 1 (15 May, 1865), inside front cover.
5. 'On the Anonymous in Periodicals', *New and Monthly Magazine and Literary Journal* 39 (Sept. 1833), 4–5.
6. The standard overview of the anonymity debate in the nineteenth century is Oscar Maurer, jun., 'Anonymity vs. Signature in Victorian Reviewing', *Texas Studies in English*, 27 (June 1948), 1–27.
7. In 'Anonymous Journalism', *Saint Paul's Magazine* 2 (May 1868), 217, Leslie Stephen compares anonymity to the ballot. *Saint Paul's* was anonymous and initially edited by Trollope.
8. See the *Fortnightly* prospectus.
9. Trollope, *Autobiography*, 190.
10. There were important exceptions and women were increasingly involved in running periodicals: Bessie Rayner Parkes at the *English Woman's Journal*; Emily Faithfull at the Victoria Press in London; the all-woman Caledonian Press in Edinburgh; Mary Braddon at *Belgravia*, and others.
11. Quoted in M. H. Spielmann, *The History of 'Punch'* (Cassell & Co. London, 1895), 53.
12. Ibid., 93. For more discussion of the *Punch* dinners and the club-like social formation, see ibid., ch. 3.
13. Charles Morgan, *The House of Macmillan (1843–1943)* (Macmillan: London, 1943), 50.
14. See Rosemary Ashton, *G. H. Lewes: A Life* (Oxford UP: 1991), 198.
15. 'The Positive Philosophy of M. August Comte', *Edinburgh Review*, 127 (Ap. 1868), 305.
16. Auguste Comte, *Correspondence generale et confessions, 1846–48* (Ecole des Hautes Etudes en Sciences Sociales: Paris, 1981), 194: 'I am delighted that my recent *Discours* has so pleased you. This is a good sign for the moral and social success of positivism, which, in your country, also corresponds to its intellectual success' (my translation).

17. This letter at the Maison Auguste Comte in Paris is quoted in T. R. Wright, *The Religion of Humanity: The Impact of Comtean Positivism on Victorian Britain* (Cambridge UP: 1986), 52.

18. Auguste Comte, *A General View of Positivism*, tr. J. H. Bridges (Trubner: London, 1865), 225–6.

19. Ibid., 248.

20. Ibid., 277–8.

21. G. H. Lewes, *Biographical History of Philosophy*, 2 vols (John W. Parker: London, 1857), Vol. 1, 662.

22. Editor [G. H. Lewes], 'Comte and Mill', *Fortnightly Review*, 6 (1 Oct. 1866), 385–406. See also Lewes's 'Auguste Comte', *Fortnightly Review*, 3 (1 Jan. 1866), 385–410 and review of Bridges' *General View*, *Fortnightly Review* 1 (1 June 1865), 250–1.

23. Positivist Papers, British Library, ADD MS 45.259, ff. 1–2.

24. Richard Dellamora, *Masculine Desire: The Sexual Politics of Victorian Aestheticism* (University of North Carolina Press: Chapel Hill, NC, 1990), 16–41.

25. Christopher Kent, *Brains and Numbers: Elitism, Comtism, and Democracy in Mid-Victorian England* (University of Toronto Press: 1978), 89.

26. Positivist Papers, British Library, ADD MS 45.227, f. 21. See Kent, *Brains and Numbers,* 88: 'most of the Comtists were devoted clubmen'. The Reform Club's membership books indicate that in the mid-1860s the following *Fortnightly* contributors were members: E. S. Beesly, Sheldon Amos, Robert Bell, James C. Morison, Marmion Savage, Joseph Charles Parkinson, Charles MacKay, Frederic Harrison. See *The Rules and Regulations, with an Alphabetical List of the Members of THE REFORM CLUB with Dates of Entrance* (Thomas Brettel: Westminster, 1866). My thanks to Simon Blundell, librarian at the Reform Club, for his assistance.

27. Richard Congreve, *The Propagation of the Religion of Humanity: A Sermon Preached at South Fields, Wandsworth* (John Chapman: London, 1860), 13.

28. *International Policy: Essays on the Foreign Relations of England* (Chapman & Hall: London, 1866), v (my emphasis).

29. E. S. Beesly, J. H. Bridges and Richard Congreve, *Religion of Humanity, Republic of the West: Papers on the War between France and Germany* (Edward Truelove: London, 1870).

30. See Walter Houghton (ed.), *The Wellesley Index to Victorian Periodicals 1824–1900*, 5 vols (University of Toronto Press and Routledge: London, 1966–89), Vol. 2, 189.

31. There were 243 articles (not including book notices, the 'Public Affairs' section or the 'Causeries') during Lewes's tenure.

32. See Dickie A. Spurgeon's entry on the *Fortnightly* for an opposing view that seems to me unwarranted, in Alvin Sullivan, *British Literary Magazines: The Victorian and Edwardian Age, 1837–1913* (Greenwood Press: Westport, CT, 1984), 132.

33. John Dennis, review of John Malcolm Ludlow, *Woman's Work in the Church*

in *Fortnightly Review* 1 (1 June 1865), 252. See also, for examples, two *Fortnightly Review*s: A. R. Vardy, *Half a Million of Money* in 3 (15 Jan. 1866), 654–5; and Robert Buchanan's review of Sarah Tytler's *Citoyenne Jacqueline: A Woman's Lot in the Great French Revolution* in 3 (1 Feb. 1866), 781–2.

34. Mary Lyndon Shanley, *Feminism, Marriage, and the Law in England, 1850–1895* (I. B. Tauris: London, 1989), 50–1. See ch.2 on the Married Women's Property Act of 1870.

35. During Lewes's absence abroad in June and July 1866 Trollope edited the periodical. No 'Causerie' appeared in July, August and the first fortnight of September 1866.

36. Editor [Lewes], 'Comte and Mill', 406.

37. Ibid.

38. Trollope, *Autobiography*, 196.

39. Trollope to Lewes (30 May 1865) in N. John Hall, *The Complete Letters of Anthony Trollope*, 2 vols (Stanford UP: 1985), Vol. 1, 304.

40. Editor [G. H. Lewes], 'Criticism in Relation to Novels', *Fortnightly Review*, 3 (5 Dec. 1865), 353.

41. Ibid., 355.

42. Editor [G. H. Lewes], 'The Principles of Success in Literature – the Principle of Vision', *Fortnightly Review*, 1 (1 June 1865), 187.

43. Trollope to Lewes (30 May 1865) in Hall, *Letters*, Vol. 1, 304.

44. In 1865–6, the *Revue* published articles on foreign affairs and England; its cover lists the cities where it could be purchased, emphasising its internationalist base; Lewes's 'Public Affairs' section provides an ongoing narrative of events in Europe and America.

45. *London Review*, 12 (3 Mar. 1866), 260.

46. Trollope, *Autobiography*, 196.

47. *Athenaeum* (3 Feb. 1866), 166.

48. Anthony Trollope, *The Belton Estate* in the *Fortnightly Review*, 1 (15 May 1865), ch. 1, 29. All subsequent references will be noted parenthetically in the text by chapter, *Fortnightly* volume number, and page number.

49. Frederic Harrison, 'The Limits of Political Economy', *Fortnightly Review*, 1 (15 June 1865), 366–7.

50. See, for example, the pamphlet *Positivist Articles, Reviews, and Letters reprinted from the Bengalee* (Bengalee Press: Calcutta, 1870), 105–6.

51. 'Capacities of Women', *Westminster Review*, 56 NS (Oct. 1865), 359.

52. 'The Laws of Marriage and Divorce', *Westminster Review*, 52 NS (Oct. 1864), 458.

53. Shanley, *Feminism, Marriage and the Law*, 14.

54. Ibid., ch. 2. See also [Helen Taylor], 'The Ladies Petition', *Westminster Review*, 31 NS (Jan. 1867), 66.

55. See, for example, *The Belton Estate* (ch. 24, II, 664–5). Will's disavowal of the estate is linked inextricably with his relationship with Clara and her relationship with Captain Aylmer.

5

MATTHEW ARNOLD AND PUBLICITY: A MODERN CRITIC AS JOURNALIST

KATE CAMPBELL

Matthew Arnold's criticism in the journals of his day solicited attention in being timely and polemical. A measure of its success, in his lifetime and up until World War One many novels engaged with his ideas directly – among the more well-known, *Daniel Deronda*, *Jude the Obscure* and *Howard's End*.[1] Arnold's criticism still invites academic attention through raising questions of continuing importance and the cultural capital of its allusions.[2] Since it is also in turns careless, emotive, ironic, mnemonic, rude and a fount of oppositions, it can almost seem programmed for publicity – a model of journalistic flair.

When the Newbolt Report of 1921 misquoted Arnold as writing 'Culture unites classes' instead of using his actual words on culture wanting to do away with classes it was, then, in a sense taking a leaf from his journalistically derived books, its misreading encouraged by his own carelessness and flair.[3] Arnold's persona, ideas and catchphrases recurred frequently in his day and subsequently. Henry Sidgwick pointed to his publicising ability in 1867 in his 'doing not a little to exasperate and exacerbate' (*CH*, 224) antagonisms despite wishing for, and being capable of, their reconciliation; Richard Garnett noted in 1901 how 'references to him in contemporary literature are endless, and he is the subject of innumerable critiques'.[4] T. S. Eliot registered the publicist talent in describing him 'a propagandist for criticism rather than a critic'.[5] This chapter challenges established views that neglect Arnold's involvement in publicity by exploring his activity as a journalistic writer.

An index of his extraordinary success as a publicist has been the frequent citation of his reading of the end of Edmund Burke's *Reflections on the Revolution in France*. Here, writing on 'The Function of Criticism', he presents disinterested liberal criticism in a powerful image of open-mindedness:

> That return of Burke upon himself is one of the finest things in English literature,
> or indeed in any literature. That is what I call living by ideas: when one side of a
> question has long had your earnest support, when all your feelings are engaged,
> when your party talks this language like a steam-engine and can imagine no other, –
> still, to be able to think, still to be irresistibly carried, if so it be, by the current of
> thought to the opposite side of the question . . . (*SP*, 140)

But as Arnold in fact acknowledges, Burke's final words, declaring the
perversity and obstinacy of those 'opposing this mighty current in human
affairs', were not referring to his own opposition to the Revolution in
France at the close of his book about it (although some extended
application is possible), as Arnold broadly makes out. Rather, taking
up his question 'What is to be done?', considering 'the best means of
combating it' (*SP*, 139), Burke's words look forward to mounting
resistance to the spread of sedition: 'this mighty current' appears to
be on his side.[6] Arnold's reading is to this extent careless, 'journalistic' in
the pejorative sense – his desire father of the famous conservative's trip on
thought's current. It was in comparable terms, of Arnold's travesty of
John Bright's and Frederic Harrison's understanding of culture to suit his
own ends, that the *Morning Star* condemned 'Culture and Its Enemies'
(*CH*, 201–4). Given his academic credentials, it seems Arnold's reading of
Burke constitutes an early instance of 'the *temptation of the media*' where
intellectuals neglect academic precision in trying to exert pressure
through the press.[7] The image of a disinterested Burke entertaining
the possibility of his own perversity was nonetheless a publicising *coup* – a
kind of 'poetry in history', such a shining image of questioning mind and
disinterest as to have been exempt from questioning itself.

In his apparent openness Arnold's Burke could serve as an icon of mid-
twentieth-century liberal criticism.[8] Following the development of ideological criticism in the 1980s, Eliot's oxymoron, a 'propagandist for
criticism', more obviously related to Arnold's hegemonic role, 'the
propagation of high culture in the service of an organicist nationalism'
resting on a disinterested self.[9] Chris Baldick's account of his centrality in
academic English was instrumental in this. Here too, though, Arnold's
publicising ability seems involved, in the singular importance granted his
views. Thus Baldick discusses Arnold's concern with prematurity without
reference to the many other political analysts similarly engaged with the
phenomenon of political form running in advance of a people's capacity to
sustain it and ideas taking hold without being thoroughly compre-
hended.[10] In general Baldick's Arnold is disconnected from political
discourse – his personal authority greatly exaggerated. Despite *Culture
and Anarchy*'s subtitle, *An Essay in Social and Political Criticism*, the
three 'recognizable phases' Baldick discerns in Arnold's writing exclude

the political altogether, comprising 'early, more "classicist", literary-critical writings, the social and theological works of the late 1860's and early 1870's, and the later literary works'.[11] Away from main currents of nineteenth-century political thought, Arnold is demonised, with elitist aspects that were widespread then unduly foregrounded, contrary movements in his thinking eclipsed. In fact, substantially qualifying the high cultural identity, by the mid-1860s Arnold was subject to class discrimination from contemporaries and something of a downmarket familiar – 'Matt Arnold' on the news-stand, 'a favourite comedian', an 'elegant Jeremiah', 'Mr. Kid-Glove Cock-Sure' (CH, 210).[12]

The labels show a distinct and provocative persona emerging from writing in serious forms. Far from straightforwardly elitist they suggest populist tendencies: something of a hybrid and tease, bringing 'high' culture down, heretically pitched towards readers deemed responsive to entertainment. Hostility to the word 'culture' dates from controversy surrounding Arnold's views, and in a sense the Arnold-bashing of recent years simply perpetuates an antipathy to elite culture that Arnold himself fuelled by contravening its hierarchical norms. Yet academic constructions of a modern in Arnold tend to be elevated, from the sentimental poet haunted by purity who later urged 'control' and distance over modernity's 'vast multitude of facts' (1857) to the critic championing disinterest and Oxford in Culture and Anarchy (1869).[13] His criticism of modern journalism (the Daily Telegraph especially) feeds into Leavisite criticism, elaborating a foundational myth of the modern in the project of culture holding back seas of anarchy in the form of the modern mass media.[14] These roles variously neglect Sidgwick's 'comedian' 'titillating' his audience with 'airs and graces' (CH, 210) and the paradigmatic journalist at whom Fitzjames Stephen scoffed: a 'very clever man, always brilliant', 'with quick sympathies and a great gift of making telling remarks', who 'really does work himself, at any rate for the time being, into an esoteric enthusiasm for the particular point which he enforces'.[15]

The critic now identified with high culture and the elevation of the public sphere could thus be seen as instrumental in their decline. The neo-Kantian Sidgwick inadvertently aligned him with the public sphere's degradation: the movement against anonymous writing had become much the stronger on account of Arnold's writing in 'periodical literature'. Sidgwick's description of Arnold's production turns on the discrepancy between his official eminence and vulgar traits, registered in repetition of the word 'new'. He thus refers to him as 'this new phenomenon', creating 'new and exquisite literary enjoyment' by delivering profound truths and subtle observations with all the dogmatic authority and self-confidence of a prophet; at the same time titillating the public by something like the airs and graces, the playful affectations of a favourite comedian' (*CH*, 210). While there may be genuine pleasure here, intimations of a 'choice' experience and shades of patronage qualify it with suggestions of vulgarity. We may object to the archness and anxieties shadowing Sidgwick's validation. But in identifying a hybrid phenomenon overlooked subsequently, challenging 'the centred, dominant cultural norms', he highlights a source of Arnold's capacity to get under the skin of his readers and needle them.[16]

Almost all Arnold's criticism first appeared in print in journal form. Until the mid-1860s many articles were revisions of lectures but even here a periodical readership was in prospect – quite explicitly when giving a lecture on Heine in Oxford it dawned on him that his lectures were aimed at periodical readers rather than the 'dead bones' in front of him.[17] In the *OED* journalism refers to 'writing in the public journals'; as mentioned earlier the word's first appearance in English signalled a hybrid phenomenon uniting higher and lower cultural forms. Focusing on Arnold's journalism and publicity leads to both a high cultural tradition of political critique and a modern world of promotion. Both these dimensions of his writing have been neglected.

This chapter examines how his thinking in the 1860s, stressing the value of disinterest and the dissemination of ideas, corresponds to the political thought of the Enlightenment philosopher who prioritised publicity, Immanuel Kant. I suggest how Arnold broadly invokes Kantian political precepts; they even inform his much-quoted criticism of 'a new journalism' in 1887 as 'feather-brained' and lacking objectivity.[18] I argue that Arnold's criticism is also characteristic of a more modern form of publicity involving promotion and flair at reason's expense. Here Enlightenment precepts are undermined and contradicted in unstable journalistic prose, giving it the aspect of 'feather-brained' 'new journalism' itself.

A JOURNALIST AS 'WANDERER BETWEEN TWO WORLDS'?

At the outset though there is the issue of Arnold's move from poetry to journalism from the 1850s. Established generic hierarchies suggest a move from a higher to a lower cultural form. Reviews of Ian Hamilton's recent study *A Gift Imprisoned* demonstrate hierarchy and doubleness in his newspaper press – 'poetry/duty', 'worldly clubman and solemn poet', 'poetry/drudgery' and many more.[19] These often make it seem as if he turned from writing altogether in the 1850s, as if no longer producing written words involving craft, inspiration, creativity; as if the conjunction of poet and journalism is exceptional rather than quite common.

There seems, however, much overlap, beyond his understanding of literature as a criticism of life to 'illuminate and rejoice us' (*SP*, 173), straddling all his forms of writing. As glimpsed already, he acceded to a prophetic function that romantic poets had espoused, precisely through journal writing. Psychologically and culturally this entailed a magisterial, upbeat quality. Arnold expressed a desire for this personally and for his 'confused' age but it escaped him in epic poetry, its customary site: 'the mass of men' want 'something to animate and ennoble them not merely to add zest to their melancholy or grace to their dreams. – I believe a feeling of this kind is the basis of my nature – and of my poetics'.[20] Another index of consanguinity and journalism's attraction is his regretting in prose 'the *articulations of the discourse*: one leaps over these in Poetry – places one thought cheek by jowl with another without introducing them and leaves them – but in prose this will not do' (*SL*, 90). While prose in general is here seen as exacting, it seems that in journalism the onus of 'articulations' may be relaxed through its distinctive temporality.

A related index of continuity, impossible to pursue here, is the deployment of a constant geographical arsenal of winds, rivers, streams, currents and the like whereby throughout his career Arnold conceptualised the activity of writing and thinking in terms of inspiration and movement: if the forms of writing change, the activities are seen fairly steadily in this respect. It seems the criticism of no other writer except Jonathan Swift – poet, journal-critic, political observer also – is so imaginatively engaged by language and thought's capacity for carrying their users away. Both positive and negative forms – the hard-earned landing on the opposite side of things for Burke, the glib rhetoric of liberal politicians – are important in Arnold's criticism. His turn to journalism is to a form singularly accommodating of such transports of the self through its informality. Arnold's characterisation of prose especially appreciates the flexibility it offers: 'In prose the character of the vehicle for the composer's thoughts is not determined beforehand; every composer has to make his own choice of vehicle' (*SP*, 159). The increased commercialisation of all levels of journalism after the abolition of the Stamp Duty in 1855, and the beginning of the end of anonymity in the 1860s, each potentially gave contributors much greater opportunity to publish and develop distinctive traits through their 'own choice of vehicle', utilising the expressive potential of the form to elaborate identity through particular serial publications.

The poet who renounced a high literary form that frustratingly tossed him in language and tradition's swell thus elected in critical journalism

another implicated in movement. Journalism's etymological root apper-
tains to the daily, and all forms of it tilt towards the quotidian and
contingent – if only in resolve to master them. Historically identified with
circulation and exchange rather than production, it has prompted numerous analogies between the journalist and the prostitute. These form an
undercurrent in Arnold's own critical reception stressing his impropriety
and hollowness (as in Sidgwick's reference to his 'titillating'); they
culminate in Georg Lukàcs' identification of the two as the apogee of
capitalist reification.[21] As 'literature in a hurry' (Arnold's apocryphal
definition) journalism comprises both an opportunity for, and a test to,
integrity – a sort of pressing invitation to go go, losing or finding oneself
in 'expression'. The testing is compounded by the constraints of editorial
policy, making it psychologically fraught for aspirants to strict self-
possession. Max Weber saw journalism as a scapegoated form, customarily judged by its ethically most reprehensible practitioners; this presumably derives from the sense of something inherently abject in a
practice so implicated in the passing moment – an ultimate parasitism
confounding humanism.[22]

Writing has of course itself in a logocentric culture always been
susceptible to such derivative, inferior status. Its association with prostitution extends beyond the journalist in a tradition dating back to
Aristotle. Arnold famously evidences anxieties about criticism's own
derivative status in 'The Function of Criticism' and when young he
acknowledged dispossession in utterance itself: 'No man can express more
than one side at once . . . but he can have a feeling for the whole if he will
not always be labouring after expression and publicity'.[23] More personally, 'I have never yet succeeded in any one great occasion in consciously
mastering myself . . . at the critical part I am too apt to hoist up the
mainsail to the wind and let her drive' (SL, 58). But one crude gauge of
the difference between the earlier Arnold and the later is that being
carried away fades as a complaint from within and becomes rather more a
criticism made by others against him, as in the earlier quotation from
Fitzjames Stephen about Arnold 'working himself . . . into an esoteric
enthusiasm'. Or else, as we will see later, a failing Arnold recurrently sees
in others.

The change of form, from poetry to journalism, seemingly redirected
an attempt at mastery, from the self to intellectual grasp of the world and
getting others to shift their viewpoints. Here one must repress a 'modern'
melancholy feeling for an 'adequate' grip on the world's multitudinousness – developing one's own nature 'in a number of directions, politically,
socially, morally, religiously', so as to reckon with 'the world in its fullness
and movement'.[24] The famous 'Arnoldian' ideological gravitation to

distance and mastery appear functions of, and in tension with, such 'fullness' – a 'culture of integration' and multiplicity where, as we will see, boundaries are repeatedly crossed. As his private letters demonstrate, Arnold's career became metaphorically dedicated to repeating the achievement of getting his poem '*Empedocles* to the railway bookstall at Derby' (*SL*, 91): crossing boundaries, impinging on his contemporaries.

The bonus of placing the identity of self and world so much in consciousness is that it allows leeway in behaviour, even a personal multitudinousness befitting modern times. For within the framework of the non-identity of the self with its 'manifestations', all behaviour becomes performance and so ironised – leaving the modern mind to sort out what's what. Arnold's exasperating insouciance signals such 'Indian detachment' hazarding impregnability. The cognitive self can thrive on the plurality confronting it, delighting in his own textual irregularity, instances of 'esoteric enthusiasm' and the windiness of others carried away in language it exposes.

In other words, agonistic quests for originality through seas of poetic tradition could be abandoned for swirling journalistic currents of contemporary criticism. Registering his personal investment in the form makes his erratic prose appear less a function of the form itself than his will. Resigned to contingency, letting himself get 'worked up', he has higher journalism's defence, of 'seeing things as they really are' from within.[25] This warrants setting the present times on the right tracks using any prevailing breeze, in the many discursive models available to him. In short, private subjectivity licenses public plurality in the 'fascinating and exciting' (*SL*, 187) habit of newspaper-writing. Here Hamilton's understanding of the post-poet as having ' "renounced renunciation" to become a solid, public-spirited man' rather misses the textual point – an exploitation of renunciation rather, which seems to have public-spirited dimensions but certainly is not solid.[26] Emphasis on the drudgery masks the flair, the franchise of desire and plurality. The goals of lucidity in language and effectivity in the world – with a private, obscure self in the wings, an enabling device for variety and defence against criticism – supplants the earlier, heavier goal of truth to an asocial self.

Demoting language as expressive resource for instrumental usage and performance thus allows more resourceful language. In its range and heterodoxy it reaches out to those outside polite culture in blatant distaste towards Philistines, vulgar expressions like 'stopping their mouths' (*CA*, 50), 'familiar' expressions such as 'a rough time of it' (*CA*, 108). The language of the street connects with a politics antagonistic to 'a condition of splendour, grandeur, and culture, which they [persons without extraordinary gifts or exceptional energy] cannot possibly reach, [and which] has the effect of making them flag in spirit' (*SP*, 105). Through such directness, familiar words and sensory appeals, as explored later, it accommodates unassuming, common modes of expression proscribed in orthodox political thought.

Much of Arnold's 1860s' publication was in the *Cornhill* and *Macmillan's*. These new magazines typified the spread of periodical journalism – with relatively wide middle-class audiences and contribution lists – and the modification of its standards and tone through their relative lightness and entertainment value, mixing fictional and non-fictional prose, for instance. They were among the first to abandon anonymity. Both helped to alter the contours of the public sphere – *Macmillan's* especially including a large proportion of non-university men among its contributors.[27] An *Economist* of 1861 (9 March) saw it as a 'kind of "Chambers Journal" for the higher classes of society'. The *Cornhill* prioritised worldly 'brilliance'. Both magazines sought the extension of existing readerships. Their lack of strong political affiliations made them particularly serviceable for free-playing minds. Arnold also wrote extensively in the *Contemporary Review* and, later, the *Nineteenth Century*, leading 'organs of opinion' known to 'look out for big names, not for good articles'. The latter pioneered the staging of debate in a single issue in the form of a symposium – the formal institutionalisation of the free play of mind within a single journal.[28] The hybridity and contradictoriness in Arnold's prose seem symptomatic of, and more intelligible in the light of, not just his writing journalism but also such historical movements within it.

Arnold thus disregards consistency and boundaries between 'higher' and 'lower' cultural spheres, alternating between desire, duty and reality, and high and low genres and idiom: a certain mutinousness informs his journalism's multitudinousness. Parts of his Homer lectures apparently contravening accepted notions of professorial identity prompted Fitzjames Stephen's charge of 'low buffoonery', their being 'not the sort of things which an Oxford Professor ought to deliver officially before the University'.[29] The security of Stephen's public sphere is vested in 'official' delivery; Arnold's breaking ranks threatens loosening things up. The reflexivity and mobility he practises, and his 'irony' in general, are symptomatic of subjectivities and societies turning away from accountability, as elsewhere in modern therapeutic and confessional modalities. Certainly his choice of form enabled extensive revisions – a subject apparently in dialogue and process, ad libbing *ad infinitum*. In this provisional approach apologies proliferate – frequently to individuals, for instance back-handedly to Mr Wright in the Preface to *Essays in*

Criticism (*SP*, 126–7), and in other ways too. An apology as to its 'sketchy and generalizing mode of treatment' prefaces the eventual publication of 'The Modern Element in Literature'.[30] The self-deprecatory posture of 'a man without a philosophy' recurs in *Culture and Anarchy* (*CA*, 98).

Sidgwick registers the lapse from reason's protocols: he judges of 'religious organisations as a dog judges of human beings, chiefly by the scent'. With this most atavistic of the senses went an 'imperturbable cheerfulness' (*CH*, 211) others saw as superciliousness, insouciance – implying some transgression of boundaries and authority. This suggests a self very actively asking for the world's criticism, ostensibly on the strength of knowing the true self it doesn't; but the criticism may be solicited to glean the parameters through which knowledge is produced. The effect of a centre may thus derive from the busy circumference of the public sphere. Both public and private writing show a selfhood pronounced through the world's reflection. This makes a virtue of the prosthetic identity demanded in public – the artificial, proper self needed for 'public' life – by jettisoning its desired sincerity and singularity while exploiting the theatricality (here anticipating Oscar Wilde). Later we will see this in close-up, as Arnold repudiates the 'the drab of the earnest, prosaic, practical, austerely literal' (*SP*, 127), performing a succession of roles in a heady 'self-difference'.[31] The plurality and performance are foregrounded in *Friendship's Garland* (*SP*, 301–39). Here, in a mock correspondence in the *Pall Mall Gazette* running before and after the *Culture and Anarchy* articles in the *Cornhill* satirising the English middle class especially, contradictory tendencies of the self and nations are staged between a sometime Arnoldian-like Prussian commanding 'Get Geist' and a *Daily-Telegraph*-reading Englishman going by the name of Arnold. The virtuosity, satire and slippages as the self and others were uncertainly staged alienated many.

ON ARNOLD'S SOCIO-POLITICAL CRITIQUE AND *CULTURE AND ANARCHY*

The term 'Arnoldian' widely refers to ideals of 'disinterest', the 'best self' and high culture, assuming an Enlightenment public sphere of political and social progress. Leaving aside its relation to Sainte-Beuve, the emphasis on 'disinterest' and critical reason in *Culture and Anarchy: An Essay in Social and Political Criticism* in particular suggests Kantian values. Disregarding the other thinkers whose presence is evident in his thinking, Arnold's affiliation to a tradition dating back to Immanuel Kant's political writings and theorised by Jürgen Habermas will now be explored through his more politically minded texts of the 1860s, especially

Culture and Anarchy. My aim here is to heighten awareness of the socio-political identity of Arnold's criticism and its departures from Enlightenment norms as publicity began to assume its current signification and centrality. I argue that in Habermas' terms Arnold embraces both Enlightenment 'critical publicity' and the 'manipulative publicity' of a media society emerging in 'new journalism', advertising and modern party political machinery; relatedly, a movement from a 'Culture-Debating' to a 'Culture-Consuming' Public.[32] The instability, range and versatility that have just been glimpsed in his writing are indicative of such a shift.

'Critical publicity' was the normative mode or principle of the Enlightenment public sphere classically expounded by Kant. Kant in fact usually refers just to publicity in his political writings. There is only glancing notice, in *The Contest of Faculties* (1798), of a specific (spurious form) – 'a mendacious form of publicity' (an early sort of public relations exercise) operating in George III's Government (*KPW*, 186). The principle of publicity, elaborated in Kant's article 'An Answer to the Question, "What is Enlightenment?"' (1784), assumes disinterest in citizens scrutinising the actions of the state through critical reason. The conclusions reached through disinterested reason in the public sphere are by definition right and in this sense there is a principle of publicity. For when in the public sphere citizens putatively abandon their particular interests as private citizens and civil servants. Instead they accede to reason's universal order and protocols: 'by the public use of one's own reason I mean that use which anyone may make of it *as a man of learning* addressing the entire reading public' (*KPW*, 55). Being a 'man of learning' requires conformity with established protocols of reason and language use. The outrageous citizen making 'presumptuous criticism' of 'taxes, where someone is called to pay them', boding 'general insubordination', is in effect rehabilitated through distance from the occasion and 'if, as a learned individual, he publicly voices his thoughts on the impropriety or even injustice of such fiscal measures' (*KPW*, 56).

The abstract, universalising language discretely upheld here by Kant, of 'fiscal measures' (rather than the vulgar need 'to pay' 'taxes') and 'impropriety or even injustice' (suppressing particular instances), offers a textbook illustration of the linguistic derealisation of the world identified by the French sociologist Pierre Bourdieu in traditional political discourse. Widely 'enabling speakers to speak without thinking what they speak', it 'discredits and destroys the spontaneous political discourse of the dominated';[33] in this respect it promotes 'sweetness and light', shrouding shrill details of complaints and injustices. For Bourdieu in his major work of the 1980s, *Distinction*, the 'essential problem of politics' is precisely the transmutation and distancing required from the assembly of habits, tastes, sensibility, sensations and 'spontaneous discourse' comprising a particular habitus for observance of the conventions of accredited political discourse. Specific interests and the norms of the dominated are both alike censored in the 'sanitised words of official discourse': 'Political analysis presupposes distance, height, the overview of the observer who places himself above the hurly-burly, or the "objectivity" of the historian.'[34] But while much of Bourdieu's socio-political analysis is hostile to disinterest, distance, universalism on account of the dominant interests served through them, on occasion in proper Kantian mode even in *Distinction* he concedes their utility for freedom – the choices and leverage and dignity they bring.[35]

Kant's public sphere is predicated on separation from the private sphere and also the state. And yet its telos is the end of this: reason being integral to mankind's moral nature, public and private will eventually be integrated as morality is realised through it with people subscribing in all their affairs to the freedom that is self-enacted law, so retiring the state. To the end of this realisation the 'public use of one's reason' runs on missionary tracks, disseminating 'the spirit of rational respect for personal value and for the duty of all men to think for themselves' (*KPW*, 55): these are the bases of maturity. The political warrant for free intellectual activity or critical reason is the assurance that its findings *are* intellectual and appertain to the public sphere, not civil society. Indeed, since it means the state is not threatened on any account, freedom of mind is precisely a function of the unfreedom of civil society under Frederick the Great, whose motto might be 'Argue as much as you like and about whatever you like, but obey!' (*KPW*, 59). Ripeness is all; on the road to freedom instrumental uses of reason are clearly proscribed for individuals capable of reason: 'Dogmas and formulas, those mechanical instruments for rational use (or rather misuse) are the ball and chains of his permanent immaturity', 'Men will of their own accord gradually work their way out of barbarism' (*KPW*, 55; 59).

Approximately eighty years later Arnold's critique of contemporary cultural forms focuses particularly on party equivalents of 'dogmas and formulas'. Approaching things rather differently from the philosopher's apparent appeasement of Frederick the Great, he all the same echoes the Kantian proposition in notably Kantian idiom: 'a state which is author-itative and sovereign, a firm and settled course of public order, is requisite if man is to bring to maturity anything precious and lasting now' (*CA*, 204). He is similarly vague in that culture involves subtle and indirect action, 'a frame of mind' (*CA*, 200) like Kant tending to efface the instrumentality of ideas as such beside enlightened subjectivities. Para-

doxically – and in human affairs considered 'in the widest sense . . .
nearly everything is paradoxical' (*KPW*,59) – for both writers only the
respectful, distant, freedom-permitting pathway of disinterested, objective truth, disdaining practical effects as such so as to preserve individual
agency, has the moral authority to effect change: telling 'silently upon the
mind of the country', keeping 'up our own communications with the
future' (*CA*, 62) is for Arnold what it is about. Increasingly modern
literature would be identified with such objectivity, disdaining proximate
material ends. Little seems more obviously Kantian than Arnold's
concern with 'expansion' and disinterest that phylogenetically connect
the history of the individual to that of the polis. The equivalence of
Arnold's 'best self' and the state is indicative of this mode of thought.

Habermas proposes that when 'critical publicity' yields to 'manipulative publicity' a series of structuring oppositions upholding the Enlightenment public sphere starts to crumble: public and private, reason and
desire, ideas and practice, principle and commerce all become confused.
Publicity regresses to a quasi-feudal condition, being represented before a
public rather than constituted by it – a masquerade of openness belying
prior private agreement. An anarchic mêlée ensues in the mass media's
'culture of integration', offering a mixed bag of 'human interest' in
entertainment and relaxation with the distance, difficulty and reason-
ableness of the proper public sphere dissolved in appeals to the senses.[36]

Habermas's theorisation is known for avoiding the actual blur of
historical processes. Most of Kant's work and other contemporary
philosophers' reached a wider audience through discussion in literary
reviews that facilitated reading and knowledge.[37] Such mediation necessarily qualifies Habermas' key distinction between the early 'access-
increasing' and 'transmitting' functions of journals and the facilitation
in a 'culture-consuming' public sphere: typically, then as now, learning of
philosophers' work through reviews is easier going. The neglect of Kant's
political writings seems in part a function of their appearance in the
relatively light-weight form of journals.[38] The neologism 'journalistic'
(*OED*, 1829) and James Mill's remarkable critique of the early periodical
form (1824) identifying its hegemonic role were themselves indicative of
consumer-cradling practices early in the nineteenth century.[39] Regarding
Habermas's important distinction between theory and practice, for
Edmund Burke, Francis Jeffrey and many others the founding event
of modernity, the French Revolution, was very much related to the power
of the press, where theory demonstrated performative capacities officially
denied it.[40] This points to a key lacuna in theorisation of a disinterested
public sphere, that utterance is not exterior to social relations where it is
necessarily implicated in networks of power.[41] However, despite such

weaknesses Habermas's engagement with changes identified at the time, taken warily, offers a useful template when considering broad historical shifts.

Kant was seen as 'the philosopher of the French Revolution' (*KPW*, 3), the most arresting event in Arnold's and many others' historical imagination. For Arnold the Revolution taught the ineluctability of political 'expansion' tending to 'mass-democracy' and change as the salient facts of modern life: his office is to alert others to their importance. The range of Arnold's allusions, eclecticism and instability clearly preclude simple association with any one writer; yet examining Kant's political thought, in particular his *Berlin Monthly Journal* article 'An Answer to the Question: "What is Enlightenment?"' (*KPW*, 54–60), establishes significant discursive antecedents of Arnold's thinking, howsoever they had been mediated in other political writings and through more informal processes described by Bourdieu, whereby 'philosophical doxa [are] carried along by intellectual rumour – labels of schools, truncated quotations, functioning as slogans in celebration or polemics'.[42]

Arnold's stated political and cultural values remained fairly constant: progressivism, didacticism, idealism, Europeanism, voluntarism, outreach, dedication to disinterested reason and ideas, preoccupation with prematurity, respect for the existing order, ambivalence to authority, teleological understanding, antipathy to mechanism and formalism, commitment to expansion and free play of the mind, distinction between thought and action, fixation with the French Revolution, attraction to a strong state, concept of 'aliens' and other tenets and lexical indexes such as 'tutelage', 'maturity', the categorical imperative and 'geist' are scattered throughout his 1860s' essays, marking them those of a post-Kantian man. In the general configuration of liberalism and authoritarianism, high moral tone and an extraordinary number of specific instances – echoes, allusions, exact phrasing, specific propositions, qualifications and emphases – they exhibit a Kantian commitment to reason, human autonomy and dignity disdainful of differences augmented by the aesthetic that allows them (associated with Schiller): a Kantian polis seems a crucial reference point in his thinking. This most obviously exceeds the terms of Kantian analysis in its concern with class but even here Arnold's attitude, declining particularity for a universal humanity, has Kantian overtones. By the time of *Culture and Anarchy* the sense of a necessary class dialectic evident in 'On Democracy' (*SP*, 99–125) had faded to an extraordinarily ahistorical account in which the different classes are almost structurally identical, making them little more than groupings of differing qualities.

Its fierce antipathy to subordination and notion of the English democracy 'throwing off the tutelage of aristocracy' (*SP*, 113) links 'On

Democracy' to 'What is Enlightenment?' A relatively straight, vigorous political account compared with later texts, its acuity and honesty are striking concerning the effects of inegalitarian relationships. Here it seems Arnold is himself daring to know, in conformity with Kant's motto of Enlightenment, '*Sapere aude*! Have courage to use your *own* understanding!' (*KPW*,54). This entails theorising politically, phylogenetically, from the individual to the state, with conviction – seemingly his own experience not masked by irony, shaped in the light of Kantian precepts mediated most obviously by John Stuart Mill:

> Now, can it be denied, that a certain approach to equality, at any rate a certain reduction of signal inequalities, is a natural, instinctive demand of that impulse which drives society as a whole, – no longer individuals and limited classes only, but the mass of a community, – to develop itself with the utmost possible fulness and freedom? Can it be denied, that to be heavily overshadowed, to be profoundly insignificant, has, on the whole, a depressing and benumbing effect on the character? (*SP*, 104)

A Kantian emphasis on human dignity and autonomy persists in Arnold's criticism alongside a prescriptivism implicated in class interests that tends for many critics to void it.[43] In recent discounting of the egalitarianism Arnold is less seen as a political writer now than in earlier liberal criticism such as Lionel Trilling's. This seems related to an antipathy in poststructuralist thinking to broaching egalitarian sentiment, communal values and, in general, politics as it has been. Yet it is recurrently in this area of critique that Arnold, often so vague, is at his most trenchant. 'My Countrymen' thus indicts the false-seeming of a nation's touting progress and superiority on the grounds of its actual incapacity for reason and ideas with a keenness at times redolent of Swift and the 'moral desperado' in Carlyle:

> if any one says to you, in your turn: 'The English system of a great landed aristocracy keeps your lower class a lower class for ever, and materialises and vulgarises your whole middle class,' you stare vacantly at the speaker, you cannot even take in his ideas; you can only blurt forth, in reply, some clap-trap . . . (*SP*, 193)

Here the severity, almost bludgeoning, is somewhat mitigated by 'airs and graces' in the form of literary devices – an ironic footnote respecting Jacobinism; the sustained ironic structure of foreigners' viewpoints. Distancing Arnold from this radical vision, these seem prompted by personal dialectics of empathy and estrangement and anxieties over a 'trenchant authoritative style' (*SP*, 177), with intensity defused in a polite reach for urbanity. The critic who sees 'My Countrymen' so severely nicely corroborates Carlyle's conception of the press as heir to the pulpit,[44] with the literary devices functioning as emollients and sweet-eners.

In subsequent 1860s' texts other Kantian political motifs recur: 'The Function of Criticism' (*SP*, 130–57) looks back to Kant's 'free teachers of right', forward to *Culture and Anarchy*'s aliens. Its celebration of the French Revolution as demonstrating people's capacity for disinterest echoes Kant's qualified approval on the same ground (*KPW*, 182). In its attack on the Philistines 'My Countrymen' (*SP*, 175–201) exudes the question of enlightenment: 'What is the modern problem? to make human life, all through, more natural and rational' (*SP*, 189). However, despite this political backdrop, some nudging as to its Prussian credentials in *Friendship's Garland*, and the subtitle announcing *An Essay in Social and Political Criticism*, *Culture and Anarchy* has seldom been regarded as a text of political thought.[45] In Stefan Collini's recent edition of *Culture and Anarchy and Other Writings* in the series, 'Cambridge Texts in the History of Political Thought', political dimensions are appropriately considered but recede before the social since 'we do not turn to him for that kind of intellectual architectonic, based on rigorous analysis of the nature of the state or the logic of political obligation' characterising Western political theory.[46] 'Other Writings' marks the architectonic abyss.

But while formal theoretical analysis is clearly absent, the assumptions just indicated point to a coherent Enlightenment political framework variously taken up by liberals in the nineteenth century, indeed registered by Arnold's critics in accusations of his 'transcendentalism' (for example, *SP*, 175). Inasmuch as Arnold presents 'rather, works of social criticism' concerned to 'cajole, mock, provoke, and persuade', as we will see in the next section, they appear founded on this theoretical structure, hardly lacking in ideas as to political obligations.[47] It seems that the subsequent blurring – an increasing non-specificity – of the historical and political analysis seen in 'On Democracy' may even be a defensive response to criticisms of an absence of motivation in his political scheme. Frederic Harrison remonstrated 'what am I profited unless I learn how this same fiddle-stick, or sauerkraut, or culture (call it as you please), comes to a man?' (*CH*, 229): persuading, cajoling, provoking, mocking, even despis-ing attempt to establish the human connection and take-up of the ideal that Kant's notoriously dry work fails widely to inspire. A strict 'logic of political obligation' is thus neglected as a socio-psychological induction of it is attempted. Absence of motivation inducing men to 'dare to know' and be high-minded is a central criticism of Kant's work; Harrison's criticism suggests Arnold's footnote to 'My Countrymen' (and other utterances to the same effect), that 'Philosophy has always been bringing me into trouble' (*SP*, 175), is not altogether ironic.

As much as in 'On Democracy' and 'My Countrymen', the central problematic in *Culture and Anarchy* is the promotion of reason and order in an expanding body politic – enabling it to *be* enlightened and modern – bequeathed from the Enlightenment. Kant actually circumvents the problem of motivation by conflating reason and morality in human nature; with persons inherently tilted towards the good, motivation is dispensed with on an ideal level. Arnold's cultural criticism in *Culture and Anarchy* in effect comes in at this point of weakness in Kant's theory – both qualifying Kant's voluntarism and displaying 'literary' features which seem, as just noted, politically motivated. The weakness in Enlightenment theory seemed demonstrated in the 1860s' run-up to electoral reform in 1867 when 'critical publicity' seemed feeble given contemporary disturbances; and all the more urgent given the development of party machinery and the political press.

At points echoing Alexis de Tocqueville's analysis and John Stuart Mill's, Arnold's sustained engagement with this changing political landscape has been mostly considered in terms of the contemporary public disturbances and accordingly attenuated. For the alliance between modern newspapers and political parties during the expansion of the newspaper reading public and democracy were crucial features of the English political scene from the 1860s. Together these innovations inaugurated a modern cultural politics, exploited by Gladstone in particular, where the image of leaders, publicity and party organisation are crucial.[48]

Arnold's critique of political leaders, particular measures and press representations relate exactly to these developments, as the enormous specificity of their reference argues. So from his *Essays in Criticism* he repeatedly objects to the 'world of catchwords and party habits' (*SP*, 139) binding those subject to them in a state of immaturity; criticises numerous individuals and developments in public life (a whole article which became a chapter in *Culture and Anarchy* argued with measures favoured by 'Our Liberal Practitioners': *CA*, 165–201); and repeatedly criticises newspaper representations for partisanship.[49] Time and again he objects to proposals not based on universal criteria of reason and justice but rather specious private interests of the party machine as in Liberal support for disestablishment of the Irish Church, which he sees as motivated by party political expediency in securing nonconformist support (*CA*, 166–174).

On a notorious occasion he attacks Sir Charles Adderley and Mr Roebuck for pious political rhetoric and Anglo-Saxon triumphalism as they manifest racism, extolling 'the old Anglo-Saxon race . . . [as] the best breed in the whole world'. Again here catchwords and political slogans are undercut on point of their discrepancy with realities of poverty, child murder and brutality in the case of 'a girl named Wragg' taken into custody following her child's murder (*SP*, 144–6). Disinterested, critical reason is required in the electorate and political leaders alike to see through the 'dogmas and formulas' (or the 'sanitised words') of those using a rhetoric of progress that enables 'speakers to speak without thinking what they speak'.

To categorise this and other analysis as 'social' (or 'personal'), more than political, seems to prioritise the interests of organised political bodies and/or theory over the agency of individual subjects: Arnold traces the generalising language back to circumstances that contradict them. Here modern political life appears to start with Enlightenment ideals and the requirement that political subjects exercise 'resolution and courage to use . . . [their understanding] without the guidance of another' (*KPW*, 54), exercising a base-line democratic political function in vigilance towards those in authority.

Arnold's insistent message, focusing recurrently on representations, that political leaders, the electorate and the press generally need to be more critical, becomes less banal than timely given the take-off of a modern media society and politics increasingly conducted through party organisations and cultural forms. Even his confession of his earlier misguided worship of Benjamin Franklin and Jeremy Bentham in 'Sweetness and Light' (*CA*, 67–8) has a timely edge. For this underlines the outmodedness of Carlylean hero-worship in a modern, disenchanted age, at precisely the point at which politics threatened its revival in the cult of particular leaders. Repeatedly Arnold fastens on 'mendacious' forms of publicity where public figures use universalist Enlightenment terms to promote private interests. His repeated deflation of the rhetoric of political speeches reported in the press – as in the case of Wragg – amounts to exercises in practical criticism and elementary semiotic awareness exposing the politicians' hype through reference to actuality. The grounds of his critique, urging the public sphere's plane of disinterest, free play of mind and critical reason as the test of all, appear consistently and turn on the 'manipulative publicity' outlined by Habermas. In these respects, then, it seems Arnold straightforwardly echoes Enlightenment tenets and applies them reflexively in his analysis of contemporary political phenomena and discourses; in doing so he points to the Enlightenment genealogy of cultural studies.

THE 'NEW PHENOMENON': ARNOLD AND 'MANIPULATIVE PUBLICITY'

Culture on the one hand and a strong and interventionist state where appropriate were Arnold's quite opposed solutions to the present ills in

Culture and Anarchy. Notwithstanding its engagement with contemporary political developments, the call 'to see things as they are' (*CA*, 46), distancing political action, and the aesthetic emphasis on 'sweetness and light' can eclipse the interventionist strand. This, and its many 'literary' features, seem a factor in its invisibility as socio-political discourse. But with a Kantian backdrop *Culture and Anarchy* is more remarkable for insisting that culture entails the Hebraic 'passion for doing good' and the related interventionism. While Arnold at times specifically resists the idea that at present 'the world wants fire and strength more than sweetness and light' (*CA*, 205), the intensities of his prose and the role of his state problematise this proposition.

A pressing problem when reading it are the lapses from reason's protocols. Detachment, disinterest, curiosity, urbanity are often absent, most notably in rudeness towards Philistines and intensities where the prose veers towards all-out utterance. An early instance is the gross objectification and sustained sneer at the Philistines beginning, 'Culture says: "Consider these people, then, their way of life, their habits, their manners, the very tones of their voice; look at them attentively"' (*CA*, 52). Later, Arnold defends a non-manipulative public sphere, condemning 'the ordinary popular literature' and those who try 'to give the masses, as they call them, an intellectual food prepared and adapted in the way they think proper for the actual condition of the masses' (*CA*, 69). But soon after he works up a quasi-racist frenzy of righteousness and religious imagery concerning culture and 'the division of light from darkness' (*CA*, 71) that cannot be exonerated from comparable manipulative intent.

Yet the proliferating definitions, joining 'spontaneity of consciousness' and 'strictness of conscience', 'seeing things as they are' and 'the passion for doing good', Hellenic and Hebraic principles in culture, aspire to make this intensity like all departures from equanimity a non-problem. The particular purchase of the Hebraic here seems its justification of a heavy-handedness that departs from the reason and voluntarist ethos of the public sphere. Admitting into it the authoritarianism that Kant (and Arnold too) approves outside it in the state as the very condition of the public sphere's freedom, the Hebraic principle apparently licenses local textual violations of reason to pressure readers into assent. Its extra-textual action is similar, urging state intervention into civil society to the end of ultimately realising perfection. Both textuality and its referent thus see norms of the public sphere contravened with rational protocols and separation of state and civil society suspended. By means of the Hebraic, in short, history's destination may be hastened. Here it seems significant that, much like Bourdieu's understanding of the role of 'intellectual rumour' quoted earlier, Arnold's perception of the public sphere's functioning at times deprecates the importance of books as such and other forms of polite society besides rougher modes boding more expansive and vital communication – 'a current of ideas' beyond books making society 'in the fullest measure . . . intelligent and alive' (*SP*, 135).

Hardly fortuitously, then, as the enabling principle of Arnold's textual versatility and contradictions the Hebraic is at one (neglected) point privileged over Hellenic 'sweetness and light': 'culture has one great passion, the passion for sweetness and light. It has one even yet greater! the passion for letting them prevail' (*CA*, 69). Here in this 'touching' self-correction, with Arnold seemingly yielding to some sweet impulse within, readers encounter a paradoxical passion, for letting 'sweetness and light' prevail; or *faux naïveté*. The repetition and punctuation marks insinuate passion in exclamation and self-correction – apparently evidencing the very priority being upheld with the critic 'carried away' into an exclamation mark. At this 'familiar' point perhaps undermining readers' critical faculties, morality interestingly loses its usual imperative cast, becoming a matter of 'letting' sweetness and light prevail, rather than 'making' and 'doing', the customary locutions. Again hardly fortuitously, the moral impulse is relayed as 'passion' – that is, naturalised, so affiliated to the Hellenic.

Such textual manœuvring, especially the sweet spontaneity of the exclamation mark, presumably exemplifies the 'airs' and 'low buffoonery' Sidgwick and Fitzjames Stephen protested. The seeming spontaneity and ingratiating facility evidence a shortfall in reason's norms of distance and difficulty. They try to cajole readers into a mood of acceptance. Often elsewhere Arnold resorts to confessional discourse, writing in the first-person singular, with similar significance attaching to personal display. The public sphere's boundaries required in contrast impersonality and self-collection: 'free teachers of right' 'do not address themselves in familiar tones to the *people* . . . but in respectful tones to the state' (*KPW*, 186).

Soon after the fiercely partisan prophetic voice appears dividing 'light from darkness', looking to 'the revolution of the times; for the old order is passed, and the new arises' (*CA*, 71). Again, as often, highly charged prose seemingly aspires to abolish Kantian critical distance in heavy-gunned Hebraic appeal to tastes and senses which might also be construed as spontaneity of consciousness. Howsoever, it hijacks signifiers of Christianity for its secular substitute, in accordance with the promotional practices of modern journalism and advertising: W. T. Stead's investi-gative journalism 'The Maiden Tribute of Modern Babylon' is an obvious example of such sensational deployment of religious language and imagery.[50] Here again the types of the Hellenic and Hebraic are not distinct. A rationale appears in a later quotation from the French religious philosopher Joubert:

> 'Just what makes worship impressive,' says Joubert, 'is its publicity, its external manifestation, its sound, its splendour, its observance universally and visibly holding its sway . . . the same devotion', as he says in another place, 'unites men far more than the same thought and knowledge'. (*CA*, 171)

Appreciative of the functions of ritual, this passage underscores the instrumentalism and appeal to the sensorium in the overblown passages. It makes Arnold's purposeful periodic recycling of religious language seem a kind of necessary softening muzak for the harmonious relations identified with culture: in the method, if seldom the precise means, a flagrant publicist of modern times. The emotive prose seemingly presumes people's responsivity to a hard sell – the 'devotion' generated – will enlist them to the cause of culture that ostensibly stands for something else. Arnold was caricatured by Frederic Harrison in terms of 'Culture [sitting] high aloft with a pouncet-box to spare her senses aught unpleasant' (*CH*, 233) – an apotheosis of dandyish fastidiousness, preparing the way for Wilde – and the negative response of distaste is a standard feature of his public image. But much of the distinctiveness of *Culture and Anarchy* lies in fulsome orchestration of the senses with appeals to reason.

The Preface of *Culture and Anarchy* entertains something of this internal anarchy in urging the Hellenic be given a top-up of Hebraism's energy that gives 'to man the happiness of doing what he knows' (*CA*, 38). Here, when you do what you know, the boundaries between thought and action and the separate identities of the Hellenic and Hebraic collapse, under the distracting smile of happiness. All in all there seems substantial interpenetration of the Hellenic and Hebraic, contrary to the racial dialectic Robert Young elaborates in which each remains distinct.[51] Most obviously, there is 'our race' (*CA*, 38) at their confluence – much as Arnold himself was a product of interracial union of Saxon and Celt.

The instability and permeability of the terms may be part of their attraction for a writer persistently balking at the authority he calls for.[52] They insinuate 'clear' distinctions and their fusion too, graphically: embodiment stretches to what logic cannot reach, granting benefits of identity and non-identity too. What is more (when apparently speculation as to the resemblance of the English and Jews was common) the racial binary of the Hebraic and Hellenic is somewhat homely and suited to teaching the Puritans a lesson – constituting a sort of allegory with scant narrative, outdoing them on their own ground.[53] After all, all that 'is said about Hebraism and Hellenism, has for its main result to show how our Puritans, ancient and modern, have not enough added to their care for walking staunchly by the best light they have' (*CA*, 11).

The discursive potency of race has already been glimpsed in the Anglo-Saxon triumphalism Arnold attacked through the case of Wragg. The typologisation of class within *Culture and Anarchy* seems to proceed on a similar basis, capitalising on the publicity of the group identities in a particularly flagrant way. For Arnold's descriptions and exhortation to disinterest utilise the popular discourse and methods of opponents such as John Bright.[54] Notwithstanding the fact that the call for 'the best self' is philosophically specious, it seems to have had widespread appeal related to its accessibility and, again, a 'homeliness' emanating from 'familiar words'.

I have used them with reference to the first chapter of *Culture and Anarchy* but the Hellenic and Hebraic do not appear until later. This points further to their importance as publicising devices: referring variable assortments of mental traits to two racial types offers an easy handle on them. It braces the criticism with quasi-anthropological terms while proceeding as if on the level of a family romance in which different characteristics descending from different family lines are discussed. It is in accord with the practice of personalisation central to modern news discourses and the flight from abstraction Arnold sees the French religious philosopher Joubert commending in his *Essays in Criticism*. As glimpsed already, the personal – in the form of Arnold's persona, prolific reference to others and general gravitation to embodiment – figures prominently throughout his work, further marking it off from the impersonal abstract discourse of critical publicity. Other boundaries – most notably between feeling and reason – are repeatedly crossed: as if he demarcates identities, and binary oppositions, for publicist ends, only to refuse them authority also. In this most fundamental respect, it seems Arnold undermines the Enlightenment public sphere through ultimately refusing its binary structure and authority.

One of the most instructive passages in this respect involves another key moment of publicity, the virtuoso Preface to the *Essays in Criticism* culminating in a set-piece on Oxford. Disdaining replying to his critics as such as his essays are collected in a book, Arnold in general terms here defends his playfulness in the name of non-violence, humility, righteousness:

> To try and approach truth on one side after another, not to strive or cry, nor to persist in pressing forward, on any one side, with violence and self-will – it is only thus, it seems to me, that mortals may hope to gain any vision of the mysterious Goddess, whom we shall never see except in outline, but only thus even in outline. He who will do nothing but fight impetuously towards her on his own, one,

favourite, particular line, is inevitably destined to run his head into the folds of the
black robe in which she is wrapped. (*SP*, 126)

The lines tread pre-Raphaelite territory with murky emotions, gender
anxieties, a black-robed Goddess, also an ambience of Sunday School
tracts about naughty boys – a defence of plurality and freedoms through
their exercise. Again hypercharged prose anticipates 'new journalism', in
particular the religious and classical imagery saturating 'The Maiden
Tribute of Modern Babylon'; and here as often in Arnold's writing there
is more than a scent of parody – and/or a wind got up – in the symmetry,
emphasis, allusions. Suggestions of parody and extreme theatricality are
intensified in the essay's virtuosity as it rushes from the lyrical and neo-
chivalric to the neo-classical and *The Dunciad* and then on to a trio of
magicians, the Woodford Branch of the Great Eastern Line and the black
comedy of a murder. The densely allusive lines celebrate distance and
variety over contact and singularity; but the writer who celebrates
plurality so energetically comes as close to saying nothing as saying
all. His proclivity for performance admits a plural, heterodox self
flagrantly at odds with the 'drab of the earnest' and straight ways of
the happily named Mr Wright (*SP*, 127).

Further arguing the staginess of the whole, there is a notable redun-
dancy in 'inevitably destined' and a self-refuting insistence in the whole
passage that is partly a function of so many pressing monosyllables. So we
may ask, exactly whose and what interests are being defended? Why ever
does the *head* of the impetuous fighter run 'into the folds'? And why is
goddess truth (if she is it) robed in black? The intertextuality of hymn,
prayer, poetry – all the chivalric non-fighting echoing Donne, St Ignatius
Loyola, Bunyan – seems another attempt to recuperate the energy of the
absolute for the cause of plurality; the soft 'folds of the black robe'
awaiting that head suggest even the absolute may have abandoned
rigidity. In the next paragraph the versatility of the writing argues
directly against rectitude and absolutism in the form of that Mr Wright
and strict correspondence in a Philistine rule-bound society – 'the drab of
the earnest, prosaic, practical, austerely literal future' (*SP*, 127).

From such a mixed environment the outlines of Oxford ('the myster-
ious goddess' transformed, it seems) emerge at the end of the Preface's
climb towards it: 'home of lost causes, and forsaken beliefs, and unpopular names, and impossible loyalties' (*SP*, 130), an ideal centre
centred in ex-centricity and plurality. Hardly surprisingly given the
paradoxes and opacities on the run-in, the prolongation of the attack
on more worldly contemporaries associated with the place – such as
Fitzjames Stephen and other *Saturday Review* contributors hostile to
Arnold – tends to be overlooked. But 'lost', 'forsaken', 'unpopular',

'impossible' characterise 'this queen of romance' and should not be so entirely deprived of their frequent evaluative load as to have an entirely positive accent. The possibility of barbed criticism and ambivalence is heightened given the preceding comedy: casually we meet three well-known theatrical performers using 'the honourable style of Professor' 'a title I share with so many distinguished men, – Professor Pepper, Professor Andersen, Professor Frickel, and others, – who adorn it, I feel, much more than I do' (*SP*, 127–8). The extent of Arnold's attachment to the university is problematised in the essay; his prose actually implicates 'her' in the 'fierce intellectual life of our century' that he upholds as her antithesis. Readers may be led to take Oxford's refulgence – 'her' role as a beacon of culture – unambiguously partly through sensory and intellectual repletion, the 'Preface' comprising a particularly dazzling instance of prophet and comedian in concert.

The mobility journalism's informality seems to have excited in Arnold is particularly apparent in oppositions, definitions and catchphrases whose reference shifts and numerous contradictions. Arnold thus famously deplores animosity ('culture hates hatred', *CA*, 69) excepting his own – approving the passions mentioned above and recurrently lapsing into savagery, as for instance on middle-class religion, 'the very lowest form of intelligential life . . . [offering], for a great treat, a lecture on teetotalism and nunneries'. Even in the act of enunciation, though, this slips the blade of savagery – the bathos of nursery idiom ('a great treat') soliciting its targets on their own ascetic ground to do without and see bigger. The humorous move, appealing to asceticism, weakens the case against it: glimpses of absolutes may even with Philistines be qualified. Indeed it seems disinterest – in the form of a sharing and a sense of commonality where differences are dropped – may be better induced in readers through humour than reason, and the arresting power of virtuosity. Appropriately, given the sliding prose, 'sweetness and light' has the distinction of hardly acceding to the referential at all – a catchphrase that is taken as such, a rallying-cry of taste and disposition, whose usage has become invariably ironic.

George Eliot registers the Philistinism in fact attaching to Arnold's culture in a joke in *Daniel Deronda*. University will give Deronda 'a passport in life', 'a little disinterested culture to make head against cotton and capital, especially in the House'.[55] Here in Eliot's awareness of the Philistine within a critic critiquing the same, and more generally, Arnold's ostensibly 'lucid' oppositions and 'key' categories founder, apparently contributing to his success as a publicist. For if the sense of 'lucidity' or 'clarity' largely derive from the drawing up of succinct formulations, vivid oppositions and types, catchphrases, familiar words, images and strong feeling in what were then termed Arnold's 'vivacities' (as in the animus against the *British Banner*, *CA*, 111), generating a succession of momentary strong effects above 'the confusion which environs' (*CA*, 202) the reader, they seem to enact the project of culture as a whole in presenting a defence against anarchy. In the face of language's repeated slippages and contradictions the determinate beckons as, say, an idealised Oxford: 'he [Arnold] says a few things in such a way as that *almost inspite of ourselves* we remember them' (*CH*, 149). The 'high standard' or 'authoritative centre' culture broadly implied for Arnold seems locally enacted for Henry James here in words and notions salvaged from time and, apparently, the unconscious, since '*ourselves*' drag against it.

Arnold cherished the general currency his phrases achieved. Writers often deal in 'memorable' phrases, few though – excepting writers of aphorisms, poetry, advertisements – with such virtuosity where what stands out is the standing out, as in 'sweetness and light'. As performance, outdoing ordinary, 'literal' language use, they are a variant of the virtuosity and playfulness already observed in Arnold's criticism. This playfulness is usually taken as relieving the high seriousness and authoritarian tendencies rather than undermining them. But a performative rather than a cognitive or aesthetic office even informs Arnold's famous definition of culture. This invokes routine journalistic functions of taking knowledge out of closets, as it were, and putting it into circulation. Even so, with distinct circularity, 'the best' appears a function of being 'the best that is known and thought in the world' – a feat of publicisation primarily:

> The great men of culture are those who have had a passion for diffusing, for making prevail, for carrying from one end of society to the other, the best knowledge, the best ideas of their time; who have laboured to divest knowledge of all that was harsh, uncouth, difficult, abstract, professional, exclusive; to humanize it, to make it efficient outside the clique of the cultivated and learned, yet still remaining the *best* knowledge and thought of the time. (*CA*, 70)

The rather plaintive culminating insistence – 'yet still remaining the best knowledge' – acknowledges the question the exposition chronically begs: exactly what remains of 'the best' (or of anything?) post such rigorous remodelling? 'The *best* knowledge and thought of the time' appear here, like the 'best self', like culture itself, absolutely constituted by the negatives and particularities they escape. Swinging from the margins to the citadels of culture with the divestment of the disconcerting, unprepossessing, complexity, difficulty, abstraction, exclusivity (all particularities or provincialisms of the mind), the retention of identity as 'the best knowledge and thought of the time' after such an overhaul seems an acute instance of consuming resources of singularity and critical challenge and reclaiming their value too, on an impossible 'familiar' basis. Here it seems that identity is forfeited for exchange value and utopianly retained too.

The famous passage suggests Arnold's criticism endorses a journalistic dedication to 'writing for the public' where the best writing stands out by standing out – sufficiently detached for time and space travel, like 'Empedocles on Etna' on Derby station. This postmodern image enacts hybridity, crossing boundaries and defying authorities, bringing a staging post on the high cultural tour in poetry to the provincial railway passenger; an exotic place-name to bookstalls selling 'familiar words', which it will join. Its excitement exceeds the mixing of aristocrat and likely middle-class reader for in railway technology the vista of mass publicity and the future open up.

'Currency in the world' is upheld against exclusive scholastic usages and difficulty in Arnold's article/essay on 'Joubert' that anticipates the famous passage above. In part a manual for writers in manipulative publicity, it offers clues to Arnold's publicist abilities. For instance, Arnold includes Joubert's dictum, 'It is by means of familiar words that style takes hold of the reader and gets possession of him'. The essay also suggests a philosophic rationale for Arnold's highly inhabited and topical prose in Joubert's quarrel with metaphysics' preferring abstraction over 'the sensible' world most people relate to: 'Distrust, in books on metaphysics, words which have not been able to get currency in the world.'[56] In this context Arnold's pose of 'plain man' suggests an egalitarian strain and rhetoric: what matters in the world is of it and has purchase within it. He attempts a common appeal through variety, the senses, declaration of preferences, 'familiar words', a teasing persona, cajolery. These features corresponded with changes in contemporary newspaper journalism invoking worldly 'human interest' and egalitarianism. But they share a tendency to buttonhole readers, reducing distance and making dissent more difficult, like the entertainment – the variety act – of a successful comedian. There are obvious calls for, and objections to, associating such strategies with democracy.

This account has drawn on Habermas' study. But since his structuring distinctions were never as clear-cut as he suggests, the question of a historical break in Arnold's criticism is problematised. I have argued that his criticism is politically grounded in Enlightenment theory assuming expansion of the body politic, where reason, the public sphere and journalism are all pivotal. Neglect of this political framework seems to have involved both English hostility to idealism and literary disregard of journalistic form.[57] But Arnold's transgression of the norms of 'critical publicity' needs also to be emphasised, since it situates him – and the 'objective' line of journalism he represents – within the modern practices he denigrates. His journalism thus evidences internally an opposition between two models of journalism customarily located externally, in a bifurcation within journalism at the time he was writing.[58] His own attack on 'a new journalism' in 1887 was indeed instrumental in the currency of the idea of bifurcation by identifying 'a new journalism' which neglected journalism's obligation to 'get at the state of things as they really are'. Yet Arnold ignored this obligation himself, crudely linking 'the democracy' to 'feather-brained' journalism as part of his attack on Irish Home Rule.[59] His 1860s, criticism is unstable and manipulative – emotive, dismissive, careless, personal, confessional: blurring Enlightenment boundaries between public and private, ideas and practice, reason and senses.

His exhibition of typical attitudes among the dominant cultural grouping he belongs to (in scathingly dismissing 'Mr. Wright''s earnestness, for instance) highlights the particular class interests in 'disinterest' and in this respect undermines the project of disinterested reason. Since it supplies critics with plentiful social grounds for objecting to Arnold's critique it points to his partial complicity with attacks on a disinterested sphere. But his high-handed dismissiveness also functions rhetorically by showing fallible humanity. This enhances the vision of a 'best self' and culture through an inoculation of 'human' shortcomings. The many references to Arnold's 'humanity' indicate its centrality to his publicity.

The alternatives show a modern identity charged through performance and publicity: hardly the discrete self of official liberal humanism. The playfulness extends to self-difference and undecidability, so that while it apparently serves serious ends it also tends to their subversion: if Arnold historically represents a new, hybrid kind of critical seriousness in entertaining, mobile prose reaching beyond conventional norms in the public sphere – a sort of seriousness that dare not show as such – he also undermines serious criticism in prose that contradicts key precepts in his criticism and is notably unhinged. My account has argued a fairly orthodox critic of propaganda and journalism, upholding the role of a critical public in modern democracies, but with a keener political edge than 'Arnoldian' usually suggests; also a neglected 'propagandist for criticism', whose own practice resembles 'a new journalism' and subverts Enlightenment norms. Arnold's writing on Joubert not 'trying to fit his ideas into a house' points to journalism's importance here: 'I doubt whether, in an elaborate work on the philosophy of religion, he [Joubert] would have got his ideas to *shine*, to use his own expression, as they shine when he utters them in perfect freedom'.[60] It seems time Arnold's modernity and significance are revised so as to register the interrelationship of ideas and 'expression' and the freedoms and 'shining' journalism enabled in his case, encapsulated in the notion of an unhoused form. Here 'high culture' is qualified in a street act of sorts where critical reason is jostled in 'free' expression.

ABBREVIATIONS

Page references from Arnold's criticism and letters, contemporary criticism and Kant's political writings appear within the text in brackets, abbreviated as follows:

CA   Matthew Arnold, *Culture and Anarchy*, ed. J. Dover Wilson (Cambridge UP: 1988).

SL   Clinton Machann and Forrest D. Burt (eds), *Selected Letters of Matthew Arnold* (Macmillan: Basingstoke, 1993).

SP   P. J. Keating (ed.), *Matthew Arnold: Selected Prose* (Penguin: Harmondsworth, 1987).

CH   Carl Dawson and John Pfordresher (eds), *Matthew Arnold, Prose Writings: The Critical Heritage* (Routledge & Kegan Paul: London, 1979).

KPW   Hans Reiss (ed.), *Kant's Political Writings*, tr. H. B. Nisbet (Cambridge UP: 1970).

NOTES

See also H. Super (ed.), *The Complete Prose Works of Matthew Arnold*, 11 vols (University of Michigan: Ann Arbor, 1960–77).

1. Late Arnoldian concerns appear in Virginia Woolf, *The Voyage Out* (Penguin: Harmondsworth, 1992 [1915]), for instance 36.

2. On cultural capital see Pierre Bourdieu, *Distinction: A Social Critique of the Judgement of Taste*, tr. Richard Nice (Routledge: London, 1994); Pierre Bourdieu, *The Field of Cultural Production*, ed. Randal Johnson (Polity Press: Cambridge, 1993).

3. On the Newbolt Report and social classes see Chris Baldick, *The Social Mission of English Criticism* (Oxford UP: 1983), 95.

4. 'Arnold, Matthew', *Dictionary of National Biography* (Smith, Elder & Co.: London, 1901), suppl., Vol. 1, 70–5, 75.

5. T. S. Eliot, *The Sacred Wood* (Methuen: London, 1920), 1.

6. Edmund Burke, *Reflections on the Revolution in France* (J. M. Dent: London, 1967), 330.

7. See 'An "Interview" with Jacques Derrida', *Cambridge Review*, Oct. 1992, 131. Arnold's disclaimers (*SP*, 127–8) scarcely detract from his academic authority.

8. It seems more extensive research would establish that Arnold's Burke *was* an icon of this criticism; Keating (*SP*, 11) registers the passage's celebrity.

9. Robert Young, *Colonial Desire: Hybridity in Theory, Culture and Race* (Routledge: London, 1995), 55.

10. Baldick, *Social Mission*, 31–2; acknowledging limitations owing to the exigencies of tracing a 'particular "line"', 16. For early concern with prematurity see Kant, *KPW*, 55.

11. Baldick, *Social Mission*, 26.

12. See Nicholas Murray, *A Life of Matthew Arnold* (Hodder & Stoughton: London, 1996), 229; Sidgwick, *CH*, 210–11.

13. See Perry Meisel, *The Myth of the Modern* (Yale UP: 1987), 39–53; Arnold, 'The Modern Element in Literature', in Miriam Allott (ed.), *Selected Poems and Prose: Matthew Arnold* (J. M. Dent: London, 1993), 135, 130; Tony Pinkney, 'Matthew Arnold and the Subject of Modernity', *Critical Survey*, 4:3 (1992), 226–32.

14. See Meisel, *Myth of the Modern*, 39; on the Arnold–Leavis line see Baldick, *Social Mission*, 193 (final résumé) and *passim*, 162–93.

15. [Fitzjames Stephen], 'Matthew Arnold and His Countrymen', *Saturday Review*, XVIII (3 Dec. 1864), 683. Keating is exceptional in noting 'the humorist' (*SP*, 10) but relates this to literature as distinct from the 'social thought'.

16. On the contestatory force of hybridity see Young, *Colonial Desire*, 22–6.

17. Quoted, Murray, *A Life*, 201.

18. The term 'new journalism' is widely attributed to Arnold with reference to the work of W. T. Stead: see 'Up to Easter', *Nineteenth Century*, May 1887, 638–9; also in Fraser Neiman (ed.), *Matthew Arnold: Essays, Letters and Reviews* (Harvard UP: Cambridge, MA, 1960), 347.

19. Ian Hamilton, *A Gift Imprisoned: The Poetic Life of Matthew Arnold* (Bloomsbury: London, 1998).

20. Quoted, Murray, *A Life*, 141.

21. Georg Lukàcs, *History and Class Consciousness* (Merlin Press: London, 1971), 100.

22. Max Weber, C. Wright Mills and H. H. Gerth (eds), *Essays in Sociology* (Kegan Paul, Trench, Trubner: London, 1947), 96.

23. Letter, August 1849/50?, in S. O. A. Ullmann, *The Yale Manuscript* (University of Michigan Press: Ann Arbor, 1989), 171.

24. See Allott (ed.), *Selected Poems and Prose*, 135, 138. Meisel, *Myth of the Modern*, 39–53, elaborates Arnold's attempts at self-mastery in poetry and continuities in the prose without registering the importance of journalistic form.

25. See Christopher Kent, 'Higher Journalism and the Mid-Victorian Clerisy', *Victorian Studies*, Dec. 1969, 181–98.

26. See Claire Tomalin, 'In His Father's Shadow', *Sunday Times*, 15 Mar. 1998.

27. For Arnold's range see Walter Houghton (ed.), *Wellesley Index to Victorian Periodicals*, 5 vols (Routledge, Kegan Paul: London,1966–89), Vol. 5, 31–2.

28. Sir John Robinson, *Fifty Years of Fleet Street* (Macmillan: London, 1904), 222.

29. [Fitzjames Stephen], 'Homeric Translators and Critics', *Saturday Review*, XII 27 (July 1861), 95.

30. Allott, *Selected Poems and Prose*, 129.
31. Dependence on others appears in *SL,* 141; the 'prosthetic body' of the public sphere in Michael Warner, 'The Mass Public and the Mass Subject', in Bruce Robbins (ed.), *The Phantom Public Sphere (*University of Minnesota Press: Minneapolis, 1993), 236–43.
32. Jurgen Habermas, *The Structural Transformation of the Public Sphere*, tr. Thomas Burger, asstd. Frederick Lawrence (Polity: Cambridge, 1992), 141–222.
33. Bourdieu, *Distinction*, 462.
34. Ibid., 460; 462; 444.
35. Ibid., for example 446. Bourdieu's allegiance to Enlightenment values is encapsulated in his later expressed goal, 'to universalize the conditions of access to the universal', in Bourdieu, *On Television and Journalism*, tr. Priscilla Parkhurst Ferguson (Pluto: London, 1998), 1.
36. Habermas, *Structural Transformation*, 175.
37. Giuseppi Micheli and Rene Wellek, *Kant in England 1793–1938* (Routledge: London, 1993), *passim*: see Micheli, 4 ff., on 'trivialisation in the reports' of Kant's writings. My thanks to Gareth Stedman Jones for the Wellek reference.
38. Hans Reiss points towards the significance of different material forms: 'the fact that Kant's great works of critical philosophy are so formidable makes his less exacting political writings appear very much less weighty' (*KPW*, 3).
39. [James Mill], 'Periodical Literature', *Westminster Review*, Jan. 1824, 206–49.
40. Burke, *Reflections*, 294; [Francis Jeffrey], 'Mounier, de l'influence des philosophes', *Edinburgh Review*, I (Oct. 1802), 1 ff.
41. This point can be laboured philosophically in terms of the non-distinctness between constative and performative modes of utterance.
42. Bourdieu, *Cultural Production*, 32, presents this heterodox intellectual transmission. Extensive reading, mid-century Oxford interest in Kant (see Micheli, and Wellek *Kant in England*, 261 ff.) and friendship with the Kantian John Duke Coleridge all presumably contributed to Arnold's absorption of Kantian tenets.
43. Reiss is not alone in his view that 'the problem of human freedom was at the very core of his [Kant's] thought' (*KPW*, 3).
44. See, for instance, 'The Hero as Man of Letters', in Thomas Carlyle, *On Heroes, Hero-Worship and the Heroic in History* (University of California Press: Berkeley, 1993), 140.
45. Omission of the subtitle in J. Dover Wilson's edition [1932] contributed to this disregard.
46. Stefan Collini (ed.), *'Culture and Anarchy' and Other Writings* (Cambridge UP: 1993), xxvi.
47. Ibid.
48. See Stephen Koss, *The Rise and Fall of the Political Press in Britain*, 2 vols (Hamish Hamilton: London, 1981) Vol. 1; A. J. Lee, *Origins of the Popular Press*, (Croom Helm: London, 1976); D. A. Hamer, 'Gladstone: The

Making of a Political Myth', *Victorian Studies*, 22:1 (1978), 29–50; Patrick Joyce, *Democratic Subjects: The Self and the Social in Nineteenth-Century England* (Cambridge UP: 1994).

49. Walter Houghton, 'Periodical Literature and the Articulate Classes' in Joanne Shattock and Michael Wolff (eds), *The Victorian Periodical Press: Samplings and Soundings* (Leicester UP: 1982), 3–27, broadly contests Arnold's criticisms of the press.

50. See *Pall Mall Gazette*, 4, 6, 7, 8, 10 July 1885; also Judith Walkowitz, *City of Dreadful Delights: Narratives of Sexual Danger in Late-Victorian London* (Virago: London, 1994), 81–120.

51. Young, *Colonial Desire*, 87.

52. Neglected in the writing itself, the irresolution towards authority is otherwise much remarked – for example in Michael J. Levenson, *A Genealogy of Modernism* (Cambridge UP: 1992), 24–7.

53. Young notes ideas of English Jewish resemblance, *Colonial Desire*, 84; and the heterosexuality of hybridity (25–6; inadvertently suggesting more homeliness).

54. See Joyce's controversial *Democratic Subjects*, 124–46.

55. George Eliot, *Daniel Deronda* (Penguin: Harmondsworth, 1983), 217.

56. Arnold, 'Joubert', in his *Essays in Criticism*, first series (Macmillan: London, 1910 [1865]), 281, 283.

57. See here Micheli and Wellek, *Kant in England*, passim.

58. Invoking the 'bifurcation' in the 'journalistic field' in the nineteenth century see, for instance, Bourdieu and the sources he mentions, *On Television and Journalism*, 70, 93–4.

59. Arnold, 'Up to Easter', 639.

60. Arnold, *Essays in Criticism*, 285, 286.

6

'THE PROFESSION OF LETTERS': WALTER PATER AND GREEK STUDIES

LAUREL BRAKE

JOURNALISM AND LITERATURE

There is a good deal of airy talking nowadays about the difference between Literature and Journalism; and there is no easier or more effective way of depreciating a friend's work than to praise it for very good Journalism, but hardly Literature. But in truth the line is not easy to draw; one is conscious of a difference, but the two really melt almost indistinguishably into each other; and to lay your finger on the precise point where the one ends and the other begins would have puzzled that great maker of definitions, Samuel Johnson himself.[1]

But . . . consider how many famous names in Literature have within this century of ours worked in this way. Scott and Southey, Hazlitt and Lamb, Coleridge and DeQuincey, Carlyle and Macaulay, Thackeray and Dickens.[2]

This anonymous account of the relationship between literature and journalism is unsurprisingly that of an editor of a monthly periodical, Mowbray Morris, who contributes a series of three articles on 'The Profession of Letters' to his own periodical, *Macmillan's Magazine*, between August 1887 and March 1888. It was Morris who published the vast majority of Pater's contributions to *Macmillan's*, the house journal of the publisher of Pater's books: these, with one exception, largely consisted of pieces previously published in periodicals. In Pater's career, like that of many of his contemporary writers after mid-century,[3] material which appeared in journals routinely reappeared to constitute his books; the transfer of format from periodical to book – a difference of cultural 'manufacture' – was the means by which Pater's journalism became literature, and ephemera permanent.

The traffic between periodicals and books, and journalism and litera-ture, is the subject of wider contemporary anxiety about the threat of the 'other' on the part of journalists and authors alike. Morris's assertion of the porosity of literature and its compatibility with journalism are for example bitterly contested by George Gissing in *New Grub Street* (1891) and by much other writing. In this debate about the relation of relatively popular literature to Art, recurring issues included the socio-economic class of journalists, authors and audiences; conditions of production; and the criteria for quality. For Morris and the period the article/essay was far more prominent in the galaxy of Literature than it is today, and this strengthened the overlap between literature and journalism. Half of the literary authors Morris quotes – Scott, Southey, Hazlitt, Lamb, Coleridge, De Quincey, Carlyle, Macaulay, Thackeray and Dickens – are, like Pater, essayists (a literary term) or writers of articles (the journalistic term); moreover, the 'novelists' (Scott, Dickens, Thackeray) and 'poets' (Southey, Coleridge) each served as founder and editor of more than one periodical, and as a contributor of articles and reviews as well as poetry or fiction.

GREEK STUDIES

Pater's Greek studies largely comprise articles/essays pertaining to classical texts, art and architecture: if in the nineteenth century they fell into that period's capacious category of literature, in the twentieth they might be as easily claimed by art history, archaeology[4] and classics as by English. They appeared in three monthly periodicals and eventually in two books, *Plato and Platonism* and *Greek Studies*, the first initiated by the author in 1893, and the second by the author's literary executor in 1895. I want to make visible the processes of production of this prose work – lectures, articles, essays, chapters – as it was shaped, variously, for different audiences for different textual occasions at different periods. I am particularly interested in why the essays on classical subjects in *Plato and Platonism* were published in volume form by Pater while the articles in *Greek Studies*, almost all of which were written and published earlier, were not.

The cultural production of these texts is, like that of all texts, related to their subject and how prose work is constituted; Greek studies in the 1890s as a field and a discourse is thick with gender markers, and Pater's texts are often transgressive,[5] for example in their celebration of the male youth and his body, their focus on myths of incest and ecstasy, and their pleasure in violence and the bestial grotesque. My assumption throughout, which I have argued elsewhere,[6] is that Pater is pursuing a self-conscious and sustained project: the creation of a concerted opus which, drawing as it does on same sex traditions of masculinity within Western culture, I deem 'gay'. The permissiveness of the periodicals and publishers with respect to these pieces is notable, particularly in comparison with the censorship of prose fiction by periodical editors, circulating libraries and publishers of the day. The maleness of the audience and authors of classical studies[7] and the inclusion of women among the audience for fiction seem crucial in accounting for the gendered space[8] which Pater's work on classical studies was allowed.

Greek studies was a field that, after an article of March 1877, was explicitly gender-marked among the audiences Pater's work addressed; it was liable to be associated with the covert circulation of discourse about male sexual preferences and practices, which are labelled 'unnatural' by Richard St John Tyrwhitt:

> These pages are a rebellion against nature as she is here, in the name of nature as described in Athens.
>
> [. . .]
>
> Socrates' purity, and indeed his asceticism of life are freely and fully vindicated elsewhere by Plato, and will never be disputed here. The expressions put in his mouth are, no doubt, typically Hellenic. But they are not natural: and it is well known that Greek love of nature and beauty went frequently against nature.[9]

Tyrwhitt's gloss on the field of classics appeared in the upmarket monthly magazine the *Contemporary Review*, in 1877, just after it had purged itself of a liberal editor and refashioned itself as more explicitly Christian. This March number was the first under the new regime; Tyrwhitt's attack on the writings of J. A. Symonds and his candidature for the post of Professor of Poetry at Oxford served as a launch pad for a more general censure of 'The Greek Spirit in Modern Literature'. Tyrwhitt was Rector of St Mary Magdalen in the city of Oxford when 'The Greek Spirit' appeared, and the combined forces of the *Contemporary* and Tyrwhitt caused Symonds to withdraw his candidature.[10]

These events affected Pater too, who also withdrew from the competition at Oxford. His first edition of *Studies in the History of the Renaissance* had been attacked in 1873 on moral grounds; the second edition, with its title altered to take account of criticism and its 'Conclusion' safely removed, appeared three months after Tyrwhitt's onslaught.[11] That, and Ruskin's moral victory over Whistler and Impressionism in court in November 1878, probably combined with other factors to convince Pater that it was not safe or desirable to publish his proposed volume, *Dionysus and other Studies*;[12] that was the first time Pater cancelled the book publication of his Greek studies, two of which had already been published by 1878 in the *Fortnightly Review*. Pater did not, however, stop writing classical studies, his subject at Oxford.

That he could continue to place such pieces in the periodicals apparently with impunity and without undue censorship, even after

Tyrwhitt's warning, is remarkable since many of Pater's articles pushed the limits of straight readers' tolerance and confirm Tyrwhitt's worst case scenario of the alliance of the 'Greek Spirit' with the homosocial.[13] All of the editors Pater dealt with in connection with the publication of these studies were Oxbridge men – John Morley, editor of the *Fortnightly* (1863–82); Percy Bunting, editor of the *Contemporary Review* (1882–1911); and Mowbray Morris of *Macmillan's Magazine* (1885–1907). By virtue of their education in the mid-Victorian period these men had been initiated into classical texts as schoolboys and studied Greek and Latin routinely. This male Oxbridge network constituted a significant portion of the readership of the periodicals in which Pater published as well; together with the authority and status of classics as a subject,[14] they allowed the kinds of publishing spaces afforded Pater – that of family firms such as Macmillan's, family periodicals such as *Macmillan's Magazine*, Christian periodicals such as the *Contemporary*, as well as more liberal periodicals such as the *Fortnightly*.

GREEK STUDIES (1895)

The history of the articles collected to make up *Greek Studies* shows three clusters of periodical publication: 1876 (three articles); 1880 (three articles), and 1889 (two articles). Only 'The Age of Athletic Prizemen' appeared on its own, in February 1894 in the *Contemporary Review*. The 1876 group, on the myths of Demeter and Persephone, and on Dionysus, and the 1880 cluster, on Greek sculpture, were both published in the *Fortnightly*, while the 1889 pair treated Greek drama in *Macmillan's Magazine*. Pater's death in July 1894 and illness just before probably prevented any finished successor to the 'Prizemen' essay, but among Pater's literary remains were found several manuscripts relating to Greek studies, including a draft 'Introduction to Greek Studies', which could mean that he had planned at some time to publish a collection of his work in this field. This surmise is substantiated by Shadwell's account of the state of his copy texts in the Preface to *Greek Studies*, in which he explains that both of the two-part essays ('Demeter and Persephone' and 'The Beginnings of Greek Sculpture') had been revised 'with the intention, apparently, of publishing them collectively in a volume', and that 'Hippolytus Veiled', one of the drama essays, was likewise rewritten after publication 'with a view, probably, of republishing it with other essays'.[15] He identifies the essays on Greek sculpture as what 'remain[s] of a[nother] series which, if Mr. Pater had lived, would, probably, have grown into a still more important work'.[16] It is to this projection of an apparently separate volume on Greek art that Shadwell attaches the manuscript 'Introduction to Greek Studies'.

If we look at 'Hippolytus Veiled' and its publishing history, some of the links between periodical work and the authoring of books in the nineteenth century may be seen. This article appeared first in *Macmillan's Magazine* in tandem with another, like most of the other articles that go to comprise *Greek Studies*. If this series dimension was unique in Pater's work, or even in this volume, it might go unremarked, but this clustering of articles is common to the structures of periodicals and of Pater's books. Periodicals by nature are series which function as individual issues and as parts of an ongoing serial, and embedded in particular issues are serial articles, fiction and features which both originate before and continue after the issue to hand. These function as devices to create appetite and expectation in the reader to read the magazine serially, to return, to subscribe. Ideally, serial parts follow monthly, as did the two parts of Pater's 'The Myth of Demeter and Persephone' and 'The Beginnings of Greek Sculpture'. Although from the periodical editors' point of view these serialised pieces are optimally published in successive issues, Pater was not a full-time periodical journalist, and he more commonly produced looser clusters of related work that was an acceptable form for non-fiction.[17] Thus, 'Hippolytus Veiled' was paired with 'The Bacchanals of Euripides' which appeared in the same periodical three months before in May 1889. They were linked by the subtitle Pater appended to the August article, 'A Study from Euripides' and of course by signature, *Macmillan's* being one of the Victorian periodicals in which even non-fiction normally carried a signature. What is telling about this particular pairing is how clear it is, retrospectively, that it is artificial, constructed for the requirements of its particular form of publication, to foster the appearance of continuity between numbers, or the serial nature of serials.

So far I have foregrounded the ways in which serialisation serves the demands of the periodical as a form, but the other part of this negotiation between article and essay, periodical and book, journalism and literature, is how the author of the book utilises the periodical to sustain her or his completion over time of a book-length manuscript. In the periodical the link in Pater's writing appears to be the drama of Euripides. But in this case the contemporaneous publication of these two articles and the drama link belie the writing history and the destination of these pieces. According to Shadwell in the Preface of *Greek Studies*, the piece on the Bacchanals was written 'long before' it was published in 1889, probably 'as a sequel to the "Study of Dionysus"' which appeared in December 1876, both being listed in Pater's letter of 1878 stating his intention 'of publishing them collectively in a volume'.[18] When 'A Study of Dionysus' was printed in the *Fortnightly* in 1876 it began with a number and the subtitle 'I. The Spiritual Form of Fire and Dew' and ended '(to be continued)', and in the letter of 1878 'The Bacchanals of Euripides' is clearly listed as part 2 of 'The Myth of Dionysus'. However, neither the volume nor the essay was published in the late 1870s.[19] Indeed, Pater's dissatisfaction with the proof of the volume which impelled him to have the type broken up was most likely to have been occasioned by the Bacchanals essay, which only appeared in print eleven years later.

Regarded as an essay of 1877–8, its similarities of subject and style with the essay on Dionysus are striking. This is not news to readers of Pater's work after 1895 when *Greek Studies* appeared with its explanatory Preface; however, the earliest readers of the articles in *Macmillan's* in 1889 were positively encouraged to view the 'Bacchanals' as one of two studies from Euripides and as contemporaneous in date and type. The identification of the 'Bacchanals' essay with the missing second part of the *Fortnightly's* 'A Study of Dionysus' published over a decade before was obscured by the author, in the interests of the new series of which the 'Bacchanals' article was a part. But Pater's longer-term writing agenda and publishing plans also figure in this equation.

The pairing of these articles in *Macmillan's* also implied that their genre is identical – critical articles on classical drama. But there is reason to suppose that Pater regarded 'Hippolytus Veiled', the genuinely later essay in *Macmillan's*, as one of his fictional 'imaginary portraits': in a letter to Arthur Symons of December [1888] Pater describes it as 'a new Portrait'.[20] What we have here is Pater's manipulation of the structural unit of the periodical form, a short piece – irrespective of whether it is an article, a short story, or a chapter of a novel – to accommodate both the changed direction of his work and the serial dimension of periodical publication. Moreover, in the same month, August of 1889, he makes precisely the same manœuvre in the *Fortnightly*, where he publishes part of his unfinished novel *Gaston de Latour* disguised as a historical article entitled 'Giordano Bruno'.[21] Although this is unprecedented in Pater's periodical work, the hybridity is characteristic.

It may be argued that, from the first, the overlap between Pater's 'articles' on historical figures such as Michelangelo, Leonardo and Botticelli with elements of fictional narrative was considerable, and that his intensive experiment with fiction in the 1880s – in which he attempted two novels and two volumes of 'imaginary portraits' – was a foreseeable outcome of his previous work. His sleights of hand in August 1889, in which he presents fiction as criticism and history, inscribe this generic doubling, and indicate the kind of accommodation Pater was prepared to make to the exigencies of periodical journalism. 'This article', he writes privately about 'Giordano Bruno', 'is really a chapter from an unfinished work, and had to be cut about for insertion in the Review'.[22] Indeed, his creation and pursuit of the 'imaginary portrait' itself may be regarded in part as a response to the voracious market for the short story which the late nineteenth-century periodical presented to would-be contributors.[23]

However, in ordering the posthumous collection of the Greek studies, Shadwell reunites 'The Myth of Dionysus' with 'The Bacchanals of Euripides' without making them explicitly part of the same historical project. Honouring Pater's last version of the aborted 1878 book,[24] Shadwell situates the Dionysus piece as the opening essay, although it is not chronologically the earliest, and follows it with 'The Bacchanals of Euripides' which, still carrying its ambiguous reference to the Euripidean drama, is left to be construed as drama criticism. But 'The Bacchanals' is then separated from 'Hippolytus Veiled', with which it appeared in *Macmillan's*, by the two-part 'Myth of Demeter and Persephone' (1876). *Greek Studies* thus realises the plan for *Dionysus and Other Studies*. The remainder of the articles revert to chronology. While the volume makes an attempt at restitution of the project and contents that Pater was unable to realise in 1878 by abrogating the publishing history of the periodical articles, Shadwell does not 'restore' 'Hippolytus Veiled' to the status of fiction although he does separate it from 'The Bacchanals'. This is perhaps because 'Hippolytus Veiled' is the only imaginary portrait he collects in *Greek Studies*, leaving the other two published but uncollected pieces – 'The Child in the House' and 'Emerald Uthwart' – to make up *Miscellaneous Studies* which appeared ten months later. The remainder of *Greek Studies* is devoted to essays on Greek art. Shadwell is complicit with Pater in masking hybridity in a volume which unites, under the term 'Greek studies', three separate projects of Pater's: the *Dionysus* book, a second volume of imaginary portraits, and a book on Greek art. Although Shadwell makes a point of announcing that his copy texts for these early *Dionysus* essays are revised versions of the periodical texts and thus more finished than 'journalism' might imply, *Greek Studies* bears the marks of Pater's trafficking in the rich marketplace of the press.

The structure of generic interchange in which these two pieces are implicated attaches to other of Pater's Greek studies, for example those articles such as the two on the myth of Demeter and Persephone that began as lectures (to the Birmingham and Midland Institute); and the whole of *Plato and Platonism* has its origins in Pater's lectures to the university. In the latter case, instead of transforming one kind of series into another, and obscuring the lecture origins of the 'chapters', Pater and his publisher advertised the volume as a series of lectures, and used the authority of the university lecture to validate the book's transgressive contents.[25]

The periodical articles from *Plato and Platonism*, like the relation of

'Giordano Bruno' to *Gaston de Latour*, are a spin-off from a larger project, involving book publication of a series of chapters (of fiction) or essays; but unlike 'Bruno', they are not written backward into periodical versions, but 'forward', from lectures to be heard into versions of lectures to be read. Interestingly, what emerges on this occasion are distinctions Pater makes between the reading audience of the periodical press and of the book. Pater's labours in this regard are detailed clearly in an unusually fulsome correspondence in the *Letters* around a publishing project.[26] Here Pater writes both to the editor of the *Contemporary Review* and more especially to his assistant (Percy Bunting and William Canton respectively), about editorial revisions to his academic lectures on Plato, whom he claims to have 'treated . . . in as popular a manner as I could',[27] to adjust them to the tolerances and expectations of a general reader. He agrees to break up long paragraphs on the prompting of the editors,[28] and to 'lighten and popularise my paper, at all points'.[29]

But the attempt to make the graduated transition from lecture to periodical article to book chapter does not succeed to Pater's satisfaction with 'The Doctrine of Plato' which finally appeared only as chapter 7 of *Plato and Platonism*. After examining the proofs from the *Contemporary Review*, Pater dithered and eventually decided against periodical publication – first withdrawing, then relenting, but finally declining – although both Bunting and Canton seemed to have wanted it for the monthly. This was the last essay Pater submitted to Bunting from the *Plato and Platonism* series, and the portion of the volume published on 9 February 1893 which had appeared previously in the press was unusually small – less than a third.

I can offer no explanation of this anomaly, except to observe that for the writing of this book Pater was in the unique position of having a freshly considered and completed draft to hand, consisting of a coherent group of manuscripts of a recently delivered lecture series. The time involved in preparation of this material for volume publication was singularly brief, perhaps a year. The thought and preparation which had gone into the academic series was transferable to the publishing project unlike, for example, the compilation of *Appreciations* in 1888. There the principle of selection of the book, from a broad range of uncollected pieces written over twenty years, and the reconceptualising of review material into 'Style' for example, typified a more amorphous and daunting task, shaping a work – an essay or a book – out of an eclectic range of materials.

The reason Pater gave Bunting on 1 November [1892] for his final decision against publication of 'The Doctrine of Plato' was its intractable length. What is surprising is his association in this letter between the 'average readers' of the periodical 'whom it might prejudice [against] my volume and your review' and the potential readership for his book. Clearly for Pater, whose book was to appear in three months, there was an overlap between these two reading publics as well as a distinction. Pater was implying that the context of a piece changes its perception: the same average reader would see a long article as distended in a periodical but not in a book of 'lectures'. If Pater is alert here to a calibration of print in the public sphere, he is also alert to the taste and sales-potential of his audience in ways which echo the new journalism, with its canny enthusiasm for the new market of the 'millions'.

The periodical publication of the three Plato essays in the year preceding the publication of the book served the author and publisher of the projected book in a number of ways: first, as a concrete incentive to the author to work up his lectures into written, publishable form gradually over time; secondly, as a means of the author keeping his name in view of the potential readership of his book; thirdly as a trailer for the book, by spreading the essays over two periodicals and a five-month period – 9 February (*Contemporary Review*), May (*Macmillan*), and June (*Contemporary Review*) of 1892; and lastly as a source of additional income.

The fluidity of Pater's texts which this generic indeterminacy implies is echoed in the collection of Pater manuscripts at Harvard, in which a number of extensive if unfinished fragments seem to indicate a degree of uncertainty about their destinations; a different way of putting this might be to emphasise the openness or porosity of Pater's published and unpublished texts. Bill Shuter's essay on *Plato and Platonism* in which he discusses numerous instances in which Pater has 'reshuffled' images and fragments from earlier work to reappear in his later work bears this out; one example shows Pater quarrying ideas and wording from the as-yet-uncollected Greek study, 'The Marbles of Aegina' (*Fortnightly Review*, 1880) for chapter 4 ('Plato and the Sophists') of the 1893 volume.[30] The point here is not only the aesthetic one – that Pater returned and returned again to familiar ideas to rework them, or to relocate them verbatim in different contexts – but also the materialist one, that this is a textual and commercial economy whereby certain discarded texts are reintroduced into the textual and commercial economy to acquire added value.

THE PERIODICALS AND GREEK STUDIES

I now want to explore the three periodicals in which these Greek studies appeared – the *Fortnightly Review* of the 1870s, *Macmillan's Magazine* of the 1880s and the *Contemporary Review* of the 1890s – and how Pater's contributions fitted in with the discourses of these titles at the time in which the articles appeared. *Plato and Platonism*, although the earlier volume, contains more preponderantly later work in terms of periodical publication, so I shall treat it last. *Greek Studies* includes a majority of essays from the decade 1870–80, seven in all, and they are all from the *Fortnightly*, in which period Pater published eleven essays in total.

If largely political, and responsive to parliamentary and foreign news, John Morley's *Fortnightly* did publish critical essays on literature, art, philosophy and classics by risky authors, such as Swinburne and John Addington Symonds, on risky subjects such as Baudelaire and Gautier. The dominance of current political and economic affairs and the sparseness of fiction in the *Fortnightly* 1871–80 suggest that the principal and targeted audience was educated men. However, Morley's *Fortnightly* does make some address and offer openings to educated women readers at this period; nearly every issue contains articles pertaining to areas of cultural life which include women, and some issues print articles by women which address, to varying degrees, the woman question: Maria G. Grey writes part I of 'Men and Women' in November 1879, and in May 1880 Edith Simcox publishes 'Ideas of Feminine Usefulness'. When one looks at the contents lists of single issues it becomes clear how such articles comfortably open to women readers are embedded in predominantly male space.[31] In this context, these articles by Pater appear appropriate reading for women interested in travel, art and the new museum culture. That is, in the context of the *Fortnightly* Pater's pieces on Greek art had a different, cross-gendered readership than they later, in the mid-1890s, were likely to attract in a volume dedicated to the announced, gendered topic of Greek studies.

Pater's two pieces, on the Bacchanals and 'Hippolytus Veiled', appear far more out of place in Mowbray Morris's *Macmillan's Magazine* in 1889. Pater was a Macmillan author, and if the *Fortnightly* was the dominant single title for Pater's publications in the 1870s, *Macmillan's Magazine* held that position in the 1880s. All of Pater's publications in *Macmillan's* pertained to fiction, either his own or in book reviews; he placed both the four imaginary portraits and five parts of *Gaston* there in the 1880s.[32] This identification of Pater with imaginative literature in *Macmillan's* reinforces the way that these two pieces are framed as literary studies of Euripidean drama, whereas they might be construed and presented quite differently in a different context: the 'Bacchanals' as allied with Pater's studies of Greek myth published in the mid-1870s in the *Fortnightly* and 'Hippolytus Veiled' as a lone imaginary portrait, heralding a new series. These are the implications of Shadwell's wording and ordering in *Greek Studies*.

However, despite the packaging, the contents of these two articles make them seem anomalous in the gilt-edged parameters of the house magazine of Macmillan's, a firm that was a byword in the trade for quality publishing. The contents of the two numbers in which Pater's articles appear make clear the distinction between Morley's *Fortnightly*, with its quantity of demanding reading, and *Macmillan's* fare, larded with popular fiction at this period, and otherwise stocked with travelogues, memoirs, belles lettres, poetry, and the very occasional critical or political essay. May and August 1889, the two numbers which carry Pater's articles, are very similar in this respect, except that the August issue carries two serialised novels rather than one: May offers *Marooned* by W. Clark, and August *Marooned* and *Kirsteen* by Mrs Oliphant.

If the character of *Macmillan's Magazine* seems to require some special explanation of the publication of these essays by Pater, so does the character of Mowbray Morris, the editor who agreed to publish them. According to Charles Morgan, the official historian of the firm, Morris's adverse and violent opinions as a Reader for the firm – on works by Hardy, Yeats and Meredith, all of whom were or became Macmillan authors – were indicative of 'a closed mind'.[33] Likewise, by Morris's own account, one might expect him to have made a shrewd estimate of the nature of his readership, and to satisfy it in his selection of material for the magazine:

> Literature, you must always remember, is in the eyes of nearly all editors, and must be, before all things a commercial speculation. They are not the patrons but the clients of the public taste; and the dictates of that taste, though they may sigh as critics, they must as editors obey.[34]

Given the readership that the contents of *Macmillan's* implies, and given Morris's view of the editor's position, it seems that some characteristics of the presentation of Pater's pieces would successfully prevent their being read by readers who might be offended by them. This might be some combination of Pater's signature, the generic topic of classical drama, or the specific references to Bacchus and Hippolytus which, to more knowing readers of *Macmillan's*, might signal potentially licentious material, fit for (male) readers of the classics. Of course, all of the Greek studies appearing in the periodicals were signed, but the signifier 'Walter Pater' in the *Fortnightly* of the 1870s, *Macmillan's* of the 1880s and the *Contemporary* of the 1890s produced different meanings among different kinds of readership. However, the 'Hippolytus' essay in *Macmillan's*, which treats incest and the rapacious sexuality of a female protagonist, seems to me to have pushed the limits of the magazine: this is the reason, I would suggest, that Pater published nothing there again for nearly three years. When he does, it is 'A Chapter on Plato', which as Greek philosophy carries clear gender markers, so that female readers were likely to be culturally aware of the risks they would be taking in reading Pater on Plato. Moreover, Pater's treatment of Plato here is (silently) sanitised to some extent by its origin in public, university lectures. It was, however, the last of Pater's publications in *Macmillan's*, and itself published only after a considerable gap.

In the 1890s, Pater turned to a number of new periodical outlets such as the *New Review*, the *Contemporary Review* and the *Nineteenth Century*, all of which were more intellectually adventurous than *Macmillan's*. His publication pattern was more eclectic than in any other decade, but again there is a dominant title, Percy Bunting's *Contemporary Review*, the third magazine involved in the publication of Pater's Greek studies. Although from its inception the *Contemporary* had a theological remit which persisted with variable intensity throughout the century, Pater's three articles on Greek topics were part of its abiding interest in all aspects of classics, and in particular the excavations of the remains at Troy.[35] The other characteristic of the *Contemporary* which might be seen to harbour Pater's Greek studies was its implication in the free debating structures of the Metaphysical Society, which James Knowles, its first editor, structurally embedded in the *Review* in the form of symposia, in which various positions on a single subject were explored by a number of renowned or expert contributors. Knowles's disinterestedness also took other forms, structurally less visible but equally strenuous.

Percy Bunting, who became editor in 1882, seemed to have retained the journal's openness to most subjects and extremes of opinion which permitted him to print the risky 'Lacedaemon' in June 1892, one of Pater's most outspoken explorations of love between men and the culture of the male body in ancient Greece. And the willingness of Bunting's *Contemporary* to publish discussion of the homosocial was repeated just after Pater's death, when his friend Edmund Gosse selected it as the most suitable place of publication for his frank obituary article which made plain the degree of Pater's commitment to 'Apollo'.[36]

But, again, this open forum policy cut both ways in the *Contemporary*: vituperative, homophobic articles appeared throughout its history, such as those by Robert Buchanan and Richard Tyrwhitt which scourged the 'fleshly school' (1871) and the 'Greek spirit' (1878). Indeed, it is likely that publication of these two articles helps explain the late date of Pater's first contribution to the *Contemporary*, long after Bunting had mollified the evangelical strain of Strahan's *Review*, and ownership had passed from Strahan and Co. to Isbister. The *Contemporary*'s liveliness throughout its run is notable.

Of course, any single number of a periodical can tell us only a limited amount about a series. But the salient aspect of the *Contemporary* – its commitment to structured controversy and topical questions of the day is evident in the contents of the number in June 1892 which included 'Lacedaemon'. As a social reformer and journalist Bunting produces an issue which balances a symposium on women's suffrage with an article on the male field of Greek studies. If the symposium attracted women readers or put off male traditionalists, 'Lacedaemon' – with its focus on male-male bonding, and its allusions to what in 1893 Alfred Douglas was to call 'the new culture'[37] – provided scholarly clerics and classicists with equally controversial male discourse.

It may seem odd that the lecture status of this essay was not invoked to bolster its institutional authority, but it had been a long-standing policy of the *Contemporary* under Knowles that it did not publish lectures. If Percy Bunting was not aware initially that Pater's proffered list of potential contributions stemmed from his lectures, as Bill Shuter observes,[38] his assistant William Canton is unselfconsciously informed by Pater in January and March 1892 first that they are 'parts of a book' and then, with the returned proof, that 'Lacedaemon' 'was written for delivery as a lecture'.[39] That this did not stop Bunting and Canton from urging Pater to publish a third lecture, 'The Doctrine of Plato' in October, suggests that Knowles' interdict was no longer in force, and casts doubt on any efforts by Pater to hide the origins of the articles from the editors. That they were hidden from the readers is likely to have been an aspect of the popularisation that Pater was undertaking through revision for the press.

It is notable that Pater's three contributions to the *Contemporary* are confined to the 1890s and to classical Greece;[40] only two of them were published in *Plato and Platonism* in February 1893, the third and last – 'The Age of Athletic Prizemen' – appearing a year later in February 1894. There it formed part of an irregular series constituted thematically as well as authorially and initiated by Pater's earlier articles of 1891 and 1892; it also functioned as a follow-up to Pater's book of 1893. Thus, it figured in the publishing timetable of both the journal and the author/journalist as part of the *Plato and Platonism* series. However, its subtitle – 'A chapter in Greek Art' – identified it to Shadwell as part of Pater's alleged plan for a book on Greek art, a project which Shadwell went on to construct in *Greek Studies* by printing the 'chapter' as the last part of the series of three essays on Greek sculpture, which Pater had published in the *Fortnightly* fifteen years before. Here the units of prose are construed to produce different generic meanings according to the requirements of two mediums (the periodical and the book), two discourses (journalism and literature) and two timescales.

TEXT

The capacity of the periodical press primarily, but also of the Macmillan volumes, to publish the kind of homosocial and homoerotic discourse found in this work by Pater, in a period allegedly prudish in which publishers, distributors, editors, legislators and readers are significantly preoccupied with policing print, may seem remarkable. It is, but I want to discuss some exemplary passages to show the power of classics as a field to command space which is successfully ring-fenced: defying censorship and prohibition, and evoking no criticism beyond sniping, the field survives as the hegemonic sign of educated male authority, even in family periodicals such as *Macmillan's* and within the theological remit of the *Contemporary*, as well as in the more open *Fortnightly*.

Though the reader of 'The Bacchanals of Euripides' in *Greek Studies* is prepared for its violence, sadism and homoeroticism by the essays preceding it in the volume, the prose is so heated and intense and the episodes so grotesque that the essay is nonetheless disturbing and haunting. In the context of *Macmillan's*, an unwitting reader might well find it unexpected and offensive. Early in the essay Pater makes the twin nature of his subject clear, it is the god himself as well as his female followers: 'Himself a woman-like god, – it was on women and feminine souls that his power mainly fell'.[41] In his selection of this play of Euripides, Pater utilises an opportunity to write what is now called gay discourse, invoking text and events from Euripides and myths around Dionysus to validate his own textual tastes. Selecting episodes and phrases for translation, he creates an exotic narrative that derives its authority and apparently its voice from 'the object of study'. This is characteristic of Pater's positioning of himself as a writing subject, as a ventriloquist for some authoritative referent outside the text, normally another text. The extended erotic introduction that Pater affords Dionysus, for example, forcibly calls to mind Aubrey Beardsley's drawings of Pater's period as well as Homer and Euripides:

> In the course of his long progress from land to land, the gold, the flowers, the incense of the East, have attached themselves deeply to him: their effect and expression rest now upon his flesh like the gleaming of that old ambrosial ointment of which Homer speaks as resting ever on the persons of the gods, and cling to his clothing – the mitre binding his perfumed yellow hair – the long tunic down to the white feet, somewhat womanly, and the fawn-skin, with its rich spots, wrapped about the shoulders. As the door opens to admit him, the scented air of the vineyards (for the vine-blossom has an exquisite perfume) blows through; while the convolvulus on his mystic rod represents all wreathing flowery things whatever, with or without fruit . . .[42]

The sexual suggestiveness of Pater's rendering of the 'darker stain' of the myth is unmistakable as the sensuous description above is reinforced:

> Yet, from the first, amid all this floweriness, a touch or trace of that gloom is discernible. The fawn-skin, composed now so daintily over the shoulders, may be worn with the whole coat of the animal made up, the hoofs gilded and tied together over the right shoulder, to leave the right arm disengaged to strike, its head clothing the human head within, as Alexander, on some of his coins, looks out from the elephant's scalp, and Hercules out of the jaws of a lion, on the coins of Camarina. Those diminutive golden horns attached to the forehead, represent not fecundity merely, nor merely the crisp tossing of the waves of streams, but horns of offence. And our fingers must beware of the thyrsus, tossed about so wantonly by himself and his chorus. The pine-cone at its top does but cover a spear-point; and the thing is a weapon – the sharp spear of the hunter Zagreus – though hidden now by the fresh leaves, and that button of pine-cone.[43]

It is clear from these passages that the classical figure of Dionysus gives Pater permission to write the phallus, erotically and playfully, and to limn the titillating characteristics of a male who is both fecund and dangerous, the *homme fatal*.

Pater hardly disguises his glee at the scope the events and language of Euripides' drama offer him:

> The singular, somewhat sinister beauty of this speech, and a similar one subsequent – a fair description of morning on the mountain-tops, with the Bacchic women sleeping, which turns suddenly to a hard, coarse picture of animals cruelly rent – is one of the special curiosities which distinguish this play; and, as it is wholly narrative, I shall give it in English prose, abbreviating here and there, some details which seem to have but a metrical value . . .[44]

This is followed by over two pages of translation which culminate in a scene in which the Maenads wildly attack some grazing animals, tearing them apart with their bare hands, 'with knifeless fingers'. Pater goes on to assure us, 'A grotesque scene follows',[45] which he does not resist describing:

> Full of wild, coarse, revolting details, of course not without pathetic touches, and with the loveliness of the serving Maenads, and of their mountain solitudes – their trees and water – never quite forgotten, it describes how, venturing as a spy too near the sacred circle, Pentheus [who is dressed as a woman] was fallen upon, like a wild beast, by the mystic huntresses and torn to pieces, his mother being the first to begin 'the sacred rites of slaughter.'[46]

It is perhaps clear from this small sample of the heated prose of 'The Bacchanals of Euripides' why Pater hesitated to publish it in 1878 in periodical or book form, but it is as interesting if less clear how by 1889 he felt it both safe and suitable to submit it to *Macmillan's Magazine*. Now although I have been quoting from the book, none of these passages I have quoted, nor the many comparable that I have not, have been

censored in *Macmillan's*. That has to be deemed remarkable in a period
when, for example, Hardy's novels involving heterosexual explicitness
were promptly (and routinely) cut for periodical publication, on the
assumption that readers of periodicals were buying a title which they
could rely on to guarantee the respectability of the contents through
selection and editing. Buyers of books, however, were their own agents.

I think we can venture several propositions from the presence of these
uncensored pieces of Pater's in *Macmillan's Magazine*. First, classics was
a protected, and gendered area which meant that homosexual discourse
might be fairly freely circulated within the normal reading locations of
educated men, notably the reviews and magazines; secondly, that Victorian women readers of *Macmillan's Magazine* did have access to material
that, should they risk reading it, would make them far more informed
about masculine sexuality than most Victorianists acknowledge such
nineteenth-century middle-class women readers to be. And 'Hippolytus
Veiled', with its treatment of incestuous love between stepmother and
son, and its unmistakable depiction of female desire, may have been closer
to the experience of female readers than 'The Bacchanals', and thus more
accessible to them.[47]

These Greek studies of Pater's might have exemplified a fault line
between journalism and literature, in so far as they were censored by the
editor or self-censored for periodical publication, to be restored in the
book edition. But they were not, and we may conclude, curiously, that
whereas 'Aesthetic Poetry' and the 'Conclusion' (both originally part of
'Poems by William Morris') were removed from his books by Pater in an
act of self-censorship, such extremes were not required by the Greek
studies because the field of classics to which they belonged was largely
protected and validated in ways that the study of contemporary and
English literature was not. But it is of course true that Pater made a
distinction between periodical and book publication for the Greek studies
essays, having never republished them in his lifetime. Because principal
weeklies – such as the *Athenaeum* and the *Saturday Review* – were not
reviewing the monthlies as a matter of course in 1889 when 'The
Bacchanals' and 'Hippolytus Veiled' appeared, Pater could hope that
any notices might appear in smaller, 'class' periodicals out of sight of the
wider public.

The profound overlap between Pater's journalism and book publication,
and the consanguinity of his work as a lecturer, journalist and author were
dependent to a considerable degree on both the general character of a
certain class of mid-and late Victorian monthlies and the nascent state of
specialisation in the universities, in journalism, and in the culture more

generally. That such a space as these journals afforded was coming to an end in 1891 is seen in an American journalist's attempt to exclude them from 'journalism proper'. 'It is necessary', W. J. Stillman writes in the *Atlantic Monthly* 'to distinguish between journals':

> They divide themselves specifically into three classes: the daily newspaper, the journal of culture (including periodicals other than daily, and incorrectly called journals), and the paper devoted to moral reforms, like The Liberator of William Lloyd Garrison . . . As the journal of culture leads to scholarship and the sounder and broader general education of the public, its work passes under the classification of science and out of journalism proper; it is a branch and continuation of *the university*.[48]

Stillman's professional anxiety as a journalist is inscribed here in his efforts not only to strip journalism of the taint of periodicals associated with 'the university' but also of 'class' journals such as *The Liberator* – which he decides to 'leave out of consideration'.

What is at issue is the definition of the word 'culture' as well as the category of journalism; we are witness to the painful split of high culture from popular culture that was dramatically accelerated by 'the new journalism', a development that Matthew Arnold recognised even as he denounced it in 1887. By 1943 in *The House of Macmillan* Charles Morgan positions 'the journal of culture' as a subject for nostalgia, and regrets its passing. Assessing *Macmillan's Magazine* he writes:

> that the list is not to be organised into groups and movements, that the great critics – Arnold, Pater, Symonds, Whibley – are all there with the theologians, the preachers, the men of science, the historians, the Laureate, the young lions, the great story-tellers and the good story-tellers, reveals a catholic prospect closed to us since we allowed Austin Harrison's *English Review* and Squire's *London Mercury* to perish. A magazine in this liberal tradition, seeing literature as a wisdom and a delight . . . is a civilized asset of which we have strangely deprived ourselves. *Macmillan's* is gone, *Cornhill* is gone, *Scribner's* is gone. We have specialised in this as in all else.[49]

Pater's publishing years, the period between 1866 and 1894, precisely correspond with the existence of such journalistic space, augmented prodigiously and updated following the removal of the Stamp Duty in 1855, a period which saw the founding of the shilling monthly in *Macmillan's Magazine* in 1859, the origins of the *Fortnightly Review* and the *Pall Mall Gazette* in 1865, and the creation of the *Contemporary* a year later. The confluence of journalism and literature in Pater's case is entirely a product of this epistemic moment in the latter part of the nineteenth century which permitted journalism to beckon Pater and many other university men into a productive contact with the larger and more heterogeneous world, the 'millions' as Stead called them. Pater's work on

Greek studies furthered the move of the subject out of the schools, academy and scholarly volumes into the public sphere, into greater visibility and scrutiny, and there is evidence that he attempted to make his classical studies publishable in a form that the broader audience of the periodical press would find accessible. It was the confluence too of the general character of the periodicals in question and the inclusive spectrum of Greek studies that resulted in the dissemination of homosocial and homosexual discourse to reaches of Victorian readers, women as well as men, who might never otherwise have had first-hand knowledge of such writing.

NOTES

1. [Mowbray Morris], 'The Profession of Letters', *Macmillan's Magazine*, 56, (Aug. 1887), 305.
2. Ibid., 307.
3. Francis Jeffrey first collected his *Edinburgh Review* essays in 1843.
4. See Lewis R. Farnell, *An Oxonian Looks Back* (Martin Hopkinson Ltd: London, 1934), 76–7; quoted by Samuel Wright, *A Bibliography of the Writings of Walter H. Pater* (Garland: New York, 1975), 99.
5. This term relates to the concept of the carnivalesque developed by Mikhail Bakhtin: see P. Stallybrass and A. White, *The Politics and Poetics of Transgression* (Methuen: London, 1986), 6–16.
6. See Laurel Brake, *Walter Pater*, *Writers and Their Work* (Northcote House: Plymouth, 1994).
7. For public debate about the suitability of women's study of classics see *The Guardian*'s correspondence columns, spring 1884 for instance, 'we think that even the general study of the classics, such as is required for Moderations Honours alone, is most undesirable for women': *The Guardian*, 19 March 1884, 427.
8. On this term see L. Brake, 'Gendered Space and the British Press,' *Studies in Newspaper and Periodical History* 1995 (1997), 104.
9. Richard St, John Tyrwhitt, 'The Greek Spirit in Modern Literature', *Contemporary Review*, 29, (1877), 557.
10. See Phyllis Grosskurth, *John Addington Symonds* (Longmans: London, 1964), 171–2.
11. The edition and revisions had been planned since November 1876, well before Tyrwhitt's article in March: see Lawrence Evans (ed.), *Letters of Walter Pater* (Oxford UP: 1970), 17–24.
12. See L. Brake, 'After *Studies*: Walter Pater's Cancelled Book', in Peter Liebregts and Wim Tigges (eds), *Beauty and the Beast* (Rodopi: Amsterdam and Atlanta, 1996), 115–26.
13. For this term see Eve K. Sedgwick, *Between Men* (Columbia UP: New York, 1985).

14. See Linda Dowling, *Hellenism and Homosexuality in Victorian Oxford* (Cornell UP: Ithaca, New York, 1994). Dowling links Hellenism with the tradition of classics in Oxford where Pater lived, and explains classics' homosocial parameters.

15. C.L. Shadwell, 'Preface', W. Pater, *Greek Studies* (Macmillan: London, 1895), vi–vii.

16. Ibid., p. vii. Unfortunately, Shadwell does not comment on the state of the relevant copy texts. The strongest indication that Pater had again considered collecting some of the Greek studies since his first attempt in 1878 (which could account for the revisions of the three 1876 essays) is Shadwell's claim that 'Hippolytus Veiled' was 'rewritten' after its 1889 publication.

17. Pater's one attempt to sustain publication over consecutive months ended abruptly after five parts, with no explanation. His novel *Gaston de Latour* appeared in *Macmillan's Magazine*, June–Oct. 1888: see L. Brake, 'Doing Time', *Nineteenth Century Prose*, 24 (Fall 1997), 19–27.

18. Shadwell, 'Preface', vi; Evans, *Letters*, 32.

19. See Wright, *A Bibliography*, 12; Evans, *Letters*, 32.

20. See Evans, *Letters*, 29 Dec. [1888], 90.

21. It appeared as chapter 7 in Shadwell's posthumous edition of the novel: see Brake, 'Doing Time'; Gerald Monsman (ed.), *Gaston de Latour* (ELT Press: Greensboro, NC, 1996).

22. Evans, *Letters*, 12 Nov. [1889?], 102.

23. See Brake, 'Doing Time', 21–3.

24. Pater's second title was *Dionysus and Other Studies*. See Evans, *Letters*, 18 Nov. [1878], 34.

25. See William Shuter, 'Pater's Reshuffled Text', *Nineteenth Century Literature*, 43 (1989), 524.

26. See Evans, *Letters*, between 21 Dec. [1891] and 1 Nov. [1892], 124–35.

27. Evans, *Letters*, 21 Dec. [1891], 124.

28. Evans, *Letters*, 17 May [1892], 129.

29. Evans, *Letters*, 12 Oct. [1892], 133.

30. See Shuter, 'Pater's Reshuffled Text', 504.

31. See *Fortnightly*, Feb. and Apr. 1880, for example.

32. The last published serialised part, on Giordano Bruno, appeared in the *Fortnightly*. See Brake, 'Doing Time', 22.

33. See Charles Morgan, *The House of Macmillan* (Macmillan: London, 1943), 144.

34. [Morris], 'Profession', *Macmillan's Magazine*, Aug. 1887, 309.

35. See, for example, *Contemporary Review*, Apr. 1877–Feb. 1879, when no less than ten articles on Greek studies appeared.

36. Edmund Gosse, 'Walter Pater: A Portrait', *Contemporary Review*, 66 (Dec.) 1894, 795–810.

37. In 1893 Alfred Douglas uses the term both in correspondence with Kains-Jackson and in the *Spirit Lamp*'s May prospectus.

38. Shuter, 'Pater's Reshuffled Text', 524.

39. Evans, *Letters*, 22 Jan. and 17 May [1892], 126 and 129 respectively.

40. Pater's late turn to the *Contemporary* may reflect hostility in its 1870s' contents, his earlier concentration on fiction, the periodical's association – largely under Knowles – with Matthew Arnold, and its allegedly religious remit.

41. Walter Pater, 'The Bacchanals of Euripedes', *Greek Studies* (Macmillan: London, 1895), 53.

42. Ibid., 58–9.

43. Ibid., 60.

44. Ibid., 68.

45. Ibid., 71.

46. Ibid., 73–4.

47. Pater touches here on the feminist issue of social purity associated with Sarah Grand; but while feminists advocated their own celibacy as the answer to their husbands' culpable 'pasts', Pater attributes to Phedre a *desire* to meet lust with lust: 'with this one passion once indulged, it might be happiness thereafter to remain chaste for ever' (Walter Pater, 'Hippolytus Veiled', *Greek Studies* (Macmillan: London, 1895), 1877.

48. My italics. W. J. Stillman, 'Journalism and Literature', *Atlantic Monthly*, 68 (1891), 689.

49. Morgan, *The House of Macmillan*, 61.

7

VORTEX MARSDEN: A LITTLE MAGAZINE AND THE MAKING OF MODERNITY

HELEN MCNEIL

PRE-WAR MODERNITY AND ITS DISCOURSES

In a 1913 feminist pamphlet, the novelist Ford Madox Ford declared himself overwhelmed by the heightened dramas of 'Imperial and political consciousness' that were sweeping his country. 'Today we crown a King, tomorrow we revise a Constitution. Last year we mourned; this year we rejoice – and always there are crowds in the street, so that it is difficult . . . to think in the very moment of celebration.'[1] Writing the same year in another feminist pamphlet, the poet John Masefield looked forward to 'a raising of the national life'. He felt that heroic British women 'have flung into the world a flaming torch of beauty . . . that the new rule of human beings, of comrades, may begin'.[2]

Reviewing the scandalous 1912 Futurist exhibit at the Sackville Galleries, a journalist called Olive Hockin demanded her own 'new rule':

> shall we not – we the representatives of the Twentieth Century – have a living, moving Art of our own? . . . Let us stand upon our own feet and make what we will of our own age . . . [without clinging] in fear and despair to the threadbare skirts of the Past!

Hockin finds Futurism to be 'Revolutionary work . . . indeed'.[3] Soon after, in 1913, suffrage activist Charlotte Despard concluded a pamphlet she had written with the assertion that soon there would be 'a new race, possessing faculties higher than those enjoyed by any, save the most gifted human beings today'. For Despard:

> To man, as to woman, the voice of the wisdom is crying out: 'Take unto yourself your great power and reign, but let that dominion begin with yourself . . . Wise and strong men are responding . . . These have recognized that there must be a new departure.[4]

For Dora Marsden, writing the first editorial for the November 1911 launch of her ambitious new 'weekly feminist review' the *Freewoman*, the new departure had already taken place for some women. All that was needed was to recognise it and to seize the power inherent in naming: 'if she [woman] is an individual she *is* free, and will act like those who are free'. Marsden notes archly that some may wonder 'whether there is not danger, under the circumstances, in labelling them free, thus giving them the liberty of action which is allowed to the free'. Probably the most famous dating of the birth of a specifically modernist sensibility is Virginia Woolf's declaration that human character changed in or about December 1910, a date usually taken to refer to Roger Fry's first Post-Impressionist show, which had opened in November 1910.[5] But Woolf wrote that later, in 1924, when modernist writing and art were well established, if not always accepted, and Woolf herself had become an important bearer of that new character in art.

What is striking about the pre-war pamphleteers, journalists and editors quoted above, and dozens of others as well, is the passionate confidence with which they threw themselves into the struggle for a sexual, political, cultural or spiritual modernity which they themselves were actively in the process of creating. While the British daily press stressed international conflict these smaller-circulation journalists shared a sense that an immediate and positive change was at hand, not only for women, for culture and for the nation, but for humanity. This impending, untrammelled, exciting era, marked by technological, political and psychological advances, is 'modernity'. Each modernity announces itself with a drive against the outworn and false and an embrace of new realities: for the early modernity of the twentieth century many of these struggles concerned control of the discourse of womanhood. 'Modernism', a term coined in retrospect, stands for the complex of early twentieth-century literary and artistic movements marked by experiment, particularly fragmentation of speaker, perspective and form. Woolf is famous as a modernist novelist, Ford tends to be known as a transitional figure, and Masefield, not a modernist, is today virtually unknown. Marsden the editor is known because her magazine the *Freewoman*, transformed in 1914 into the *Egoist*, became famous as an originary site for much of Anglophone modernism. Less visible is what happened in the mingled discourses of pre-war modernity that my chapter begins to uncover, and what may happen when that historicised modernity impacts upon modernism's 'known' forms and values.

The greatest event which was about to strike the cultural centre that Ezra Pound called Vortex London was in fact the Great War.[6] The war tore apart Europe and transformed many of the discourses which had exercised cultured or politically active people in Edwardian Britain. Because these changes were so profound, the discursive field of the immediate pre-war years tends to be looked at through hindsight: looking backwards to find the origins of modernism, feminism, fascism, marxism, psychoanalysis or gender theory. Awareness of the tenacity of this drive for origins must inform any historicising of modernism and modernity: in the case of Marsden, her ideas may anticipate or parallel ideas in Michel Foucault, Gilles Deleuze, Julia Kristeva or Judith Butler, but it decontextualises her thought to credit it for resembling what we take ourselves to be. The way discourses operated in the pre-World War One era is particularly distant in a field such as sexuality, where the Freudian terminology long since used as discursive currency was not yet employed, and 'sex-consciousness' was being used to further many different agendas.

THE WARS OF THE MAGAZINES

The way an age talks to itself is heard most immediately in the many voices of its ephemera, which, for Edwardian and Georgian Britain, were the information, propaganda, entertainment and cultural press. These journalistic and editorial commentaries were culturally and economically mediated, with no text necessarily more 'true' or 'accurate' than another. Together, though, they comprised the discursive networks that were making modernity, as it was then understood, with newspapers and literally thousands of pamphlets, periodicals, printed lectures, manifestos and posters providing an unusually full picture of the range of debate. In economic terms, the dominance in this period of a conservative daily press combined with mass literacy and cheap printing to create an explosion of niche publications, of which the cultural 'little magazine' was only one type. Most new Edwardian publications were funded by public institutions or commercial firms, or were backed by a wealthy patron, but the first action of any new or breakaway group appears to have been to appoint an editor (often the leader) and seek out a compliant printer.

The *Freewoman*, *New Freewoman* and *Egoist* sequence (1911–19) formed a significant part of this modernity in the making. In the period 1907–14, when both pro and anti-woman commentators wrote as if women were on the verge of seizing the discourses of the feminine and the sexual, the *Freewoman* sequence was a self-conscious initiator of modern discourses of womanhood. In its rhetoric, its language, its associations and its enemies, it was a major combatant in what I would call the 'wars of the magazines' which immediately preceded the shooting war. There were other warriors: the *Freewoman* (1911–12) and the *New Freewoman* (1913) centred on the mind and body of woman, a highly contested and volatile field.

Ford Madox Ford (then Ford Madox Hueffer) wrote his pamphlet, ironically titled *This Monstrous Regiment of Women*, for a 'woman suffrage' organisation called the Women's Freedom League (WFL), which had broken away from the 'suffragette' Women's Social and Political Union (WSPU) in 1907, but which pursued similar policies until 1912 when the WSPU turned to criminal forms of civil disobedience. Ford's phrase 'Tomorrow we revise a Constitution' shows him thinking of Britain as a unitary entity: 'we' may finally grant women their suffrage, we may also grant universal male suffrage. And we may also revise the unwritten Constitution so that the Irish will have Home Rule. The crowds in the street Ford referred to were drawn by the funeral of Edward VII in May 1910 and the coronation of George V in 1911, but also by the unprecedented spectacles of the suffragette marches. Crowds gathered to watch women turning themselves into a political force before their very eyes. There had already been two mass marches in June 1908, the second of which had attracted well over a quarter of a million participants. The 1910 WSPU Albert Hall Franchise demonstration, one month after the king's funeral, was a 'monster procession'.[7] A year later, in June 1911, a similar 'Coronation' march attracted 40,000 female participants in a show of strength for the second Conciliation Bill (defeated in April 1912 by Asquith's Liberal government).

John Masefield's pamphlet *My Faith in Woman Suffrage*, was written for the Women's Press, the publishing arm of the militant WSPU, headed by the mother and daughter team of Emmeline and Christabel Pankhurst. Masefield prefaced his bitterly sardonic attack on judicial and social double standards with the disingenuously bland remark that: 'I am an artist, which is, as you all know, as much as to say an extremely bad citizen' (*My Faith*, 1). In his view, inward-turning 'stupidities' like artistic bad citizenship have combined with the 'hideous' rule of the practical-minded to 'make the world a bad place for women'. Masefield's Britain is a nation divided: the artist from society, women from men, poor from rich; worst of all, those who are fed lies are divided by those lies from those who are in control of information.

Olive Hockin, the otherwise unknown reviewer of the Futurist show, was writing from a less accessible mingling of modern discourses, since she wrote for *Orpheus*, the magazine of the art movement of the Theosophical Society, published from 1907 to 1914. Welcoming Futurism for its modernity, Hockin found in it the 'breezy voice and headlong philosophy of Walt Whitman' as it – and her review – celebrated 'the racing motor-car and the factories with their waving hair of smoke [as] vital phenomena of the times' (*Orpheus* 17: 55). The Futurist evolution towards accurate representation of 'mental impressions' was, however, marred for Hockin by their manifestos' assault on woman. Hockin wrote sarcastically:

> The conception of 'woman' seems to be in all alike the same – (How woman can be thus separated from man has always been a mystery! One supposes that a separate race consisting of women only is presumed . . . it is difficult to understand . . . the continual contrasting of beings, which are, in reality, simply identical) – but this it seems is consistent with their profession of faith, which announces 'Contempt for Women' as one of its axioms. (58)

This passage identifies Hockin as an equality feminist like Marsden, but one whose belief in equality is based upon the assumed spiritual likeness of all beings. From this position she mocks what she perceptively identifies as Futurist essentialism and fetishisation of 'woman'. Although she does not mention it by name, the text she is quoting and attacking is Marinetti's 1909 'Founding Manifesto of Futurism', which declares: 'We wish to glorify war . . . the beautiful ideas that kill, the contempt for women . . . We wish to destroy the museums, the libraries, to fight against moralism, feminism . . .'[8]

By 1913, Charlotte Despard was a seasoned suffrage campaigner, President of the Women's Freedom League, and also a novelist, having written *Outlawed: A Novel on the Woman Suffrage Question* with Mabel Collins in 1908.[9] Despard and Collins were, however, theosophists as well as suffragists; the passages quoted from Despard come from her booklet *Theosophy and the Woman's Movement*, published by the Theosophical Publishing House, the publishing arm of the London (Blavatsky) Lodge of the Theosophical Society.[10] 'Why is the woman's movement so powerful?' Despard asks, and then answers her own question in a rhetorical fragment: '*Because it is in the direct line of spiritual evolution*' (*Theosophy*, 12).

When Dora Marsden, a former active member of the WSPU,[11] was declaring woman free, she was launching the *Freewoman* with Mary Gawthorpe (also ex-WSPU). As a weekly, the magazine would expect to report, respond to or even lead immediate opinion. It was in and of contemporary history, not seeking to escape from history or revise its origins. The *Freewoman* was explicitly and unremittingly an organ of what it considered to be the cutting edge of modernity. Marsden founded it when she could no longer accept the discipline of the Pankhursts' WSPU and decided her commitment to women could function better through discursive debate than through direct action. As Carol Barash's researches into Marsden's background have shown, her activism involved deep personal commitment and her education forged long-term networks with other feminist intellectuals.[12] Marsden's feminism gives her individualism its characteristic shape. The freewoman is already free, Marsden argued; it is only the less fully evolved 'bondwomen', or women defined by their self-sacrificing social role, who remain unfree. The vote is only 'a rough and ready expedient, whereby the weak may be protected'. However, 'their more robust sisters' are 'relatively less in need of it' (23 Nov. 1911, 3). Marsden is, in her own terms, a modern 'feminist'; she is only a luke-warm 'suffragist', and she is definitely not a 'suffragette'.

Marsden's 'feminism' differed sharply from suffragist arguments for legislative reform or suffragette direct action. The most divisive and iconoclastic of these journalistic campaigners for modernity, Marsden privileged discourse over politics or aesthetics. She privileged the individual woman over women as a group (though she did argue for some social welfare programmes), she privileged sexual freedom over marriage, and, like many other Edwardians, she believed openly in an elite. For Ford the elite was class- and race-based, for Despard it was spiritual, for Marsden it was based upon woman's intelligence and will manifested through individualism and 'sex passion' (9 May 1912, 482). When Marsden wrote in her launch editorial that the ruling class of men felt for women 'all the natural contempt which a higher order feels for a lower when it presumes bursts [sic] out into the open', she wrote with a floating irony (23 Nov. 1911, 1). The 'fine gentlemen' whose hitherto secret contempt has been flushed out by talk of equality were certainly being mocked, but she also had little sympathy for women who have in her view chosen an unindividuated slavery. Men, in her view, oppose the freewoman because they 'fear' her 'liberty of action'. For the freewoman, however, the contempt men (men like Marinetti?) feel for women as a group 'is the healthiest thing in the world' since women as a whole 'have shown nothing but "servant" attributes'. The freewoman must refuse the comfort of continuing to be, as Marsden strikingly puts it, 'a kind of human poultice' (23 Nov. 1911, 2).

As a writer who uses Nietzschean master–slave analogies for male–female relations, Marsden is alert to the sexual *frissons* of women's struggle. When the ruling class 'of Curzons and Cromers and Asquiths' feel, as she puts it, 'all the charm of an unaccustomed sensation', an 'instinctive and primitive' passion is being roused in them. Marsden's evocation of the male beast awakened by the spectacle of 'imperious wants' coming from a slave sex contains a sly allusion to recent events. As Marsden well knew, suffragette demonstrators were sexually harassed routinely by policemen, plain-clothes men and male onlookers. The Parliamentary Conciliation Committee reporting in 1911 on police behaviour towards WSPU demonstrators during November 1910 did not mince words: 'Many of [the police] resorted to certain forms of torture.

They frequently handled the women with gross indecency'. One marcher reported how: 'Several times constables and plain-clothes men who were in the crowd passed their arms around me from the back and clutched hold of my breasts'.[13] However suitable a topic for irony such 'instinctive' and 'primitive' aggression may have been to Marsden, in 1910 political control of the female body politic was being exercised through sexual assault on women's bodies.

Marsden's 'primitive' is also mischievous because she is not on the side of the suffragettes. In the 'Notes of the Week' of her launch issue she fiercely attacks Mrs Pankhurst for continued militancy and she lashes out at what she considers specious arguments for suffrage: 'half-hearted and sentimental allusions, to prostitution, sweating, child-assault, race-deterioration, and what not' (23 Nov. 1911, 3). Although her leader reflects that women might have been 'crushed' in the past, this argument is 'beside the point' in the early twentieth century since, 'in the long run, the mind plays on its own merits'. Bondwomen enslaved through environment and labour practices are not considered here. In some 'Notes' in later issues, Marsden did advocate trade-union representation and the inclusion of domestic servants in national insurance schemes, and she offered space for other 'modern' arguments such as H. G. Wells on divorce law reform (Mar. 1912). However, at times she also took an even harder line on the power of the discourse of freedom: even the economically disadvantaged woman should be able to become free by declaring herself free.

For Marsden, the freewoman is evolving from the bondwoman: she should be 'a master', and 'find her place among the masters'. Woman is thus seen as a dualism (free and bonded) while men are unitary, referred to as 'he' or 'man'. Although Marsden is offering a challenge to those women who may feel themselves able to declare themselves 'freewomen,' her invocation of mastery supports an essentialist concept of masculinity. Her free/bond distinction parallels class divisions, but Marsden doesn't address how men oppress other men, either through class or colonialism. Taking the masculine as the norm, Marsden hopes that someday, the freewoman will 'consider her sex as incidental as men do' (23 Nov. 1911, 2). Even so, Marsden's declaration is revolutionary: by separating the female sex from feminine gender roles, it proposes a 'free' female-sexed individual who is not defined by marriage, motherhood or sexual orientation.

For freewomen, the future will be narcissistically exhilarating, since 'their freedom will consist in appraising their own worth'. The result of the emergence of the freewoman will be 'vivid new life-manifestations' (23 Nov. 1911, 2) – a phrase which would apply equally well to theosophy,

Nietzschean will to power or sexual freedom. In her fourth issue, writing on the 'New Morality', Marsden argues that women's intuition 'will make their greatest revelations of life-manifestation to the world' and 'will push open the door of the super-world' (14 Dec. 1911, 62). Four months later, Marsden called for female pleasure: 'The Over-and-Above – Joy – the Thrill' that makes life worth living (1 Feb. 1912, 201). Since 'Joy is the Life-Force', her Blakean solution to vice is 'its completer satisfaction': 'desire is not evil. It is good' (1 Feb. 1912, 202).

Sceptical about any governmental function, Marsden was libertarian in her conviction that the individual's desires – especially sexual desires – should come first (she is less explicit about rights). By mid-1912 she was willing to call herself an anarchist, but unlike other early twentieth-century anarchists and syndicalists, she did not believe in the capacities of the mass of the population to govern themselves. Because she locates power internally, Marsden is also the least politically involved of these pre-war polemicists of change. For Marsden, the economic and political systems don't have to change: in her leaders, the future is already here in the form of its discourses: all that is needed is for woman to *declare* 'that she is superior, a master' (23 Nov. 1911, 2). If Marsden's spiritual idealism sounds theosophist, her sexual vitalism may sound Nietzschean and proto-Lawrentian. Her declarations lack Nietzschean and Lawrentian sex-differentiation. In *Bid Me to Live*, an autobiographical novel about the *Egoist* set by the poet H. D. (Hilda Doolittle), the character Rico (who represents Lawrence) uses a 'man-is-man, woman-is-woman' dichotomy to make the heroine Julia feel her creativity is 'wrong' but Marsden's *Freewoman* and *New Freewoman* writings refuse this division, even in its inverted form of 'difference' feminism.[14]

In October 1912 the *Freewoman* failed. Although in her last editorial Marsden claimed that sales had been holding up, the magazine had visibly been running out of material, and energy had moved to the *Freewoman* discussion circle. Rebecca West, who had been putting together a strong review section, with emphasis on drama as well as feminism and spiritual issues, was becoming marginalised. The publisher, Charles Granville, pulled out his backing and the weekly, relatively expensive at three pence an issue, could not survive. In June 1913 Marsden relaunched it with the financial help of Harriet Shaw Weaver as the *New Freewoman*. It kept that title until January 1914, when it became the *Egoist: An Individualist Review*, with Weaver as Editor, Marsden as contributing editor and Richard Aldington and Leonard Compton-Rickett as Assistant Editors. Ezra Pound was not on the masthead in 1914 but gleefully considered himself to be in 'controll' [sic] of the 'literatchure', as he described it to Alice Corbin Henderson, associate editor of the American magazine

Poetry.[15] It is through the Pound connection that the *Egoist* became and has remained famous as the nursery of a literary avant-garde, indeed of a literary modernism which takes Pound, Eliot and Joyce and Imagism as its centres.

EGOISM, THEOSOPHY AND MODERNITY

In the history of pre-war literary and cultural 'little magazines', all except *Blast*, that other iconoclastic title, worked to provide initial platforms for publication, aimed at attracting attention to their authors' work, having it published commercially in book form and having it reviewed and sold. Attention from the mainstream press was sought, even while its philistinism was derided. In terms of the trajectory of the creative work, the magazine was the first stage in an economy of publication, sometimes followed by inclusion in an anthology, always (if successful) culminating in a single-author book. The *Freewoman, New Freewoman, Egoist* sequence, however, diverges from this pattern in ways that offer an insight into the mingling of discourses of woman in the making of both modernity and modernism.

As Marsden and these other writers show, these discourses were not in practice always distinguished or even defined as distinguishable at the time. Lisa Tickner's *The Spectacle of Women: Imagery of the Suffrage Campaign* has shown that suffragette iconography, performance and street spectacle constituted a visual modernism displayed to a huge public.[16] Using Marinetti, *Blast* and Christabel Pankhurst, Janet Lyons has argued that the suffragettes were 'making literal . . . to an astonishing degree the metaphors and metalepses of iconoclasm used by the English avant-garde'.[17] These historically detailed studies validate suffragette modernity by identifying it with types of modernist trope. In another effort at separating out strands which have been tangled by classic readings of modernism, Robert van Hallberg has warned against the 'unattractive consequences' of inferring either a narrowly 'technical' modernism or a proto-fascism from Imagist doctrine and personalities. Looking specifically for Dora Marsden's contribution to literature, he finds it in her appreciation of 'the literary implications of [Max] Stirner's antistatist philosophy'.[18] Bruce Clarke's *Dora Marsden and Early Modernism* finds that Marsden's 'individualism presents a libertarian anarchism' (I would question the specificity of that 'anarchism'), but before locating Marsden amidst the literary figures Pound, Lawrence and William Carlos Williams, he quotes Astradur Eysteinsson's warning that the critic must be aware of the contradictory pressures arising from 'divergent approaches to modernism as, on the one hand, a *cultural force*, and on the other as an *aesthetic project*.[19] The 'cultural force' is part of history, particularly when it is expressed through journalism; the 'aesthetic project' may seek to deny or break with history.

Van Hallberg finds parallels between Marsden's individualist philosophy and the anarchist and syndicalist ideas of the day (her feminism is not stressed). Marsden was broadly anti-statist, though I am not convinced of Stirner being the basis for her thinking from the start, since Stephen T. Byington's translation of Stirner's *Der Einzige und Sein Eigentum* was published only in 1912 as *The Ego and His Own* (though arguably 'der Einzige' means 'the unique'). More importantly, 'The Growing Ego', Marsden's leading article of 8 August 1912, bears the marks of something like an immediate conversion experience. She has, she writes, 'just laid aside one of the profoundest of human documents' which has 'just now' had a 'penetrative influence', and she devotes the rest of the article to expounding Stirner. Like many converts, Marsden has recognised in Stirner the articulation of something close to her existing beliefs. For Marsden, though, her individualism was worked through by means of her feminism. In the *New Freewoman* relaunch, Marsden recapitulates her dismissal of the merely political 'Woman movement'. She then reiterates the essential fact that: 'A very limited number of women have been emphasizing' that the primary fact about them is 'that they are individuals' – Marsden herself being one of these non-typed female individuals. Only then does she move on to assert a theoretical individualism of desire derived from this individualist feminism: 'The centre of the Universe lies in the desire of the individual' (15 June 1913, 5).

Stirner's 'egoism' (as distinct from mere selfish 'egotism') was not always distinguished or, for contemporary readers, particularly necessary to distinguish from other aphoristic and individualistic philosophies such as those of Nietzsche or even Schopenhauer. Marsden could have come across a summary of Stirner in *Egoists: A Book of Supermen* by the cultural journalist James Huneker, who also surveyed Blake, Baudelaire, Flaubert, Huysmans, Ibsen, Nietzsche and others as 'egoists' in the same work.[20] The terms 'ego', 'individual' and 'superman' were ready fodder for pre-war journalistic debate. Reviewing Arnold Bennett for the *Freewoman*, Rebecca West remarked that: 'We may become Supermen and Superwomen as fast as we will' (4 Apr. 1912, 387). Nietzsche was even mixed up with theosophy, when A. R. Orage, who had popularised Nietzsche in a 1906 collection of his aphorisms,[21] wrote *Consciousness, Animal, Human and Superhuman*, using a theosophy-influenced evolutionary model to outline how his new Nietzschean man could 'enter into the ecstatic world'.[22]

Marsden's vocabulary of ego is part of a post-Hegelian individualist ideology,[23] but she was also involved with theosophy, using articles, reviews and letters by theosophist writers and giving a lecture herself on 'The Free Woman' at the theosophical summer school in 1913, as advertised on the last page of the 15 June 1913 *New Freewoman*. Several of Marsden's contributors, such as Selwyn Weston, Huntly Carter, E. S. P. Haynes and Charles Granville, expressed theosophical-type views, and W. Allan Macdonald and Helen Meredith Macdonald appear to have been followers of Mary Baker Eddy's Christian Science. Both the term and the concept of 'ego' were part of theosophy's spiritual evolutionary model. When she was writing her mystical treatise *The Secret Doctrine* in the mid-1880s, Helena Petrovna Blavatsky, the co-founder of theosophy, felt that 'mankind was never more selfish and vicious than it is now', even though spirituality should be 'on its ascending arc' towards 'the Higher Ego'. This ego is not 'the selfishness of the *personality*' (a meaning closer to the dictionary definition of 'egotism') but 'the *nous* or *Mind*'.[24] In her later writings Blavatsky argued more for an evolving individual ego:

> The Ego starts with divine Consciousness . . . Only after many births does it begin to discern, by this collectivity of experience, that it is individual. At the end of its cycle of reincarnation it is still the same divine self-consciousness, but it has now become individualized Self-consciousness.[25]

Marsden's interest in theosophy was noted by Jane Lidderdale in her 1970 biography of Harriet Shaw Weaver: 'Dora, like many of the suffragettes, was interested in esoteric cults, particularly in the Theosophists.'[26] She may have been considered by the Blavatsky Institute (the London theosophical centre) to have been more than merely 'interested', since it gave the *New Freewoman* both editorial offices and space in its publishing house in Oakley Street, near the British Museum. As tenant, the *New Freewoman* could sell copies of its magazine from the Blavatsky bookstall without a payment to a newsagent. This meant that the greatest sales income came from Oakley Street[27], indicating also that the greatest identifiable readership was drawn from theosophists, a point discernible from *New Freewoman* articles, and from the letters columns well into the era of the *Egoist*. In the 1 July 1913 issue of the *New Freewoman* W. W. Leisenring (Winnifried Leisenring, the secretary of the Blavatsky Institute) wondered disingenuously whether Marsden's declaration that 'Woman as such has no reality' might be a call for 'a neuter person' or, even worse, evidence of the 'so-called Buddhist view that nothing temporal is real'. Leisenring briskly corrected Marsden: 'self-conscious knowledge of one's own individuality cannot be reached except by means of temporary male and female bodies' (35). Marsden had reason to take these critiques seriously since Leisenring was also Treasurer of the

'Thousand Club' which had raised a lot of the funds for the launch of the *New Freewoman*.

VORTEX MARSDEN AND THE AUDIENCE-TEXT

Dora Marsden had her own, highly individual life. Having been one of the very few women of her generation to gain a BA (from Manchester University), she was genuinely a member of a female intellectual elite and proudly displayed BA after her name on the *Freewoman* masthead. Petite, dark-haired and, according to her friends, seraphically beautiful, she suffered from poor health most of her adult life and turned in later years to a feminist Christianity.[28] However, the maker of the particular modernity of the *Freewoman* sequence is not so much the biographical Marsden, as it is 'vortex Marsden': the discourses she articulates, represses, reforms and de-forms through her writing and editorship. All writers are to some extent part of stronger or weaker cultural vortices, but journalism is a special kind of literary product whose text is in some sense its audience.[29] Whatever its content, the *Freewoman* sequence is always also 'about' the partitioned social space of Edwardian Britain which its designation of an audience conveys.

Vortex Marsden's discourses map out audiences, not through hunting for sales but through her exploration of a cluster of interests given their impetus by feminism. As her discourses shifted, so did her readers, who made their agreements or disagreements known through highly inter-active letters pages. Pushing out her leaders under the pressure of a weekly deadline and editing a magazine as well, Marsden didn't seek a long-term consistency of discourse. Her shifts of emphasis are not only integral to her role as editor, they evidence that cultural role of generating responsive audience-texts. Launching her magazine from a suffragette platform, she immediately split feminism off from suffragettism and so lost that audience which put the WSPU first (many left parting shots in the letters columns). After losing the symbolic capital of the suffrage struggle, Marsden's discourses designated other audience-texts, notably those of sex reform, theosophy and, later, linguistic debate. Throughout, individualism is assumed to be a given by almost all her journalists and correspondents.

When Marsden welcomed the change in the magazine's title to the *Egoist* in January 1914, she was continuing to refine her ideological audience-mapping, seeking to add 'a literary flank to her movement . . . lending cultural breadth to her brand of feminism'.[30] It is no longer possible to see the retitling of the magazine simply as an ambush by Pound, even if that was Pound's view: the Marsden of late 1913 was already an egoist, and it was she who wrote the leaders defining 'egoism'. When Rebecca West, then serving as assistant editor, sought out Ezra Pound after he had been recommended to her by Ford Madox Ford and Violet Hunt, she had Pound submit proposals for his literary pages, which she passed on to Marsden. Requiring an assurance from Pound that his intellectual position was compatible with the policy of the magazine, Marsden got one, with Pound somewhat uneasily declaring himself an 'individualist'.[31] Marsden also obtained a guarantee that he would bring in funding. This is a narrative showing careful vetting. In my view the gradual shift of editorial control to Harriet Weaver and the move forward of the literary 'back' of the magazine actually mark an expansion of Marsden's 'egoism' into literary egoism, or Poundian modernism. Pound's subsequent audience-text is what became the 'Pound Era'.[32]

Many movements of the immediate pre-war period were seeking to join, enlarge, unite and be accepted: woman suffrage, women's legal rights and sex reform are perhaps the most salient examples. In the wars of the magazines and the spectacles on the street, these campaigners were, however, perceived by their opponents as agents of chaos and disorder because a new, larger definition of the body politic and the physical body would mean a shift of power. The sense of threat crossed party lines. For A. R. Orage at the 'progressive' *New Age*, women – all women, since women argue they must marry – are seeking to double their privileges selfishly, by claiming both economic support and the vote (6 July 1911, 227), when in fact they lack reason and intelligence. In Orage's 'A Tale for Men Only' the pseudo-intellectual Marion invades the serious philosophical debates of a group of male friends and makes a fool of herself.[33] Indeed, for Orage, woman is animal, lusting after coarseness: 'She loves to be taken at spear point. Which proves that her vaunted culture is enamel, lying on the surface' (6 Apr. 1911, 550). The 'instinctive and primitive' male aggression that Marsden noted is blamed by Orage on woman's instinctive desire to be dominated. For Orage, who read German, a key source for misogynist theory would have been Otto Weininger, of whom more later.

For the conservative physician Sir Almoth Wright, in his lengthy 27 March 1912 letter to *The Times*, the male must be 'mystified' by the 'eerie feeling' caused by 'the periodically [i.e.monthly] recurring phases of hypersensitiveness, unreasonableness and loss of sense of proportion' in woman. (In later Freudian terms, Wright is describing his unconscious sense of the uncanny caused by the threatening proximity of the female sex organs.) For Wright women also invariably suffer either the 'complete alteration of character' caused by childbearing or 'the terrible physical havoc' of lost love, followed by the 'long-continued mental disorders' of the menopause. Today, these creatures are expressing their 'mental disorder' by the 'hysterical revolt' of the 'fatuous' suffrage campaign. For Wright, woman is her womb, her hysteria. Yet this dread of female action, once recognised, became a weapon for those who were its target. Thrust into the position of the abject, the suffragettes performed like the repressed, acting out the male ruling-class nightmare of anarchic hysterical disruption until granting the vote should seem a relief.

Possibly, though, the use of models of unity (or transcendent unity or higher justice) versus fragmentation – the fragmentation so pronounced in literary modernism – may have been part of the pre-war problem as well as part of the desired solution. This model must have made it harder to notice the high levels of tension between fixed, recognised entities: England, Germany, France. And some drives for change were truly divisive: Irish Home Rule was meant to soothe Irish nationalism, but the real drive was for full independence. In psychology, the notion of the unified self was no longer tenable. Meanwhile in the suffragette, anarchist, socialist and religious press of vortex London, there was little sense of impending doom, rather of vital issues which can and will be solved.

Vortex Marsden mingles the disruptive and fragmentary with the unitary. Her consistent quest for a unified 'I', ego, or self also usually – but not consistently – refuses mind–body dualism and male–female essentialism. The icons she assaulted in her iconoclastic editorials were fixities, whether male or female. Her biting critiques of suffragettism and the Pankhursts were a pre-emptive – and arguably premature – deconstruction of what she took to be a foundationalist discourse in the making: a discourse of 'woman' as undifferentiated wronged victim. In Marxist terms, she was destabilising ideology in the sense that suffragettism offered a belief system that reconciled contradictions (specifically those clustered around 'woman') through its belief that the vote was the preeminent issue. Individualism had long since been such an ideology – indeed Stirner's fellow Young Hegelian Ludwig Feuerbach was the target of Marx's polemic in *The German Ideology* - but a feminist individualism was inherently unstable because of the ambiguity of its terms. Indeed, did the category 'woman' exclude the category 'individual'?

Indifferent to literature, Marsden privileged the linguistic because she recognised its power both as interpellative pseudo-statement and as aphoristic 'truth'. Her definition of the ego takes in both an Adamic self-definition and a feminist validation of desire: 'I . . . Me, I . . . Me, the birth-song of the human soul', she wrote (28 Mar. 1912, 361). For her, the power of the substantive derives from the self-creating entity 'I'. 'We [women] lag behind in the upward thrusting of life because we have not developed "definiteness" in mind, which is individuality' (362). Women can be 'other' for Marsden because of their 'indefiniteness', but rather than going for a 'male' side of a binary as in her first *Freewoman* leader, in 1912 she uses imagery of a tightening and 'intensification of self-consciousness' as the female self moves from a material vagueness to a distinct and upward-thrusting 'life' (362). The elements are already there in women, but diffused, and women – freewomen – can raise themselves. There is little of the imagery of war or struggle here that marks Sylvia Pankhurst's memoirs of the same period, and a notable absence of mythic analogues.

Although later she had doubts, during the *Freewoman/New Freewoman* period, Marsden used substantives as entities whose interpellative and conceptual power she embraced even as she tried out her own definitions. In May 1912 she proposed a 'Select Glossary': 'Freedom . . . is clearing the way for Life' (16 May 1912, 503). 'Spirit' is not only that 'more extended and less differentiated life-force' of all existence (as in theosophy), but 'rather that self-conscious spirit of man . . . The Spirit is life-force made *self-conscious*' (502). The same article marks her effort, under pressure from a member of her audience at the Discussion Circle, to explain 'the Man-Woman idea' she had recently set forth in a talk. Marsden duly attributes 'Knowing' and 'mentality' to men, and 'Feeling' and 'intuitive faculties' to women, as if this conventional facultative psychology were a truth. Although Marsden doesn't employ this readily available terminology of the Man-Woman as her usual designation of the new female individual, any writer who accepts unquestioningly the practice of categorical interpellations would have difficulty avoiding the conventional ones. In her long 5 September 1912 leader 'The Policy of the Freewoman', in which Marsden dissociated herself from Mary Gawthorpe's campaign against forcible feeding of suffragette hunger strikers, she starts to question the practice of categorisation itself – 'We are, therefore, more concerned with the work of establishing our own mastery' – and to argue, as Gawthorpe does, that the Home Secretary is 'ungentlemanly' is, Marsden argues, a 'category mistake' – 'they fail to see that government is nothing other than coercion' (305). Here Marsden is shifting towards nouns signifying action– mastery, coercion – and against those reinforcing established institutions by their reiteration – government, gentleman.

The following week, though, continuing her analysis of government as crude power, Marsden used substantives in an uglier interpellation. Male and female emancipationists should stop whimpering 'feebly' about 'rights'. 'The object of contempt is not the slave-owner, but the slave . . . The person who is responsible for the tyrant is the slave' (12 Sept. 1912, 321). Political reformists waste their time targeting

Parliament, since '*Government rests on force*' (322). The State is a monopoly, and the Standing Army a product of 'Jewish occupation'. Once, the army was answerable to the people: 'but the Jews have changed all that'. The Boer war, says Marsden, 'was a Jews' war', and if there should be a war between England and Germany, 'It would be a war between money-lending German Jews and money-lending Jews in England' (323). The Jews, not the English, have set up the Police, and Inspectors: 'There seems to be no epithet, no word . . . that would be sufficient to rouse [the English] to revolt . . . The word has not yet been coined which can . . . sting him into revolt' (323).

Marsden may be propounding a proto-Foucaultian view of state power even while she is advancing a proto-fascist group libel. Through her calumny of Jews Marsden the feminist anti-statist individualist gleefully enrolls herself as part of a nationalist 'England' unified by its anti-semitism and thus by its difference from the Jew who might, as she vividly puts it, 'spurn [the Englishman] with his foot, lash him with thongs, and spit in his face'. Using Nietzschean terminology, Marsden hopes 'we' shall know that Britons never shall be slaves when the Jew must face the 'adequate weapons' – possibly not just epithet-weapons – of the Englishman roused (12 Sept. 1912, 323). Since Marsden speaks of trying to find the right (that is, the most virulent) 'epithet', she knows well the power of the substantive weapon she uses. In his brilliantly vicious 'Unedited Notes' in the *New Age* of 6 July 1911, which we may assume Marsden had read, A. R. Orage had turned round the suffragists' analogy between the oppression of Jews and the oppression of women. (Since many suffragists were overt racists, the 1960s' analogy between oppression of blacks and oppression of women was not employed.[34]) According to Orage, neither Jews nor women have been forced to become usurers or dependent wives, since Jews actually 'have no skill' for anything but money-making, and women only 'pretend they have no option of a choice' but to marry. To get out of such an unflattering comparison, Marsden has jettisoned the Jew and turned him into a scapegoat. Her audience-text was well-judged: in the following weeks, those active letters columns don't carry correspondence defending Jews.

Inclusion of one 'other' was achieved by abjection of another, an exclusionary anti-semitic manœuvre which was pursued by other entryist outsiders of the period. For Ezra Pound, an American, it led to active fascism, for T. S. Eliot, also American, it led to, amongst other texts, 'Burbank with a Baedecker . . .' and the essay 'After Strange Gods'. In *Deadlock* (1920), one of the later volumes of her autobiographical feminist novel *Pilgrimage*, Dorothy Richardson has her Dora Marsden-like heroine Miriam Henderson defend the 'individualist with consciousness' against the argument of Michael Shatov (a Jew) that 'the race is *clearly* more sacred than the individual'.[35]

THE WAR OF THE WORDS

In the first anniversary editorial of the retitled *Egoist* (1 Jan. 1915) Marsden (now contributing editor) declared it her new task 'to break the hypnotic spell, to blast the stupefactions of – The Word'. Then, in an important passage, she announced: 'Our war is with words and in their every aspect: grammar, accidence, syntax.' Marsden writes that she agrees with 'our friends the Imagists' in their attack on the adjective, but in her view the substantive (the noun) 'approaches much nearer the conceptual: the abstract'. Marsden is probably referring directly to the attack on abstraction in Pound's 'A Few Don'ts by an Imagiste', first published in *Poetry*, March 1913, and there is certainly an interplay of ideas between Imagism and Marsden.

Van Hallberg and Andrew Thacker have emphasised the parallels between Marsden's attack on the symbol and the Imagists' attack on abstraction, as in her comment: 'Woman . . . is an empty concept and should be banished from the language' (1 July 1913, 23).[36] (But 'Jew' should stay?) When, in 1915, Marsden attacked 'abstract substantives', she focused again on 'woman', though without a critique of the aggressive fetishisation of 'woman' by war propaganda.[37] Marsden's attack is not, however, only against abstraction, but against *all* language, and it is based, not upon a hope for a purified, more precise, or less deceiving language, but upon a sharp appreciation of the power of language in all its uses: 'words incline by capacity to deception'. As early as October 1913 Marsden had been working towards a recognition that categories thrive on empty oppositions; refusing again to identify her magazine with a single 'Cause', she wrote: 'by being critical of the static, we at least create a void' (15 Oct. 1913, 165). By 1915 she had located the ideology of interpellation in its agent, language. As a leader writer, Marsden was a rhetorician, and she knew the power of her tools, whether blunt or sharp, in other hands as well as her own.

In my view, Marsden's most significant intersection with Imagist poetics is her insistence in 1915 that the power of the image arises from its source in the ego:

> Accurately, every sentence begins with 'I' . . . when I say, 'IT moves, I mean 'I have the image of it moving', even though it may be possible 'by means of mechanical contrivances' to produce: 'the image that it moves'. (1 Jan. 1915, 3)

In this passage Marsden mentions approvingly Marinetti's loathing for the controls of syntax and his preference for the 'fluid' verb. But, continues Marsden, every verb arises from a subject. Even the first person singular verb 'represents only a passing image' of the 'comprehensive entity – the "I" '. 'The verb's purpose is to particularise the condition of the 'I' under which for the moment it shows itself' (3). Arising from the same vortex as Imagism, Marsden's theory of language is proposing that the repression of the 'I' in Imagism and its emphasis upon direct representation of 'things' does not affect the power of the ego: 'Always it is "I" which feels.' 'Scenes, sounds, smells . . . appear as qualities of the "things" sensed, but then the "things" also are but the product of and exist only in the "I".' Even 'scientific' observation of external objects is part of the ego:

> So one may pride oneself on being scientific: bent on looking at 'things', and on 'measuring things' . . . What is that [the scientific attitude] but the pressing of more egoistic power into that one particular effort of the scientist's 'ego', by which means he may hope to call out from himself and for himself a more clear and full image . . .

Scientific objectivity must be the product of the scientist's ego because the ego makes the image. Since image is an aspect of ego, Imagism's syntactic suppression of the pronoun 'I' actually foregrounds the ego by displaying its image-making act. In Imagism, the poem and the external or internal 'thing' it manifests are fetishised as hard definite entities, with the poet's 'mastery' evident in his or her control. Marsden's argument points up the process in Imagism where, as in the classic operation of fetishisation, the power attributed to the object has been imputed to it by the subject, the ego, whose agency can then be denied, not least by the ego itself, even while its effects are performed in the ego's poem.

SEX, BODY AND EGO IN THE VORTEX

In historic terms the feminism of the pre-World War One period has slid like a tectonic plate under the powerful image of the suffragette. To this day, images of marching suffragettes look glorious, and the metaphor of the 'Cat and Mouse' poster still conveys the agony of the repeated imprisonments and forced feeding of suffragette demonstrators. These women put their bodies on the line for their beliefs. In pre-war modernity, both pro- and anti-suffrage groups were heavily engaged in using the female body, that visible and material mark of difference. What the suffragettes did was to materialise that discursive object through their own bodies, and publicise that physicality through the WSPU magazines *Votes for Women* and *The Suffragette*, edited by Christabel Pankhurst. The symbolic marches soon became a middle ground between two other, even more extreme, poles: the aggression of property damage, and the physical sacrifice of hunger strikes by imprisoned suffragettes, followed by forcible feeding through a tube pushed into the nasal passage. Forcible feeding created for a horrified public an analogy between political and bodily integrity on the one hand, and anti-suffrage policies and physical violation on the other (via the nasal rape of the hunger strikers). Suffrage and suffering were united at the physical level.

At the same time, at the *Freewoman*, Marsden was physicalising the goals of her new woman. Partly because of Marsden's 'open' editorship, partly because she had trouble filling the magazine on a weekly basis, the magazine rapidly became an important forum for radical ideas on sexuality, given their impetus by feminism but often breaking new ground. Mainly, though, the impetus came from Marsden's increasing conviction that the ego becomes what it is through desiring. The range of sex-related topics covered in the *Freewoman* and *New Freewoman* testifies to immense cultural pressure needing the outlet of public debate. Among the topics were: marriage as breeding contract, marriage as prostitution, free love, neo-paganism, 'old maids', 'Aethnic' (celibate) union, maternity allowances, divorce, the effects of sexual abstinence before marriage, 'white slavery' and prostitution, venereal disease or the 'social evil', the rights of illegitimate children and mistresses, sex-passion, 'Neo-Malthusianism' (contraception), and male and female homosexuality. When Marsden began a five-part editorial on 'The New Morality' for issues 4 and 6 through 9, her views initially sketched out a Nietzschean binary, though without crediting Nietzsche: 'Men are pagan . . . Women are wholly Christian . . . Women themselves are very different from men' (14 Dec. 1912, 62). Almost immediately, though, Marsden moved to an 'us', a kind of desiring community, sometimes elite, sometimes apparently not, which became the hallmark of her subsequent writings about sex. For 'us' sexual passion offers communication between subject and object. By 1915 the external love-object has been absorbed in the ego, but at this earlier stage of Marsden's theorisation, an object is present to be desired.

For vortex Marsden, desire and creativity follow the same path: the 'riveted attention' of sex passion is 'the open avenue along which creative vibration communicates'. And for most of us (Marsden here includes herself) 'the Open Gateway . . . must be the gateway of sexual passion'. Marriage is disconnected from passion: monogamy is a monopoly, she argues in 'Woman: Endowed or Free' (29 Feb. 1912), following Friedrich Engels, Charlotte Perkins Gilman and Olive Schreiner. The 'endowed' wife is supported by her husband in a lazy concubinage while freewomen earn wages. Furthermore, apparently progressive proposals for maternal benefit allowances would simply increase 'endowment', as she notes in the course of a lengthy debate with H. G. Wells, Upton Sinclair and others on maternity benefits, marriage and divorce.

Marsden's resistance to the strongly sex-differentiated gender theory of her day was based on a political and economic analysis as well as a philosophical one. As her 4 April, 1912 response to Sir Almoth Wright's letter to *The Times* shows, Marsden understood perfectly that protection of male economic domination underlay the biological differentiation argument. 'We seek to work alongside men, receiving equal pay for equal work', she says, while Wright has argued that men and women in the workplace would destroy 'the modesties and reticences upon which our civilization has been built up' (4 Apr. 1912, 392).

Perhaps sensing its intractability, Marsden let the economic linkage go once she had pointed it out. In a four-part leader essay 'Interpretations of Sex', which ran during May 1912, Marsden advanced a transcendent and inclusive theory of sex, which deliberately sought not to be physically explicit (for which some correspondents criticised her) and which also deliberately separated sex from its material aspects of breeding, hygiene and social policy. While Christabel Pankhurst was using her platform in the *Suffragette* to deny the usual association of woman's sexuality with pollution, indicting male sexuality instead, Marsden was using the *Free-woman* to establish a sexual woman without using gender binaries. She knew that connecting women with sex and attributing desire to women – even an intelligent desire – was dangerous at a time when these attributes were routinely used to denigrate women. Marsden's articles were in fact written in response to Otto Weininger's misogynist sexology, *Sex and Character* (1903), whose last (and least offensive) chapter she reprinted over a period of weeks in order to have her opponent available for refutation.

Weininger's influential argument was based upon an absolute sex-distinction, with woman merely 'sex', incapable of reason or truth, her only belief that of a coital cult. In 1894, Havelock Ellis's *Man and Woman* had argued a soft version of binary gender destiny, hoping for 'equal freedom of both the masculine and feminine elements of life',[38] elements which he considered to be biologically determined rather than cultural. Weininger, however, argued passionately against such fusion; for him, no matter what the conditions, there could be no moral relations between the sexes and no relaxing of absolute gender binaries. Translated in 1906, *Sex and Character* became a formidable anti-feminist weapon in the English-speaking world.[39]

Weininger and Marsden were both sex radicals. Weininger pushed the masculine–feminine binary to its logical limit, with absolute man in his positive form as genius and absolute woman as negative, or 'absence of

intelligible ego' (*Sex*, 202). For Weininger: 'the ego
intelligible existence' and he cites Nietzsche, Stirnei
sources at various times for Marsden) as proving tha\
towards oneself' (158). For Weininger, as for Marsden, slav
because of 'their servile dispositions' (338); for both, the c
marital 'pairing' should be resisted. Both are anti-semitic. In
fourteenth chapter, the one reprinted by Marsden, he oppose\
women but hopes for the 'emancipation of woman from herself', c   .g
that 'woman, as woman, must disappear' (343). This categorical imperative
looks as if it may have influenced Marsden's attack on the category
type in her 1913 declaration: ' "Woman" is doing nothing – she has,
indeed, no existence', but Marsden wants a desiring individual while for
Weininger the disappearance of 'woman' is also the behavioural disappearance
of sex: 'Women must really and truly and spontaneously
relinquish coitus'.

By reprinting a chapter from Weininger over four issues of her
magazine, Marsden makes him into a leader writer like herself, blurring
possible distinctions between the 'professional' academically trained philosopher
and the journalist. She too is academically trained in Kantian
philosophy, she too is a polymath who can establish categories, and then
thunder and ironise. In the decadence of the Kantian idealist tradition,
these discursive similarities between philosophical treatises and weekly or
monthly philosophical speculations by journalistic figures such as Marsden,
Orage, Ford (Hueffer), Wells, Allan Upward, Guy Aldred and others
ummasked philosophy as a rhetorical practice perpetuating arbitrary
nominative abstractions. This convergence may have served as an impetus
to the shaping of the more rigorous, linguistically aware, philosophical
logic by Bertrand Russell and Ludwig Wittgenstein (though there is a
continuity in Wittgenstein's admiration for Weininger).[40]

Weininger moves towards the modernity in which one's identity is
defined by what one desires (the homosexual and the pederast are defined
for Weininger by what they desire); he accepts a homosexual component
in man, defined as a constitutional bisexuality leading to desire for the
same sex, without letting it disturb the absoluteness of his gender
categories. Marsden leaves homosexuality to her correspondents to
discuss and assumes a self which may desire anything: 'Passion can take,
and rightly take, all or any forms of expression natural to it' (2 May 1912,
461). Like religion, desire can perform itself in any way, whether 'an
elaborate ritual' or 'few outward forms'. Sex is, and always has been,
about pleasure: 'From the first protozoa up through the scale of life, it has
been experienced for its own satisfaction', with 'continuing the race'
merely a by-product. For Marsden, sexual abstinence before marriage has

. the same ethical value as 'the case of a man who refuses a snack lest
.e spoil his zest for lunch' (461). (Marsden frequently associates sexual
pleasure with eating.) And sex evolves, from 'sex-instinct' to 'sex-sense'
(462), and from 'sex' to 'passion' (9 May 1912, 481). Far from dragging
the human down to the animal, 'Sex, more than any human factor, is still
to be the means of springing life higher' (23 May 1912, 2). If sex comes
from the individual ego, there is also no need to define its identity
according to its object of desire. Finally, though, to facilitate her nominal
sex/passion distinction in her last essay, Marsden reintroduces a body–
mind dualism that her first leader had avoided.

By the end of May 1912, disputes about the *Freewoman*'s treatment of
sex had erupted into the daily press. After Sir Almoth Wright's letter and
a correspondence in *The Times* initiated by the anti-suffragist novelist
Mrs. Humphrey Ward, Ward used the *Freewoman*'s apparent advocacy of
free love and irreligion as a stick to beat all suffragists.[41] With moderate
suffragists anxious to avoid the labels of hysteria or immorality, Agnes
Maude Royden of the non-militant NUWSS (National Union of Woman
Suffrage Societies) accordingly wrote to *The Times* on 21 June criticising
Ward for judging the NUWSS on the basis of 'an obscure little periodical
[the *Freewoman*] which is neither published, owned, nor read by their
members'. Indeed, said Royden, 'this nauseous publication' is as un-
representative of suffragism as Wright's misogynist fulminations are, she
presumes, of the female anti-suffragist Ward.

Although Marsden, in full editorial pursuit, triumphantly forced
Royden to admit that *Common Cause*, the magazine of the NUWSS,
had in fact often quoted the 'nauseous' *Freewoman* approvingly, Royden
did have a point. Most of the sexual discourse in the *Freewoman* has
nothing to do with suffrage and everything to do with breaking the binaries
that controlled sexuality. Reinforcing popular prejudice, Sir Almoth
Wright had declared that most militant suffragettes were 'sexually embit-
tered' and 'life-long strangers to joy' – that is, frustrated old maids, other
marchers being merely deluded. However, Marsden's frequent correspondent and sometime reviewer Harry J. Birnstingl was looking at the same
processions and seeing something rather different. When critics assume
that 'agitators' must be 'celibate and childless', Birnstingl notes:

> . . . it has apparently never occured to them that numbers of these women find
> their ultimate destiny, as it were, amongst members of their own sex, working for
> the good of each other, forming romantic – nay sometimes passionate – attachments
> with each other. (4 Jan. 1912, 128)

In other words the spectacles which so appalled Wright and others were
even more radical than they had feared: the marches constituted the

performance of a politicised lesbianism. This phenomenon Birnstingl considers 'splendid', finding it 'one of the most wonderful things of the twentieth century' that these unmarried women, condescendingly considered surplus women, actually experience deeply purposeful lives, loving each other and 'working together for the freedom of their sex' (128).

Birnstingl was the main bearer of vortex Marsden's discourse on homosexuality, defending not only lesbianism (never named in so many words) but also male homosexuality, which he termed 'Uranianism', following and developing the 'modern' view of an identity determined and designatable by its sexual preferences. Describing 'Uranians' or 'Urnings', Birnstingl uses them to refute the 'notion that any absolute sex-distinction' can be 'drawn between the sexes'. Emphasising some aspects of Edward Carpenter's defence of bisexuality in *The Intermediate Sex*,[42] Birnstingl finds Uranians 'rich and many sided', part of the 'infinite combinations' of the atoms which make up 'the normal male and the normal female'. Their desires he finds 'natural' simply by virtue of 'the very fact of their existence'. Developing his idea in later articles and in a long-running letters dispute with Dr Charles J. Whitby, a pro-suffrage gender binarist, Birnstingl proposes the homosexual (or intermediate sex, in Carpenter's terms) as the higher sex, possessing 'a peculiar universality' and '*a faculty for perceiving things from a standpoint other than their own*' (8 Feb. 1912, 235). Where Birnstingl implicitly uses the evolutionary argument for homosexuality, Whitby explicitly employs Weininger's concept of bisexual origins yielding strongly sex-differentiated ideal types, but turns Weininger's categories into an inexorable evolution from lower to higher sex-differentiated species.

Other correspondents of the *Freewoman* took positions following received sex binaries. 'Sython', a self-described effeminate homosexual, argued that 'we are women, in spite of an outward appearance' (22 Feb. 1912, 224). Sython's view of himself as 80 per cent female and 20 per cent male reflected Carpenter's view that male homosexuals are men 'who might be described as of feminine soul enclosed in a male body' (*Intermediate Sex*, 19). By offering a formula by which the female element in the 'bisexual' male Uranian was attracted to the masculine man, Carpenter preserved sex binarism while allowing for behavioural variations in desire. His bisexual is constitutionally bisexual rather than desiring both men and women.

Marsden and Birnstingl took more transcendent lines, with Marsden not using the 'intermediate sex' argument (and thus binarism) in relation to sexuality, saying instead that 'sex love' rather than lust, or 'snacking at sex', as she put it in a strong gustatory image, should be humankind's high goal (28 Dec. 1911, 212). As so often, she seems to be trying to describe qualities in women which aren't sex-related. Two years later, Marsden finally found the invention of the new sex-type of 'Uranian' to smack of 'unwisdom', since 'we are concerned to break down the conception of types into individuals [and not] create another of doubtful accuracy' (*New Freewoman*, 15 Oct. 1913, 166). Either to protect himself from the threat of prosecution for sodomy or as part of his sexual transcendence, Birnstingl asserted that Urnings 'hardly ever have sex'. Marsden may also have been protecting herself from curiosity about a personal arrangement which would have been known to her circle, since by 1914 she had moved from London back to the North-West, living henceforth for many years with fellow feminist Grace Jardine, and with Marsden's mother.

As editor, Marsden was both original and daring in promoting debate about gay rights when male homosexuality was illegal and the cultural trauma of the Oscar Wilde trial was still fresh. A unique audience-text has been established here, with 'Sython' part of a gay and lesbian constituency whose 'principal reason for [reading the *Freewoman*] is the sympathetic way in which the Uranian question was treated' (22 Feb. 1912, 224). Marsden is also being radical as a feminist theorist, in proposing a feminism whose physical base is derived through a concept of non-sex-differentiated passion as life force: 'Passion creates personality, and personality is the differentiated form of life which will not sink back into the undifferentiated'.

THE PHYSICAL EGO

When 'feminism' is separated from the women's movement, it must locate itself in the 'I' of the theorist. The ego which is female is female, however, because it is located in the female body – for the moment perhaps, as theosophy would argue, but nevertheless located there at that moment. In the immediate debates of which Marsden was so thoroughly a part, her resistant radicalism settled upon a physical ego: passion leading to ever higher selfhood. Thus, refusing one binary of masculine–feminine, she also (though inconsistently) tended to refuse another with which it is interdependent: the Western dualist division between mind or soul and body. As vortex Marsden's articles become less politically feminist, they (and their surrounding audience-text of articles, reviews and correspondence) become more engaged in addressing passion. Once Marsden had articulated this passional ego, suffragettism and workers' rights looked to her like forms of denial. In 'The Lean Kind', her first leader for the new title, the *New Freewoman* (15 June 1913), Marsden launched a contemp-

tuous and, in the contemporary context, shocking assault on the suffragette hunger strikers for their selfless 'leanness': 'To be selfless is to have
attained unto that condition of which leanness is the fitting outcome.' For
Marsden, 'The Cause' (of woman suffrage) is no more than 'the idol' for
masochistic suffering, to which the desired 'self-sacrifice' can be offered
(1). As for the worker: 'his leanness blights the landscape and *he is
responsible*' (2).

This necessity for grounding the ideal or mental in the physical was
also vehemently asserted by Max Stirner in some of the many
passages in *The Ego and His Own* where he does not use ego as
part of an antistatist argument. For Stirner, the 'free critic' (the non-
Christian critic) must deny the existence of 'something higher' 'above
the *bodily man*' because any 'idea of humanity' is doomed to remain
'unrealized' if it is not moored by the body. 'If, on the other hand, I
grasp the idea as *my* idea, then it is already realized, because *I* am its
reality; its reality consists in the fact that I, the bodily, have it.'[43] Far
from being incidental to a political argument, the egoism of Stirner's
incorporated self is distinguished by him at the outset from any
spiritualised, ideal or absolute self (one might substitute Emerson's
'imperial self' or, as Stirner does in his conclusion, substitute Fichte's
universal 'ego'). Opening his argument, Stirner declares: 'Not until
one has fallen in love with his *corporeal* self, and takes a pleasure in
himself as a living flesh-and-blood person . . . has one a personal or
egoistic interest' (*The Ego*, 14). For Stirner, this seizing of selfhood via
the physical is nothing less than the difference between the youth and
the man; the man is 'harder', 'more definite' (15). What is needed to
make the leap into maturity and 'heart's pleasure' – and, one might
add, the leap to modernity – is the assertion: 'I alone am corporeal'
(16).

Towards the end of its run the *Egoist* had long since been edited by
Harriet Shaw Weaver in a classic shift of power to the monied backer,
who in this case turned out to be also a hugely discriminating but still
'open' editor. Marsden continued to write the leader and in 1917
returned to the discourse of the body in a long series of editorial essays
on 'Lingual Psychology'. In a letter critiquing her, William Carlos
Williams pursued the sex-difference line from his double authority of
poet and physician, assuming that Marsden's 'exuberant and arrogant
power' of rhetoric must be the attack of an 'enemy', namely 'militant
female psychology' attacking 'male psychology'. Marsden, he feels, has
lost sight of the fact that: 'based upon divergent sexual experiences,
psychology . . . is capable of two very different interpretations: male
psychology and female psychology' (Apr. 1917, 46). It is cultural nurture

being paraded as nature again, and Marsden gives it only a short riposte, accusing Williams of vagueness:

> Mr. Williams's 'criticism' will be more helpful when he makes clearer what the distinction is which he draws between male and female psychology. Is it anything beyond the fact that the one is written by a man, the other by a woman? (Apr. 1917, 46)

Williams's lengthy reply to this crushing remark concludes, perhaps predictably, by citing Weininger as authority, praising his 'service' in recognising 'the psychic field to be divided into reciprocal halves, the cleavage running roughly with the division into sex' (Aug. 1917, 111).

While Williams doesn't mention it, by this time Freud was also lending weight to the masculine–feminine binary, D. H. Lawrence had published *Sons and Lovers* and the format of a monthly magazine with long literary excerpts was no longer the place for vigorous philosophical, feminist or sexological debate. Even literary journals had been dampened by the ongoing anguish of the Great War. Marsden's editorials had become more like philosophical essays, in which she tried to expound a theory of self using elements of (by then) sharply divergent phenomenological and linguistic schools of philosophy. By then, also, Pound had succeeded in realigning egoistic modernity into his own egoistic modernism, and the diverse mingling of ideas of the pre-war years was being transformed by the Great War into the modernity of guilt, mourning, impotence and ignorance which Pound was to describe in 'Hugh Selwyn Mauberley' (1920). The history of the modernist text has until recently overwhelmed the mingled and immediate modernities of those who were primarily editors, journalists or activists such as Marsden, Orage, Despard, Hockin and Royden, among others.

Writing in one of the last issues of the *Egoist* (July 1919, 34) about how much authority Egoism 'allows to the science of External nature', Marsden laid it out in a proposition. Egoism's rival formula is 'My universe = My body *plus* My external world'. This is dualism rinsed through a theoretic of the ego: it is 'my' universe and 'my', rather than 'the', external world, but the ego still assumes the body to be its possession.

According to Marsden, for Egoism the formula is 'My universe *minus* My body = 0'. Without body there is no universe to possess. The proposition ends by being strangely moving.

NOTES

1. Ford Madox Hueffer, *This Monstrous Regiment of Women* (Women's Freedom League: London, n.d. [1913]), n.p. [1]. Hueffer changed his surname to Ford in 1919 and is referred to as Ford in this chapter.

2. John Masefield, *My Faith in Woman Suffrage* (Women's Press: London, n.d. [1913]), 11, 12.

3. Olive Hockin, 'Impressions of the Italian Futurist Painters', *Orpheus* XXII (1912), 55–56.

4. Charlotte Despard, *Theosophy and the Woman's Movement* (Theosophical Publishing Society: London and Madras, 1913), 43, 47.

5. Virginia Woolf, 'Mr Bennett and Mrs Brown', *The Captain's Death Bed and Other Essays* (Hogarth Press: London, 1950), 91.

6. See Ezra Pound, 'Vorticism', in his *Gaudier-Brzeska* (Marvell Press: Hessle, 1960). *Blast* (1914–15) was to be the magazine of the 'Great English Vortex'.

7. E. Sylvia Pankhurst, *The Suffragette Movement* (Virago: London, 1977) 162, 539. See also Anna Raeburn, *Militant Suffragettes* (New English Library: London, 1973).

8. Filippo Marinetti, 'Founding Manifesto of Futurism', in Jane Heap, *Futurism* (Studio Vista: London, 1972), 9. Marinetti used the mass and 'quality' press (such as *Le Figaro*, where the manifesto first appeared), little magazines, broadsheets and performance to spread the influence of Futurism.

9. Charlotte Despard and Mabel Collins, *Outlawed: A Novel on the Woman Suffrage Question* (Henry J. Drame: London, 1908).

10. Collins had written several tracts for the theosophist 'Riddle of Life' series and had served as co-editor of *Lucifer*. Under that title and later as *The Theosophical Review*, this ambitious flagship publication featured articles on topics of spiritual, occult, or cultural interest, and a large review section. Helena Petrovna Blavatsky and Collins edited volumes 1–3, Blavatsky edited volumes 4–8 herself, Annie Besant and Blavatsky edited volumes 9–14. After Blavatsky's death in 1891, Besant and G. R. S. Mead (the only male editor) edited it until Vol. 40 (1907), changing the name to *The Theosophical Review* with Vol. 20. When Besant took up residence in India in 1907, Mead edited volumes 41-3.

11. See accounts in Les Garner, *A Brave and Beautiful Spirit: Dora Marsden 1882–1960* (Gower: Avebury, 1990); Jane Lidderdale and Mary Nicholson, *Dear Miss Weaver: Harriet Shaw Weaver 1876–1961* (Faber: London, 1970), 53–65; and Bruce Clarke, *Dora Marsden and Early Modernism: Gender, Individualism, Science* (University of Michigan Press: Ann Arbor, MI, 1996). Clarke's account came to my notice after this chapter had been drafted.

12. Carol Barash, 'Dora Marsden's Feminism, the *Freewoman* and the Gender Politics of Early Modernism', *Princeton University Library Chronicle*, 49:1 (Aug. 1987), 31–56.

13. Conciliation Committee for Woman Suffrage, 'Memorandum of Feb. 2nd 1911', '. . . gross indecency', 1; '. . . my breasts', 5. No publisher listed (parliamentary memorandum). Evidence collected by Dr. Jessie Murray and Mr. Brailford, 'sifted' by Lord Robert Cecil, KC and Mr Ellis Griffith, KC.

14. H.D. (Hilda Doolittle), *Bid Me to Live* (Virago: London, 1984), 164.

15. Letter to Alice Corbin Henderson, 8–9 Aug. 1913, Shari Benstock and Bernard Benstock, 'The Role of Little Magazines in the Emergence of Modernism', *Library Chronicle of the University of Texas*, XX:4 (1991), 76.

16. Lisa Tickner, *The Spectacle of Women: Imagery of the Suffrage Campaign 1907–1914* (Chatto: London, 1984).

17. Janet Lyon, 'Militant Discourse, Strange Bedfellows: Suffragettes and Vorticists before the War', *Differences: A Journal of Feminist Cultural Studies*, 4:2 (1992), 100–33, quote from 120.

18. Robert van Hallberg, 'Libertarian Imagism', *Modernism/Modernity*, 2:2 (Apr. 1995), 63, 66.

19. Astradur Eysteinsson, *The Concept of Modernism* (Cornell University Press: Ithaca NY, 1990), 16, cited Bruce Clarke, *Dora Marsden and Early Modernism: Gender, Individualism, Science* (University of Michigan Press: Ann Arbor, MI, 1995), 6.

20. James Huneker, *Egoists: A Book of Supermen* (T. Werner Laurie: London, 1909).

21. A. R. Orage, *Friedrich Nietzsche, the Dionysian Spirit of the Age* (T. N. Foulis: London and Edinburgh, 1906) offered a brief biography, excerpts and aphorisms; A. R. Orage (ed.), *Nietzsche in Outline and Aphorism* (T. N. Foulis: London and Edinburgh, 1911) offered aphorisms by topic.

22. A. R. Orage, *Consciousness, Animal, Human and Superhuman* (Theosophical Publishing Company: London and Benares, 1907), 83.

23. See Lawrence S. Stepelivich, 'Max Stirner as Hegelian', *Journal of the History of Ideas*, XLVI:4 (Dec. 1995), 598–617.

24. Helena Petrovna Blavatsky, *The Secret Doctrine*, Vol II: *Anthropogenesis* (Theosophical Publishing Company: London, 1888), 111.

25. Annie Besant (ed.), *The Esoteric Writings of Helena Petrovna Blavatsky* (Quest Books/Theosophical Publishing House: Wheaton, Madras, London: 1980 [reprint of *The Secret Doctrine*, Vol. 3, 1897]), 433.

26. Lidderdale and Nicholson, *Dear Miss Weaver*, 58.

27. Ibid., 69.

28. Ibid., 56 and *passim*.

29. My discussion is influenced by Jürgen Habermas, *The Structural Transformation of the Public Sphere*, tr. Thomas Burger and Fredrick Lawrence (Harvard UP: Cambridge, MA, 1981). See also Brendan Dooley, 'From Literary Criticism to Systems Theory in Early Modern Journalism History', *Journal of the History of Ideas*, 51 (1990), 470.

30. Van Hallberg, 'Libertarian Imagism', 67.

31. See Clarke, *Dora Marsden*, 107, and discussion 105–13; Van Hallberg, 'Libertarian Imagism', 66–9 and Lidderdale and Nicholson, *Dear Miss Weaver*, 70–5.

32. Hugh Kenner's *The Pound Era* (University of California Press: Berkeley, CA, 1971) precisely reproduces Pound's literary egoism: Marsden's name does not appear and Harriet Shaw Weaver is a 'Miss Weaver' who gave Joyce money (303).

33. R. H. Congreve, 'A Tale for Men Only', *New Age*, 10, 17, 24, 31 Aug. and 7 Sept. 1911. Orage used the pseudonym of Congreve. See Beatrice Hastings, *The Old 'New Age': Orage and Others* (Blue Moon Press: London, 1936).

34. In the *New Age*, Marsden's friend Emily Wilding Davison wrote about South Africa: 'The statesmanlike way to end the Black Peril is to give votes to white women' (7 Sept. 1912, 478).

35. Dorothy Richardson, *Deadlock* (Virago: London, 1979), 150, 152. See also Jacqueline Rose, 'Constructions of the Jew', in Brian Cheyette (ed.), *English Literature and Society: Racial Representations 1875–1945* (Cambridge UP: 1993).

36. See Andrew Thacker, 'Our War is with Words: Dora Marsden and the *Egoist*', in Gabriele Griffin (ed.), *Difference in View: Women and Modernism* (Taylor & Francis: London, 1994), 75–91.

37. See Jane Marcus, 'The asylums of Antaeus: Women, War and Madness – Is there a Feminist Fetishism?', in H. Aram Veeser (ed.), *The New Historicism* (Routledge: New York and London, 1989), 132–57.

38. Havelock Ellis, *Man and Woman: A Study of Secondary Sexual Characteristics* (Walter Scott: London, 1897 [1st edn 1894]), 396.

39. Otto Weininger, *Sex and Character* (AMS: New York, 1975 [reprint of W. Heinemann: London, 1906 edn]).

40. See Allan Janik, *Essays on Wittgenstein and Weininger* (Rodopi: Amsterdam, 1985), 64–95.

41. See Les Garner, *Stepping Stones to Liberty: Feminist Ideas in the Women's Suffrage Movement 1900–1918* (Heinemann Educational: London, 1984), 67 and chapter 5, *passim*. Robin Hicks's M.Phil. dissertation *Gender of the Self: Dora Marsden and 'The Freewoman': Feminist Beginnings of the 'New Freewoman' and the 'Egoist'* (Oxford 1990) argues for the feminist basis of Marsden's individualism. My thanks to Diana Collecut for directing me to this work.

42. Edward Carpenter, *The Intermediate Sex* (George Allen & Unwin: London, 1916, 4th edn).

43. Max Stirner, *The Ego and His Own*, tr. Stephen T. Byington (A. C. Fifield: London, 1912), 176.

8

THE MAKING OF A MODERN WOMAN WRITER: REBECCA WEST'S JOURNALISM, 1911–1930

LYN PYKETT

I earn my living as a journalist. People actually pay me coin of the realm to write about literature . . . I consider the profession of journalism to be at least as honourable as that of medicine.[1]

At the time of her death in March 1983 Dame Rebecca West, whose pen-name had long since obliterated her family name of Cicely Fairfield, was very much a *grande dame* of modern English letters. This status derived partly from the longevity and productivity of her literary career, and more significantly from the reputation of her post-war writings. These comprised reporting of the Nuremberg trials described in *The Meaning of Treason* (1949); anti-communist journalism; *Black Lamb and Gray Falcon* (1941), initially a travel book describing a journey through Yugoslavia, but ending up as a cultural history of that divided country; and autobiographical novels in realistic mode, *The Fountain Overflows* (1956) and *The Birds Fall Down* (1966). However, in the last years of her life, a different version of 'Rebecca West' had begun to emerge as a result of the work of a new generation of feminist literary critics and historians who were putting back into circulation the work of West's feminist and socialist earlier years. In 1980 Virago reissued West's early fictions *The Return of the Soldier* (1918), *The Judge* (1922) and *Harriet Hume: A London Fantasy* (1929), and thus made available new perspectives on the hitherto dominant texts of literary modernism. Even more importantly, for my present purposes, in 1982 Jane Marcus edited a selection of West's early writings. It is the 'Rebecca West' this selection began to retrieve which will form the focus of this chapter.

Marcus's edited selection in *The Young Rebecca*: *Writings of Rebecca West 1911–1917* directs our attention to the important fact that, like so many women writers, especially novelists from the early nineteenth century onwards, Rebecca West earned a living as an independent woman, and served her writer's apprenticeship as a prolific (and in her case controversial) contributor to the periodical and newspaper press. As Marcus has demonstrated, in the period around the First World War, 'it sometimes seemed that there was hardly a left-wing paper in England or America to which Rebecca West did not contribute'.[2] In the decade following that war West, like Virginia Woolf, extended her journalistic activity from the socialist and left-liberal and feminist journals in which she had begun her writing career. Like Virginia Woolf, she addressed a larger and more varied audience both in Britain and America, by writing for an increasingly wide range of literary, general interest and women's magazines (the latter included *Women's Home Companion*, *Woman's Journal* and *Vogue*). Something of the scale and range of West's journalistic activity during the first three decades of the twentieth century can be glimpsed in G. E. Hutchinson's *A Preliminary List of the Writings of Rebecca West* (Yale University Library, 1957). Hutchinson's bibliography, which as his title acknowledges is by no means exhaustive,[3] lists over four hundred items under 'Articles in Periodicals' between 1912 and 1935 (to take a rather arbitrary cut-off point in the 1930s).

Although derided by Ezra Pound, her associate on the *New Freewoman*, as *merely* a journalist, West has been significantly absent from the history of early twentieth-century journalism. As Jane Marcus has noted:

> Rebecca West's absence from the history of English journalism is striking. As a journalist she wrote openly and directly [in the first three decades of the twentieth century] . . . as a feminist and socialist critic of patriarchal attitudes and imperialism in literature and politics. Her work always excited controversy; her essays always brought hundreds of arguments in letters to the editor.[4]

Until quite recently this absence from the history of journalism has been matched by West's absence from the history of the literature of the early twentieth century, which for much of the post-Second World War period has been constructed around a particular version of modernism. West's journalistic networks linked her to many of the writers who identified themselves with literary modernism,[5] and she was herself a sometimes experimental writer of fiction – her story 'Indissoluble Matrimony' was first published in *Blast*,[6] and *The Return of the Soldier* (1918) and *Harriet Hume: A London Fantasy* (1929) are clearly the products of a particular moment of fictional experimentation. She was also a frequent commentator on modernist experiment in reviews and essays which expressed a great deal of scepticism about some of the social and aesthetic ideas and artistic practices of self-consciously innovatory writers, many of whom were included in the canon of high modernism.

However, despite her contemporary role in mapping both modernity and modernism for a wide contemporary audience of newspaper and magazine readers, West has (until relatively recently) largely been excluded from histories of modernism. Indeed, the designation 'journalist' was itself in many ways antithetical to emerging definitions of modernism. To be a journalist was to be part of an army of writers who offered themselves for hire in the commercial market-place. The avant-garde literary artist, on the other hand, eschewed the mass market and wrote for a discriminating coterie. While the men of 1908 or 1914 tended to confine their 'journalistic' activities to relatively (and sometimes absolutely) small-circulation little magazines, West deliberately sought a wider audience (as well as larger financial rewards) by moving out from a small-circulation 'coterie' publication such as the *Freewoman* to write for Fleet Street daily newspapers and for wide-circulation general interest magazines in Britain and America. This involvement in a rapidly changing market for 'middlebrow' and popular journalism linked West much more closely than most of her (male) modernist contemporaries to modernity and modern mass culture, and placed her on the other side of that 'great divide' which separates 'mass culture [which] is somehow associated with women' from 'real, authentic culture [which] remains the prerogative of men'.[7] In other words, any consideration of West's early work takes us back to the now familiar problematic of gender, genre and modernism.

In this chapter I want to suggest that we should look at the four hundred or more witty, incisive, iconoclastic and sometimes sensationalising reviews, essays and articles which West published between 1912 and the early 1930s not simply as the work of an apprentice novelist experimenting with a range of voices and honing her prose style. Rather, they can be seen as a distinctive form of literary work by means of which a particular writer self-consciously constructed herself as a modern woman of letters, as she took up positions on a wide range of contemporary social, political and aesthetic issues, and situated herself (both in what she said and the kind of publication in which she said it) in relation to current cultural and political trends: in short, we should view West's early journalistic writing as a form of intervention in the public sphere. I also want to suggest that a re-reading of West's early journalism complicates our understanding of early twentieth-century cultural formations, as we trace in it the development of a distinctively modern syndicalist feminism committed, unlike most of the best-known male modernists, to democracy, to social and political reform, and to modernity itself.

In the following three sections I shall give a brief survey of West's early career in journalism, examine some of her writing on contemporary social and political issues, and look at her critique of modern writers and of modernism.

I

West, the daughter of a globe-trotting journalist who deserted his family when she was only eight years old, began her career as a professional journalist with a theatre review for the London *Evening Standard* in 1911. Theatre reviewing, alongside book reviewing, became an important part of her journalistic portfolio, and provided a steady income, in the early 1920s. But her very first newspaper publication, when she was just fifteen, was a letter to the editor of *The Scotsman* (published in October 1907, the year of the defeat of a private member's Bill to give women the vote), on the subject of 'Women's Electoral Claims'. The letter denounced the degradation implied for women in the concept of 'manhood suffrage'. For the next few years West's connections with journalism continued to be through the suffrage movement, as a volunteer seller of the Women's Social and Political Union's *Votes for Women* in Edinburgh.

Four years after the letter to *The Scotsman* and following her move to London, West published the first of many pieces in the small-circulation but influential feminist weekly the *Freewoman*, edited by Dora Marsden and Mary Gawthorpe. West's debut article, a polemic on feminism in the guise of a review of a book on the position of women in India, was published under her own name, Cicely Fairfield. It was, however, typical of the work that was to become associated with the name Rebecca West, which she rapidly adopted to save the feelings of her family.[8] It began in an arresting, even sensational manner, with the words, 'There are two kinds of imperialists – imperialists and bloody imperialists', and it continued by urging feminists to become socialists:

> The Feminist must take a bolder line. If she is going to enter the labour market she must take capital with her – she must try from the first to capture the commanding fortresses of industry, from which she can dictate the conditions of her own labour.[9]

At the *Freewoman* West developed for herself the role of *enfant terrible*. She attacked cultural and political shibboleths and also writers with established reputations or a current cachet (writers as different from each other as Mrs Humphry Ward and H. G. Wells). She also wrote outspokenly in defence of the political goals of the suffragettes while criticising some of their philosophies and their methods.

In June 1912, while she was still writing regularly for the *Freewoman*, West took over the editorship of the woman's page of the *Daily Herald*.[10] West's brief was to reinvigorate this page, as she explained in a letter to Dora Marsden:

> 'The Daily Herald' has seduced me into editing the woman's page. They are tired
> of baby clothes, they say and want 'Hot Gospel' talks to women. I fear this means
> trials for sedition, so I may not long be free.[11]

West certainly succeeded in avoiding the topic of baby clothes, engaging instead with a number of pressing issues of the day, including the new Insurance Act and resistance to it (she took the Keir Hardie line that the scheme should be non-contributory and financed by high taxes on the wealthy), the problems of female homelessness, the puerility of the 'Noble Art' of politics, and the need for suffragism to return to and develop its links with socialism. West's woman's page also contained those staples of women's pages, recipes, including an extremely tactless recipe for Nesselrode Pudding ('a prima donna among ices') with which an editorial assistant filled half a column inch during a dock strike. Reflecting later, in 1924, on the cavalier spirit in which she had approached the woman's page, West confessed:

> I have realised that one form of [male] nagging [that] has taken me in for years . . .
> is the form of nagging that expresses itself in sneers at the women's papers which
> concern themselves specifically with household matters.[12]

By this time West was ready to argue the case for the seriousness of the 'specialist' function of this branch of journalism which she had previously thought of as 'foolish and unnecessary'. Woman's pages and women's magazines, West argued, merely offer women advice on the 'technical side of certain of [their] occupations', and should be seen as no more limited and partial than other specialist branches of journalism.

> *The Financial News* is deficient in references to the beauties of art or religion, but
> men are not shamefaced regarding the readers and writers of such a paper, nor do
> women use it as evidence to support an accusation against men of a sordidly
> materialist point of view.[13]

In September 1912, West was recruited to the *Clarion* by Robert Blatchford who had been impressed by West's 'exhilarating, breezy . . . irresistibly funny' attack in the *Freewoman* on Sir Almroth Wright's pamphlet on feminism.[14] The *Clarion* was a radical socialist journal described by Mary Gawthorpe as a 'sort of nation-wide club on a non-dues paying basis which united readers everywhere in an atmosphere of camaraderie'.[15] West readily developed a tone to match the exuberant version of socialism espoused by Blatchford's paper, which was:

> not in the least like the preconceived idea of a socialist journal. It was not highbrow;
> it did not deal in theoretical discussion, or inculcate drearyisms. It was full of
> stories, jokes and verses . . . as well as articles [and] . . . was written in language
> that anyone could understand.[16]

West produced a regular supply of increasingly militant articles for the *Clarion* until December 1913. Indeed, as a comparison of contemporaneous articles for the *Clarion*, the *Daily Herald* and the *Freewoman* shows, West was adept at matching both her tone and her message to the political position of the paper for which she was writing. During the summer and autumn of 1913 West also wrote occasional essays and reviews for the *Freewoman's* successor, the *New Freewoman*, until she was so marginalised by the combined forces of Marsden's metaphysics and the rising spirit of (Ezra) Poundism that she left.

In the early months of the war West began a long association with American journalism with reviews for the *New Republic* and, later, *Atlantic Monthly*. At around the same time she also started to write for the *Daily News*, a Fleet Street paper. With a northern edition produced in Manchester, this gave her access to a much wider British readership (about four hundred thousand) than she had previously reached. The *Daily News* was a liberal, free-trade paper committed to social reform and social justice. Under the editorship of A. G. Gardiner (1902–19) it had a complex relationship with the Liberal Party, not least because of Gardiner's support for the cause of women's suffrage and his attempt to forge an alliance between liberalism and labour. West reviewed a wide range of books for the *Daily News*, following her usual practice of using the genre of the book review as a means of attacking established literary reputations and entrenched social and political positions, and of developing her own socialist and feminist perspective. Her work for the *Daily News* extended well into the war, when West wrote trenchantly on women's experience of war, and particularly of women's war work.

Although West's first novel (her war novel *The Return of the Soldier*) was published with some success in 1918, she continued to rely on her journalism both as a source of income and as a means of keeping herself in the public eye while she was working on a second novel. Between April 1920 and December 1922 she engaged in a well-regarded, if exhausting, period as a fiction reviewer for the *New Statesman* during which she wrote fifty-five 2,000-word reviews of 136 novels.[17] The year 1920 was also the year of the launch of a new feminist magazine, *Time and Tide*, produced by an all-woman board of directors headed by Viscountess Rhondda, and addressed to the changed social and political situation of the post-war period and an audience of 'newcomers to the political game', the women over thirty newly enfranchised by the Suffrage Act of 1918. West was *Time and Tide*'s theatre reviewer from May 1920 until March 1922, and she also published a number of important articles on women's issues and contributed to debates about trends in modern journalism.[18]

By the mid-1920s West had become a very marketable journalist and was able to capitalise on the growing, and increasingly lucrative, market for women's writing, especially in the USA. She went to the States in 1924, following her final break with Wells, and she and her agents negotiated a series of favourable contracts in Britain and America for columns on a wide range of subjects in *The Bookman* ('A Letter from Abroad' and 'A London Letter') and the *New York American* ('I Said to Me' in the early 1930s). West also reviewed for *Herald Tribune Books* and the *New Republic*, and from 1932 for the *Daily Telegraph* in London. In this extremely prolific and eclectic period she developed a more urbane and cosmopolitan journalistic persona, but continued to return to many of the social and political issues which had preoccupied her at the outset.

I I

> I myself have never been able to find out precisely what feminism is: I only know that people call me a feminist whenever I express sentiments that differentiate me from a doormat or a prostitute.[19]

> I am an old-fashioned feminist. I believe in the sex-war.[20]

Rebecca West's entry into writing was through her feminism, which however difficult to define was (as the above quotations suggest) expressed in the combative terms of someone who was not prepared to be trampled on nor to take things lying down, and who encouraged other women to take the same line. West was involved with the *Freewoman* (later the *New Freewoman*) more or less from its inception, and her striking essays contributed quite significantly to that paper's project of 'ponder[ing] the profounder aspects of feminism'.[21] West was, however, considerably more sympathetic than its editor Dora Marsden to the continuing cause of suffragism, and she wrote a number of scathing articles in the *Clarion* in 1912–13 about the ill treatment of suffragettes and their betrayal by Liberal and Labour politicians.[22]

West's essays in the *Freewoman* were an important factor in the paper's impact, which was quite disproportionate to its small circulation. Looking back at the impact of the *Freewoman* in 1926 West argued that 'unimportant as it was in content, and amateurish in form [it] had an immense effect on its time'. It was 'a keystone of the modern feminist movement', which had been responsible for a significant 'change of outlook' in Britain. Three important aspects of the *Freewoman*'s work were noted: its defence of the economic independence of women, its frankness on sexual matters, and its smashing of the romantic conception of womanhood. West gave prominence to the paper's 'unblushingness': its 'greatest service [to] its country' was to mention sex and venereal diseases 'loudly and clearly and repeatedly and in the worst possible taste'. As a result of this 'candour' the *Freewoman* 'smashed the romantic pretence that women had as a birth-right the gift of perfect adaptation'. West also attributed to the 'strong lead given by the "Freewoman"' the mid-1920s' orthodoxy of the view that 'it is degrading to woman, and injurious to the race to leave the financing of the mother and her children to the double-barrelled caprice of the father and the father's employer'.[23]

West's retrospective assessment of the importance of the *Freewoman* would serve quite well as an assessment of her own early journalism. In the years immediately preceding and following the First World War West, like the *Freewoman*, was best known for being a feminist and for being shocking. As her articles in the *Freewoman*, the *Daily Herald* and the *Clarion* reveal, she was frequently as shocking to middle-class feminists and suffragettes as she was a shocking feminist. From her earliest articles in the *Freewoman*, right through to her work for *Time and Tide* in the 1920s, West continually stressed the need for proper educational and employment opportunities for women, and attacked the gender stereotyping that legitimated the restriction of such opportunities, denied working women fair pay, and presumed and hence perpetuated women's economic dependence on men.

West's first article in the *Freewoman* elaborated some of the central concerns which were to recur in her journalism until the late 1920s and beyond. West used this review of a book on 'The Position of Women in Indian Life' to analyse the situation of women in Britain and the shortcomings of the 'out of date' aristocratic feminism of its authors. In particular she attacked the book's perpetuation of 'that most malignant libel spoken by the rich against the poor – that the average housewife of the lower and middle classes is an ignorant incompetent'. Mounting the hobby horse on which she was to ride into numerous assaults on paternalistic, or even worse maternalistic schemes of training, West castigated this libel 'as a device to cheat poor girls of their education', and dismissed 'Domestic Science' as a conspiracy 'designed to elbow out of the school curriculum all subjects likely to develop the minds of the girl scholars, and thus leave them, irrespective of their individual gifts, fit for nothing but domestic service'. Outmoded feminism was also held to be responsible for the book's 'complaisant' approach to the underpayment of women, a failing which West attributed to the authors' misinterpretation of 'the feminist opposition to regulative legislation of women's labour'. West argued that feminists did not object to regulation, but to the fact that 'it is regulation framed according to the conception of woman held by the public-schoolboys who make up the House of Commons'.[24]

This review critiques aristocratic and upper middle-class feminism, domestic work and the exploitation and betrayal of the working class – not least through opposition to the substitution of narrow training for education in policies directed towards that class, and advocacy of women's paid employment outside the home and fair pay for women. These views are repeated again and again in West's writing, with varying degrees of irony, impatience, and contempt according to context.

West's early journalism is often passionate, and almost always sceptical and suspicious. It is passionately feminist, but it is suspicious of feminists and suffragists, especially those who seemed to West to appropriate the labels without thinking through their implications. Its pervasive scepticism about the motivations of feminists and women in general, and their lack of what West regarded as a necessary materialist and socialist political analysis, prevents it from being 'sisterly'.

West's focus on the material and economic determinants of women's condition is unsurprisingly at its sharpest in a series of articles she wrote for the radical socialist journal the *Clarion* in 1912. Here she lamented, among other things, the collusion of 'industrial women' in the structure of capitalistic exploitation by accepting low wages:

> The underpayment of women is one of those 'ninepence for fourpence' tricks that capitalists have ever loved to play on the people . . . Capitalists have said to women: 'We deduct fourpence from your wages so that we can pay men larger wages, and then they can support you as their wives. So in the end you will make at least ninepence out of it.' It is only an excuse for sweating more money out of the people. It pretends that women have no dependants . . . Women ought to understand that in submitting themselves to this swindle of underpayment, they are not only insulting themselves, but doing a deadly injury to the community.[25]

West also wrote scathingly of the failure of middle-class suffragettes to spare 'a little of their dear irreverence and blessed pluck to stir up the industrial women to revolt', and she lamented the absence of any 'women syndicalists' ('Where are our women syndicalists?').[26] Like Dora Marsden, Ezra Pound and others associated with the *Freewoman* (and its subsequent incarnations as the *New Freewoman* and the *Egoist*), West was extremely critical of a feminism that concentrated all its hopes and efforts on the suffrage issue. However, West's critique of the suffrage campaigners, unlike that of Marsden and Pound, was not based on the irrelevance of the suffrage, but on the failure of most suffragists and suffragettes to think beyond their immediate goal of the enfranchisement of women to the question of how women should use their political power. Thus, using a common label of the period, West attacked as 'parasite women' those middle-class supporters of women's suffrage who failed or refused to see that the enfranchisement of women would inevitably lead to a social revolution, either progressive or reactionary:

> Women should not concentrate their intelligences too fixedly on the vote without preparing for the tremendous issues that follow. And that is why socialists should regard the woman's movement as something more important than the fad of a few propertied ladies and women as humble beings to be satisfied by pious opinions concerning the advisability of free milk for babies. When woman came out of the home she came bringing not peace but a sword. Great things depend on how she uses that sword.[27]

Her sharpest and most frequent jibes against parasite women, however, were directed at the women of the upper and middle classes, who lived in prosperous or luxurious idleness.

Parasite women also came under attack in a review of Christabel Pankhurst's *Suffragette* article 'The Dangers of Marriage', in which West rejected Pankhurst's 'partial' view of the sexual bestiality of men. It is not the inherently depraved sexual nature of men which is responsible for prostitution both within marriage and on the streets, West argued, but rather a particular economy of sex–gender relations, in which men are constantly invited to brood on sex by us, by 'the army of rich parasite women who have nothing to do, no outlet for the force in them except to play with sex'.[28]

Despite her retrospective admiration for the *Freewoman*'s outspokenness on sex, West herself had relatively little to say on matters sexual in her early journalism. Indeed in the *Clarion* review just quoted she expressed considerable distaste for Pankhurst's anatomisation of the details of venereal diseases. When she wrote about sex it was usually to attack the sexual humbug and hypocrisy of both men and women. When she exploited the shock value of sex it was usually in order to hit another target. For example, when she wrote of the controversy about the performance of the scantily clad chorus girl Gaby Deslys in an article subtitled 'A Plea for Decency', she turned on its head the shock of bishops and social purity feminists such as Christabel Pankhurst by announcing that she herself was more shocked by the numerous ugly, care-worn, scantily clad bodies of the poor than by 'one healthy and well-nourished young woman voluntarily assuming becoming and scanty garments'.[29]

The main purpose of the Gaby Deslys article was to make a plea for the 'decent' treatment of the poor, but making her political point with a characteristic *elan*, West celebrated an aspect of popular culture even as she appropriated it. West's willingness to acknowledge the value of popular culture and mass entertainment, and her readiness to associate herself with the 'difference of view' involved in editing the *Daily Herald*'s

woman's page, anticipated Woolf's essays of the 1920s.[30] Similarly West's
pre-war journalism expounded views of women, their achievements, and
the conditions necessary for improving both women's lot and their
contributions to art and science which Woolf would develop further in
A Room of One's Own (1929). For example, in one of her early pieces for
the *Freewoman* she anticipated Woolf's analysis of the causes of women's
relative lack of achievement in the Arts:

> The worst of being a feminist is that one has no evidence. Women are capable of all
> things yet, inconveniently, they will not be geniuses. This is brought home to one
> during the publishing season . . . It would be hard to say why women have refused
> to become great writers.[31]

In this article West went on to round up the usual suspects for the crimes
against women's creativity: marriage, which 'undoubtedly . . . eats like a
cancer into the artistic development of women'; women's 'timidity
towards adventure and lack of faith in life'; their preference for safe
professions, like the Civil Service. The doctrines of certain kinds of
feminism and what one might describe as 'womanism' were also called to
account: Olive Schreiner's ascetic philosophy which 'may only be a
further development of the sin of woman, the surrender of personality',
and the 'spiritual pride' of a Mrs Pethick Lawrence with her belief in the
ability of 'the mother soul' to solve all the problems of civilisation.[32]

West also anticipated Woolf's championing of a feminism with
pleasure. 'A New Woman's Movement: The Need for Riotous Living',
for example, is a brilliant satiric attack on the various forces for the
prevention of pleasure in the lives of poor women and women in the
professions, which ends with a wonderful surrealist/utopian fantasy of a
world turned upside down by female militancy. West attacked the
enforced asceticism of women, whether it was promulgated by charitable
institutions, canons' wives (who won't permit waltzing in the local girls'
club), capitalist employers (who wish to depress women's wages), or
anti-feminists who 'want women to specialise in virtue'. She concluded
with this call to arms:

> Decidedly what we need is a militant movement for more riotous living. School-
> mistresses must go to their work wearing suffrage badges and waving the red flag.
> The ladies of Hopkinson House [a 'philanthropic' institution for women] must stay
> out till two in the morning, and then come back and sing outside till the doors are
> opened. And we must make a fuss about our food. 'The milk pudding must go' shall
> be our party cry. I can see in the future militant food raids of the most desperate
> character. I see the inmates of the YWCA . . . pelting the central offices with bread
> and butter and threatening a general massacre of hens if the boiled egg persists in
> prominence . . . And in Simpson's some day the blenching stockbroker shall look
> down the muzzle of the rifle and hand over his nice red-and-black beefsteak to his
> pale typist.[33]

Like her feminism, West's socialism was joyous and celebratory, as well as sceptical and hard-headed. Despite her sometimes protestant-sounding exhortations about the religion of work, there was nothing ascetic about West's socialism. She took pleasure in the good things of life and wished to see such pleasure, and the material conditions necessary for experiencing it, more widely extended.

Throughout the period under review West's feminist analysis remained resolutely materialist, and she rejected the 'goddess' feminism, the turn to metaphysics, and the agrarian 'new life' feminism or 'Tolstoyism' of some of her contemporaries.[34] She constantly sought 'modern' syndicalist ways of ameliorating the damage inflicted on the lives of labouring men and women by a capitalist industrialism: the suggestion that England should return to being 'a nation of amateur agriculturalists' was rejected as romantic, uneconomic and ultimately regressive.[35] Her most vigourous critique of feminists and suffragettes was directed at those individuals and groups that had become detached from working-class movements and/or had failed to pursue the logic of their feminist analysis, which in West's view would inevitably lead them to a socialist perspective.

> The real objection to the control of the woman's movement by the middle classes is the extreme danger of any disassociation between the emancipation of women and the emancipation of workers. Otherwise the emancipation of women may only mean their exploitation'.[36]

West attributed what she saw as the decline of the Women's Social and Political Union (WSPU) to its becoming detached from its origins in the community and the workplace, and exchanging 'the warmer, more intimate spirit of syndicalism, for the cold ideal of old-fashioned socialism which imagined an England governed by a central bureaucracy, which would leave no room for trade unionism'.[37] Under its 'unsuitable' London-based, middle-class leaders, she asserted, the movement 're-lapsed into timid conservatism, urging such safe though necessary reforms as equal penalties for adultery rather than the complete economic independence of women'.[38]

West continued to argue her socialist feminist case in the avowedly non-sectarian *Time and Tide*. In the article she produced for the Six Point Group she returned, with renewed vigour, to her favourite theme of equal pay for women, first developed in 'The Woman as Workmate'.[39] By 1923 the socialist feminist case for equality was made in the acerbically confident tones of a veteran of the sex-war:

> [A]ll save the few [men] who have cut down the primitive jungle in their souls want women in general to be handicapped as heavily as possible . . . They want this not out of malignity, but out of a craving to be reassured concerning themselves and the part they are playing in a difficult universe . . . A person insufficiently fed and

clothed is apt to be most satisfyingly inferior to a person who is sufficiently fed and clothed. It is this savage sex-antagonism which makes people desire that women teachers should be paid less highly than men who are doing the same work.[40]

In this essay on equality, as so often in her journalism, we also see West the fiction writer at work, as she gives examples of the effects of inequality on the lives of women teachers she has known, and fleshes out their characters so as to give a human embodiment to the abstract debate about equality.

III

Throughout her writing life Rebecca West was a prolific reviewer of other people's books. It is only a slight exaggeration to say that a re-reading of her reviews from 1911 until the late 1930s enables one to construct a cultural history of the first third of the twentieth century in England, or at least a history of that culture as it appeared to a left-leaning middle-class feminist who was often as much concerned with making a name for herself, entertaining her readers, and shocking both the bourgeoisie and the literary establishment, as she was with giving a judicious assessment of the books and trends under review. West reviewed both feminist and anti-feminist books on women and women's issues, books on other contemporary social and political questions, literary histories and books of critical essays. She also reviewed contemporary poetry, and hundreds of novels. The novels ranged from those of the 'uncles of the English-speaking world' (Wells, Bennett and Galsworthy)[41] and the middlebrow potboilers of Eden Phillpotts, Hall Caine, E. M. Delafield, and Sheila Kaye-Smith, to the attempts of James Joyce, Dorothy Richardson, Virginia Woolf and D. H. Lawrence to remake fiction for the twentieth century. It is this aspect of West's work that I want to look at in this section.

West was involved in, though increasingly marginalised by, the *Free-woman*'s metamorphosis from an outspoken freethinking feminist journal to an organ of Poundian modernism. Quite early on West encouraged the development of 'a literary side' at the *Freewoman*, representing this move to editor Dora Marsden as a 'bribe to the more frivolous minded in London'.[42] In encouraging the development of a 'literary side' West had a more serious purpose – entirely in keeping with the 'programme' of Marsden's *Freewoman* which, as West recalled much later, included a 'general whip-round for ideas which would *reform simultaneously life and art*'.[43] West was responsible for introducing Pound to the journal, and she produced an interesting early assessment of imagism to preface some of his poetry,[44] but she soon objected to the material supplied by Pound and his associates on the grounds that it failed to 'come up to a certain standard of taste and literary skill'.[45]

It seems in her post-war journalism, and particularly in her reviews of contemporary novels and novelists in the *New Statesman* and elsewhere in the 1920s, that West engaged most closely with current debates about literature and modernity, and literary modernism. Like Woolf's, West's thinking on the novel began with a rejection of Wells–Bennett–Galsworthyism, and like Woolf she was an informed but frequently sceptical and unsympathetic commentator on modernist experimentation in fiction. Her reservations about modernist experimentation were expressed most forcefully in her discussions of Joyce's methods in the title essay of *The Strange Necessity* (1928), part of which appeared as 'The Strange Case of James Joyce' in *The Bookman* (September 1928). In this essay Joyce is described as an important writer but an incompetent one; *Ulysses* is acknowledged as a work of genius, but one which is written in gibberish. Joyce's great mistake, according to West, was to confuse 'heterodox technique' with aesthetic emancipation. In her view his linguistic experimentation involved a regression from the sentence to the word, resulting in a merely reactionary and 'mincing' sentimentality.[46]

West was similarly dismissive of Dorothy Richardson's experimental method, which she described as 'the meticulous record of the secondary stream of consciousness',[47] with an unfortunate influence on other writers. For example, a rather negative review of Bryher's novel *Development* remarked on its 'pretentious' 'cerebral activity' which had 'all that solemn reverence for her own sensory impressions which is characteristic of Miss Dorothy Richardson'.[48] May Sinclair, praised as the author of 'many excellent books' who has 'attained a high level of permanent form', was similarly found wanting because of her over-preoccupation with the 'handling of a technical method': 'one of the most memorable comedies of modern letters' was that in writing *Mary Olivier* Sinclair had 'showed Miss Richardson what could be done with her own method'.[49] On the evidence of her early work Virginia Woolf was adjudged 'a supremely important writer', but 'a negligible novelist': *Jacob's Room*, which occasioned this judgement, was not a novel, but a 'portfolio' of loose leaves, marred by its failure to 'concern itself primarily with humanity',[50] a failing shared by Bryher's *Development*.

West's only unreserved commendation of an experimental fiction can be found in her uncharacteristically effusive review of Woolf's historical fantasy *Orlando* as 'a poetic masterpiece of the first rank' which combines 'the frankest contempt for realism' with 'the profoundest reality'. It is a book, West asserted, which *'demands careful reading and the completest consent to receive its novelty*' (emphasis added). The demanding novelty of *Orlando* consisted of the way it remade 'the poetic tradition' while keeping faith with it.

> [*Orlando*] illuminates an important part of human experience by using words to do more than describe the logical behaviour of matter, by letting language by its music and its power to evoke images convey meanings too subtle and too profound to be formulated in intellectual statements.[51]

West additionally found purposeful novelty in the way in which Woolf combined formal experimentation with 'experimental' subject-matter. She particularly admired Woolf's ability to 'enquire . . . deeply into fundamentals' by using a 'frivolous' form, especially in the sex–change passages in which Woolf debates 'how far one's sex is like a pair of faulty glasses on one's nose'.[52]

West was an advocate of D. H. Lawrence, although critical of many of his views. She admired the passion and vitality of his attempts to provide surgery for the novel, even when he wrote a 'plum-silly' book like *Aaron's Rod* with its 'pugilistic and exhausting' ideas upon the relationship of men and women.[53] Her critique of Lawrence, like her critique of Joyce, was based on what she saw as his misguided, inappropriate, or just unsuccessful method:

> The trouble is with Mr Lawrence that he is so much of a poet that it is difficult for him to express himself in prose, and in particular the prose required of a novel, and that he finds it impossible to express what he wants except by desperately devised symbols.[54]

West was, on the whole, anti-Eliot. Despite his 'true and splendid' poetry and the 'appearance of deliberation and trenchancy' in his earlier critical work, the spurious authoritative air and affected fastidiousness of Eliot's criticism made its influence, in West's view, a malign one: '[T]o my mind at least, the years this American author has spent in England have inflicted damage on our literature from which it will probably not recover for a generation.'[55] West objected very strongly to Eliot's 'Humanist' conception of tradition and the way in which his views had infiltrated the literary establishment. She argued that Eliot's version of tradition, which he had derived from Irving Babbitt and Paul Elmer More, 'reduced it to propaganda for a provincial conception of metropolitan gentility'. She had commended Virginia Woolf for demonstrating in the serious frivolity of *Orlando* that 'there is nothing about the mental habit of the present generation which breaks the poetic tradition',[56] but she took the view that Eliot's 'sterile' conception of tradition was likely to be damaging for new writers. It would, she suggested, induce a feeling of inferiority which they will be encouraged to

Convert . . . into a sense of superiority, not by performance, but by subscription to
a very easily held faith. One will then have a world of T. S. Eliot's who have not
achieved *The Wasteland*, who are utterly sterile and utterly complacent.[57]

Ironically, West's questioning of Eliot's authority as a critic was carried
out in her own characteristically authoritative manner. From her earliest
reviews in the *Freewoman* West cultivated a witty, authoritative and
independent voice, which some recent feminist commentators have
described (negatively) as 'masculine'.[58] Clearly, much of West's early
journalism was produced in a milieu which was still largely the preserve of
men, and there is almost certainly an element of male mimicry in the voice
she developed in her attempt to establish herself in that milieu. However,
it might also be argued that her eschewal of a conventionally 'feminine'
voice in her journalism is strategic, and that her authoritativeness of tone
is a way of challenging (rather than merely succumbing to or reproducing)
conventional gender stereotypes: she demonstrates that wit, force, vigour,
irony and rationality are not the exclusive preserve of male writers.

West's critical discourse (like that of her contemporaries, both male and
female) is a gendered one, with many of the negative terms gendered
feminine. She found mincing effeminacy, sentimentality and spinsterish-
ness everywhere, in the novels of Wells, Joyce and Lawrence, as well as
those of May Sinclair. Her critical judgements, like her feminism, were
often decidedly 'unwomanly' and unsisterly: 'It is not always with
exultation', she wrote, 'that one says, "This book could only have been
written by a woman"'.[59] She was hard on women novelists, and
persistently chided them for adhering to the romantic conception of
self-sacrificing woman. She also resisted what she saw as a feminisation of
fiction in the post-war period, observing that the fact that 'fiction is at the
present moment largely in women's hands . . . may very well be (whether
one's bias is feminist or not) a cause for anxiety'.[60] She represented
modern, and especially modernist, impressionism as a 'feminine' form,
whether it was practised by Richardson or Joyce. She also represented
modern impressionism as narcissistic and sentimental, whether it was
practised by self-consciously experimental writers such as Richardson and
Joyce, or by a 'female maunderer' such as Irene Forbes-Mosse, who,
'influenced by . . . Vernon Lee's profound reverence for her own
sensorium' and 'the coy introspectiveness' of Elizabeth Von Arnim,
produced work of 'uncorrected egotism'.[61]

On the whole, despite her scepticism about their methods, gender
politics and/or metaphysics, West valued highly those novelists who have
(it turns out) been admitted to the canon of twentieth-century fiction.
However, she also took seriously and valued highly traditional, middlebrow writers such as Eden Phillpotts and Sheila Kaye-Smith; in fact

she reviewed Kaye-Smith's *The Singing Captive* in much more enthusiastic terms than those in which she had discussed May Sinclair's *The
Romantic* and *Larry Munro* written by her close friend G. B. Stern. West
placed all three novels within the category of 'distinctively women's
books', but only *The Singing Captive* was praised as 'a book that only a
woman could have written' because it 'reveals the truth about the
specifically feminine phases of experience', and 'rises to the very extreme
of . . . veracity'.[62]

The terms in which West expressed her admiration for *The Singing
Captive* shed some light on her scepticism about some of her more
experimental contemporaries. Although she herself experimented with
impressionistic stream of consciousness forms in *The Return of the Soldier*
(1918) and *Harriet Hume: A London Fantasy* (1929), she clearly retained a
commitment to realism and to popular middlebrow forms such as
melodrama (as she demonstrated in *The Judge*, 1922). At a time when
experimental, self-consciously literary writers were seeking new forms in
which to represent a fragmented, subjective, modern reality, West
remained sceptical about what she saw as the tendency of such writing
to decline into a merely self-referential narcissism, and to withdraw into a
self-enclosed, merely literary world. As many of her reviews suggest, she
retained a preference for novels which engaged with the objective social
realities within which subjectivities are constructed and experienced.
Similarly, although she made many trenchant criticisms of the outmoded
methods and ideas of the Edwardian uncles of the English novel, she
continued to valorise novels whose characters were rooted in a clearly
delineated and analysed social environment.

It is somewhat facile to reduce the complexities of West's perspective
on, and relationship to, literary modernism as a conflict or tension
between the aesthetic, and the social and political. Nevertheless, West's
early journalism (indeed her early fiction too) plays out a version of this
conflict. One early piece from the *Clarion* provides a very arresting
example of both the problematic of representation and the tension in
West's work between the literary and the political, the private and the
public. 'A Quiet Day with the Constitutionals' is designed to rouse its
readers to anger (and action) at the treatment of the suffragettes by the
forces of law and order. However, the article's rhetoric is the very reverse
of incendiary, as West adopts the calm, rational tones of the dispassionate
observer who would prefer to be almost anywhere than at a conference on
the Cat and Mouse Act.[63] The deliberations of the participants in this
conference are succinctly described, as is the appearance and behaviour of
the police spy whose presence is exposed, before the focus is switched
back to the feelings of the writer whose day and whose view of social

relations are severely disturbed by the events which she unwillingly observes. At the centre of this article is a passage which appears to enact a conflict between pleasure and literature on the one hand and social obligation, politics and journalistic duty on the other:

> I did not want to follow that deputation. I was extremely hungry and I wanted to write a short story. The satisfaction of those needs lay on the Northern Heights, but as a conscientious journalist I went to St Stephen's and waited on the pavement . . . thinking of my tea and my heroine with melancholy intensity.[64]

In the end, however, the conflict staged in this article is not simply between literature and politics, writing and acting, but between different kinds of writing. The author's desire to give herself up to the subjective claims of fiction is relinquished for a form of journalistic writing which is an act of bearing witness that is also a keeping of the faith and an intervention in the public sphere. The resulting article is also a very carefully structured representation. It is a short story with two heroines: Margaret Macmillan, the activist who is 'thrown down a flight of stairs by half-a-dozen policemen', and the young woman who produces from the 'murder in [her] heart' a perfectly dispassionate piece of writing to combat the ' "ferment of coercion and hysteria" that has gone on for too long'.[65]

For Ezra Pound Rebecca West was merely 'a journalist', a designation which he used to place her outside of modernism: 'Rebecca West is a journalist, a clever journalist, but not "of us". She belongs to Wells and that lot.'[66] It also placed her outside of literature, since a journalist, in Pound's hierarchy of literary production (and despite his own extensive 'journalistic' activities) was a mere transcriber, not a creator. I have tried to show, in this chapter, that West's journalism was far from transcription, and neither outside modernism, nor outside literature, but engaged in a vigorous debate with and about modernism and modern literature. This lively, witty, iconoclastic body of writing is itself a significant contribution to the literature of the early twentieth century. In her best pieces West, like her modernist contemporaries, made it new, as she constructed a series of representations designed to challenge the way things are, and to rouse her audience – especially her women readers – to resist and to change traditional gender stereotypes.

NOTES

1. Rebecca West, letter to the editor, *Freewoman*, 1 Aug. 1912, quoted in Jane Marcus (ed.), *The Young Rebecca: Writings of Rebecca West, 1911–1917* (Virago: London, 1989), 49.
2. Marcus, *The Young Rebecca*, 351.
3. Joan Garrett Packer has supplemented Hutchinson's work in her

Rebecca West: An Annotated Bibliography (Garland Publishing: New York, 1991).

4. Marcus, *The Young Rebecca*, 293. West is not mentioned in Stephen Koss's *Fleet Street Radical: A. G. Gardiner and the 'Daily News'* (Archon Books: London, 1973), nor in his *The Rise and Fall of the Political Press in England* (Hamish Hamilton: London, 1984).

5. See Bonnie Kime Scott, *Refiguring Modernism*, Vol. I: *The Women of 1928* (Indiana University Press: Bloomington and Indianapolis, 1995).

6. 'Indissoluble Matrimony', *Blast*, 20 June 1914, 98–117.

7. Andreas Huyssen, *After the Great Divide: Modernism, Mass Culture, Post-modernism* (Macmillan: London, 1986), 47.

8. On the adoption of her pseudonym see Rebecca West, ' "The Freewoman" ', *Time and Tide*, 16 July 1926, 648–9.

9. Cicely Fairfield, 'The Position of Women in Indian Life', *Freewoman*, 30 Nov. 1911, reprinted in Marcus, *The Young Rebecca*, 12–14.

10. The *Daily Herald* was founded and later (1919–23) edited by George Lansbury, a supporter of the suffragettes, and Labour MP for Bow and Bromley 1910–12 and 1922–40.

11. Letter to Dora Marsden, June 1912, quoted in Kime Scott, *Refiguring Modernism*, Vol. I, 234.

12. 'On a Form of Nagging', *Time and Tide*, 31 Oct. 1924, 1052–3, 1052.

13. Ibid., 1053.

14. Robert Blatchford, quoted in Marcus, *The Young Rebecca*, 89.

15. Mary Gawthorpe, *Up the Hill to Holloway* (Traversity Press: Penobscot, ME, 1962), 175.

16. Margaret Cole quoted in Marcus, *The Young Rebecca*, 89–90.

17. These figures are taken from Carl Rollyson, *Rebecca West: A Saga of the Century* (Hodder & Stoughton: London, 1995), 53.

18. See 'The Six Point Group Supplement. Point no. 3 Equality for Men and Women Teachers', *Time and Tide*, 9 Feb. 1923, 142–3; 'Form of Nagging'; ' "The Freewoman" '; 'The Function of the Weekly Review', *Time and Tide*, 9 Dec. 1927, 1114–15; 'The Journalist and the Public', *Time and Tide*, 2 Mar. 1928, 194–6.

19. 'Mr Chesterton in Hysterics', *Clarion*, 14 Nov. 1913, 5.

20. 'Form of Nagging', 1052.

21. West, ' "The Freewoman" ', 648.

22. See, for example, 'An Orgy of Disorder and Cruelty', 27 Sept. 1912; 'The Labour Party's Treachery', 25 Oct. 1912; 'The First Result of the Franchise Bill', 17 Jan. 1913; 'Quiet Women of the Country', 31 Jan. 1913; 'The Mildness of Militancy', 28 Feb. 1913; 'The Isles of the Wicked', 28 Mar. 1913; 'The Life of Emily Davison', 20 June 1913.

23. All quotations in this paragraph are from West's essay on The *Freewoman*.

24. Cicely Fairfield, 'The Position of Women in Indian Life', see Marcus, *The Young Rebecca*, 13.

25. 'Women and Wages', *Clarion*, 18 Oct. 1912, 4.

26. Ibid.

27. 'The Future of the Middle Classes', *Clarion*, 1 Nov. 1912, 3.

28. 'On Mentioning the Unmentionable: An Exhortation to Miss Pankhurst', *Clarion*, 26 Sept. 1913, 5.

29. 'Much Worse than Gaby Deslys', *Clarion*, 28 Nov. 1913, 9.

30. Virginia Woolf illustrates her assertion that 'in or about 1910 human character changed', by referring to the maid entering the living-room and asking for the *Daily Herald*: see her 'Mr Bennett and Mrs Brown', *The Captain's Death-Bed and Other Essays* (London: 1950), 91.

31. 'So Simple', *Freewoman*, 12 Oct. 1912, 390–1.

32. Ibid.

33. 'A New Woman's Movement', *Clarion*, 20 Dec. 1912, 3.

34. See ' "The Freewoman" '.

35. 'Rachel East', 'The Normal Social State', letter to the editor, *Freewoman*, 5 Sept. 1912, 312–13.

36. 'The WSPU', letter to the *Daily Herald*, 11 Sept. 1912 (reprinted in Marcus, *The Young Rebecca*, 369–71, 370).

37. 'Feminism', *Daily Herald*, 5 Sept. 1912 (reprinted in Marcus, *The Young Rebecca*, 367).

38. Ibid.

39. 'The Woman as Workmate', *Manchester Daily Dispatch*, 26 Nov. 1912 (reprinted in *The Young Rebecca*, 373–6).

40. 'Six Point Group Supplement'. See also 'Form of Nagging'.

41. See, for example, 'Uncle Bennett', *New York Herald Tribune Books*, 10 Oct. 1926, 1, 2 and 6. Reprinted in R. West *The Strange Necessity* (Jonathan Cape: London, 1928), 199–213.

42. Undated letter to Dora Marsden, quoted in Scott, *Refiguring Modernism*, Vol. I, 44.

43. 'Spinster to the Rescue', *Sunday Telegraph*, 11 Nov. 1970, 12.

44. 'Imagisme', *New Freewoman*, 15 Aug. 1913, 86–7.

45. ' "The Freewoman" ', 649.

46. *The Strange Necessity*, 37.

47. 'Notes on Novels', *New Statesman*, 16 Oct. 1920, 50; subsequent *Statesman* references from her 'Notes on Novels' column.

48. Ibid., 7 Aug. 1920, 504–5, 504.

49. Ibid., 16 Oct. 1920, 50.

50. Ibid., 4 Nov. 1922, 142.

51. 'The High Fountain of Genius', *New York Herald Tribune Books*, 21 Oct. 1928, 1 and 6.

52. *Ibid.*, 6.

53. *New Statesman*, 8 July 1922, 388.

54. Ibid., 9 July 1921, 388.

55. 'What Is Mr. T. S. Eliot's Authority as a Critic?', *Daily Telegraph*, 30 Sept. 1932, 6.

56. 'The High Fountain of Genius', 6.

57. 'A Last London Letter', *The Bookman*, Aug. 1930, 513–22, 520.

58. Gloria Fromm suggests West wrote non-fiction 'as a man speaking to men; and men were patently more important in her eyes than women': 'The Fiction of Fact and the Facts of Fiction', *New Criterion*, 9 (1991), 45–53, 50. See also J. Marcus, 'Rebecca West: A Voice of Authority', in Alice Kessler-Harris and William McBrien (eds), *Faith of a (Woman) Writer* (Greenwood Press: Westport, CT, 1988), 237–46.

59. *New Statesman*, 1 Oct. 1921, 706.

60. Ibid., 2 Dec. 1922, 270.

61. Ibid., 1 Oct. 1921, 706.

62. Ibid., 706 and 708.

63. Following criticism of the force-feeding of hunger-striking suffragette prisoners the government passed the 'Cat and Mouse Act' of 1913. Under this act suffragette prisoners were released when they became seriously weakened, and then rearrested as soon as they had recovered their health.

64. 'A Quiet Day with the Constitutionals', *Clarion* 1 Aug. 1913, 5.

65. Ibid.

66. Ezra Pound quoted in Scott, *Refiguring Modernism*, Vol. I, 89.

9

'MONARCH OF THE DRAB WORLD': VIRGINIA WOOLF'S FIGURING OF JOURNALISM AS ABJECT

LEILA BROSNAN

> Monarch of the drab world; of the shifting shuffling
> uneasy, queasy, egotist's journalist's pobbing and
> boobling, like a stew a-simmer, asking for sympathy
> dousing the clean the clear the bright the sharp in
> the stew of his greasy complacency.[1]

Stewing in the juices of his own second-rateness, the journalist emerges from one of Virginia Woolf's few pieces of deliberate verse as a highly unsavoury character. Not only is he characterised by an 'unbaked crumpet face;|with a hole for a mouth; and a blob at the lips' (4–5), but he

> sit[s] there, sprawling, self conscious,
> conscious only of nothing, blear eyed, blubber
> lipped, thick thumbed, squirming, to be seen,
> Brown like a bug that slips out on a lodging house
> wall.
>
> (26–30)

The individual journalist, who appears initially as the nominally truncated J.B., eventually metamorphoses into 'John Bug; James Bug Bug bug bug' (30), but is denied any connection to the civilised human qualities that his forename might suggest. He surfaces from his infectious stew to sip blood, 'my blood' (33), the blood of the poet who is, presumably, a representative of 'the clean the clear the bright the sharp' (15). Unlike the 'lady of the house' (1) who writes the 'FANTASY UPON A GENTLEMAN WHO CONVERTED HIS IMPRESSIONS OF A PRIVATE HOUSE INTO CASH', J.B. is a degraded figure, a bestial parasite, sucking the poet's blood to give himself substance and life, and by his very existence impeding her creativity. Like the Muse in Pope's *Dunciad*, whose presence ensures that

Art after *Art* goes out, and all is Night.
[. . .]
Light dies before thy uncreating word:
Thy hand, great Anarch! lets the curtain fall;
And Universal Darkness buries All,[2]

J.B. puts out the light of the poet's world by

sitting there, in the chair in the spring of the year;
taking time, air, light, space; stopping the
race of every thought; blocking out with his tweeds
the branches; the pigeons; and half the sky.

(8–11)

The vampiric journalist is, this depiction suggests, the epitome of all evil,
the 'great Anarch' of the world of early twentieth-century letters.

Like Pope's attack on Colley Cibber, Woolf's venting of spleen in
'Fantasy' was based on her encounter with an actual figure. On 27 March
1937 a reporter from the *New York Times* visited Monk's House uninvited
and took notes in a green book before being escorted from the premises by
Leonard Woolf; Virginia Woolf recorded the event in her diary and then,
presumably, wrote the poem shortly afterwards.[3] The tone and content of
'Fantasy' were therefore partially conditioned by immediate circumstances, but the specific details of the actual incident do not limit the
poem's referential and analytic potential. The terms in which the incident
was rewritten in the poem, when read against Woolf's other pronouncements on journalism and journalists, and later twentieth-century theories
of literary history and subjectivity, render it emblematic not only of the
role of journalism in Virginia Woolf's imagination and self-construction,
but also of the self-construction and subsequent readings of the movement
characterised as 'modernism'. By the time the poem is concluded, Woolf's
characterisation of J.B. has raised many of the contradictions inherent in
her approach to journalists and the world of journalism. These contradictions, in turn, lead to the surfacing of new readings of Woolf's non-
fiction in which her journalism is no longer seen as simply an adjunct to
her fiction, and Woolf is read differently as a modernist writer.

As a relatively unknown item from the Woolf corpus, 'Fantasy'
symbolises the profile of Woolf's journalism in assessments of her career.
Like the poem, which forms an appendix to Quentin Bell's biography of
Woolf, Woolf's journalism is consistently relegated to the margins of

critical assessments of her life and work. This lack of critical attention derives partly from Woolf's own disparagement of journalists and her own journalism, a dismissal which critics have taken at face value; partly from a tendency to bracket her as an example of a particular literary critical movement, ignoring works which lie outside disciplinary boundaries; and partly from a tendency to deem journalism a sub-literary form, unworthy of close scholarly attention.[4] In this respect, Woolf occupies a similar position to Dorothy Richardson and May Sinclair, both of whose journalism is generally overlooked in critical assessments of their writing. In the case of Dorothy Richardson, critical attention is directed at her fiction at the expense of her journalism; in the case of May Sinclair, whose non-fiction forms a significant proportion of her literary output, the lack of attention to her writing generally bespeaks a tendency to neglect a writer whose main contributions to readings of modernism are couched in the form of journalism.[5] Ignoring Woolf's extensive career as a journalist, which lasted from 1904 to 1941, risks limiting investigations of her non-fiction to the *belles-lettres* of the occasional essay, concentrating on issue-specific assessments of the contents of various essays, divorcing them from context, or dismissing her non-fiction altogether.[6] In so doing, critics perpetuate the construction of a literary figure, and the movement she is often deemed to exemplify, as separate from a whole sphere of literary and cultural production. Investigating Woolf's understanding of her own journalism as a cultural and personal activity avoids this critical impasse and leads the way to an assessment of her status in the literary history of her time, while questioning both our and her conceptions of what exactly constitutes 'literature' and how it can be analysed. Woolf's status as a cultural icon of both modernism and feminism, and her ability both to occupy and describe 'sites of cultural contestation', as Brenda Silver puts it, points to the relevance of a critical reading of her as a journalist.[7]

Woolf's publication of her non-fiction in the periodical press positions both her texts and herself as a figure precariously at a site of cultural contestation in which the status of the texts and the self-perceived status of the author slide between the 'high' art of literature and the 'low' work of journalism. She produced the majority of her essays and reviews for journals and papers which could in no way be considered 'popular' or 'lowbrow' by the general public – John Carey, for instance, cites the *Criterion*, for which Woolf wrote, as an organ of elite high culture, 'the circulation of which was limited, even in its best days, to some 800 subscribers'.[8] Woolf herself, however, placed that aspect of her work well below her fiction, so that it enjoyed a relatively low status, regardless of the intellectual and class pretensions of the journal in which it appeared.[9] Yet as a novelist and as a member of an upper middle-class, intellectual family and the social grouping of 'Bloomsbury', she was, as Brenda Silver points out, 'clearly representative of "high art" [and . . .] on the side of an "intellectual aristocracy" or "elite." '[10] In writing both high modernist literature and journalism that she characterised as low, but which in the main was written for a cultured audience, Woolf highlights the confusion of boundaries between high and low culture, as well as the anxiety surrounding that confusion, that is often associated with the writing and reading of modernism.

Woolf's anxiety over the crossing of cultural boundaries which resulted in the writing of 'Fantasy' was initially prompted by the physical crossing of the threshold of her privacy, when a *New York Times* reporter visited her house, uninvited, in 1937. Her success as a writer of fiction led, ironically, to her commodification as an object of journalistic interest. Leonard Woolf's reaction to her status as this object of public interest – 'Mrs W. didnt want that kind of publicity' – suggests a measured official response; Woolf's own reaction, on the other hand, is less circumspect: 'I raged. A bug walking over ones skin – cdn't crush him' (*D5*, 73). The journalist as bug, as repellent, crawling and bloodsucking insect, becomes the object of her ire and the focus of the poem, as she turns away from motivation towards an intense examination of the body of the journalist. The notion of the poet as subject of distasteful publicity recedes from the poetic narrative, as the journalist himself becomes the object on view. In order to escape the gaze of J.B., the poet turns *him* into an object of speculation: 'Yes, I see; I see' (4); she becomes spectator rather than exhibit, making the journalist the subject of *her* 'piece'.

Woolf's decision to focus on the individual reporter and her choice of the bug to exemplify him reveals many of the connotations the world of journalism held for her. A lower species than the human, James Bug recalls that well-known epithet for all things journalistic, Grub Street, as well as Dickens's characterisation of the reviewer as a louse.[11] 'Grub Street' and the 'Underworld' were terms used freely by Woolf in reference to journalism and its practitioners, as was the figure of the insect and the obsession with blood. John Middleton Murry, for instance, editor of the *Athenaeum* and the *Adelphi*, whom Woolf considered 'an oracle in the underworld' (*D1*, 156), worked in her 'flesh' like a 'jigger insect' (*D2*, 249), and resembled a 'bloodless flea' (*L3*, 38) who 'had been rolling in dung, and smells impure' (*L3*, 95). Sir Jack Squire, literary editor of the *New Statesman* from 1913 to 1919, and founder and editor of the *London Mercury* (1919–34), was a 'cheap & thin blooded creature' (*D1*, 133) and 'the spit and image of mediocrity' (*L3*, 394). Other 'creatures' of the underworld like J. B. Priestley (whose initials may well have inspired Woolf to call the journalist 'J.B.'), Robert Lynd and Arnold Bennett suffered from similarly vicious descriptions, even if they did lack the specific animal appellations. Lynd was a 'second rate writer' (*D*3, 70), while Priestley, along with Bennett, was one of the 'tradesmen of letters' (*D*3, 318). As suggested by the subterranean metaphor of the underworld and her frequent reference to social position, Virginia Woolf's perception of the landscape of literary culture was premised on hierarchy, a division that was described in her writing by a rhetoric of social distinction. Her reliance on images of animality, bloodiness and consumption, in turn, connects that social hierarchy in complex ways, to notions of both gender and subjectivity.

The language of 'Fantasy' explores these connections in detail. The relationship between J.B. and the poet, figured as parasite and host, makes explicit the hierarchised distinction between the two. Not only is he a 'bug' to the poet's 'lady', but he exudes the odour and the physical signs of the lodging house – 'his eyes/streaming with the steam of some lodging house stew' (35–6) – while the lady is specifically the resident of a 'private' house (40). Journalism and the journalist threaten the hitherto bounded and secure world of the 'private house' of the 'literary' writer as well as the boundaries of her own body. The power of that threat is highlighted by the particular vigour of the language used to describe the lady/bug relationship. 'Fantasy' uses minimal punctuation, vivid imagery and frequent, almost uncontrolled, repetition, and the terms of description for the loathsome bug – 'uneasy', 'queasy,' 'greasy' and 'egotist' – startle the reader by echoing each other in rhyme and assonance. In addition, they are terms of potent abuse in Virginia Woolf's vocabulary, with egotist, in particular, being one of her most damning condemnations. In her correspondence Woolf declared that 'the mention of "I" is so potent – such a drug, such a deep violet stain' (*L*5, 193), and 'I hate any writer to talk about himself; anonymity I adore' (*L*5, 191). 'I' is 'large' and 'ugly', and, in *A Room of One's Own*, the shadow it casts leads to 'aridity' and sterility; 'nothing will grow' within its shade.[12]

The particular triumvirate of 'queasy', 'greasy' and 'uneasy' also harks back to Woolf's responses to Joyce's *Ulysses*, another occasion on which her literary judgement found expression through a vocabulary of class-inflected phrases and vivid terms of physical repulsion. Woolf noted, when reading *Ulysses*, that 'Bloom is/Editor of a paper': he is in fact an advertising canvasser, but the many connections between *Ulysses* and journalism may have contributed to Woolf's use of a similar vocabulary in condemning both.[13] Joyce's innovative prose was a threat to Woolf's newly developed literary subjectivity, and the ease with which she turned to abuse based on class distinctions suggests that when one aspect of her writing sensibility was threatened, either by journalism or a fellow novelist, she bolstered it with a return to established parameters, the security of class being the most easily available. In her most famous response to Joyce, in the diary entry of 16 August 1922, she describes her reaction to reading *Ulysses* as 'puzzled, bored, irritated, & disillusioned as by a queasy undergraduate scratching his pimples'; it was an

> illiterate, underbred book [. . .] the book of a self taught working man, & we all know how distressing they are, how egotistic, insistent, raw, striking, & ultimately nauseating. When one can have the cooked flesh, why have the raw? (*D2*, 188–9)

Reading Joyce led her, in her writing, to 'dwindle, niggle, hesitate' (*D2*, 69). He literally made her uneasy, taking the ease out of her own methods of composition. In all these passages references to social status jostle with symptoms of poisonous consumption, and the hated term 'egotist' presides over all. In reference to *Ulysses*, as in 'Fantasy', a sense of revulsion couples with a sense of threat – Joyce threatened her sense of originality and the bug of journalism threatened the privacy and bodily integrity of the poet. Reading *Ulysses* made Woolf reflect that 'what I'm doing is probably being better done by Mr Joyce' (*D2*, 69), while journalism interrupted the process of writing fiction and threatened Woolf's sense of pure artistic purpose: 'the horror of writing 1, 2, 3, 4, reviews on end [. . .] I've been groaning & grumbling, & seeing myself caged, & all my desired ends – Jacob's Room that is – vanishing down avenues' (*D2*, 35). Although the threat to her writing self as experimental and 'high art' novelist is existential, Woolf's responses are expressed in terms of a corporeal reaction: her body is attacked by a parasite, nauseated by raw flesh and caged like an animal. Joyce and the journalist join as examples of an almost bestial opponent to 'the clean the clear the bright the sharp' of Woolf's vocation as a writer.

Woolf's private writing on journalism, then, echoes this preoccupation with class and the threat such a 'low' occupation poses to the higher pursuit of writing fiction. In thus reducing journalism to a subservient position in the gradation of culture and opposing it to innovative fiction, Woolf was not an unusual figure in her time. Ezra Pound, with typical brio, condemned the conservatism of reviewers, whose professional restraint he saw as a blight on creativity:

> Let us deride the smugness of 'The Times': GUFFAW!
> So much for the gagged reviewers,
> It will pay them when the worms are wriggling in their vitals;
> These are they who objected to newness,
> Here are their tomb-stones.[14]

F. R. Leavis, too, characterised journalism by its associations with a world of vice and squalor. For Leavis, journalism 'solicits us everywhere' and even 'the academic conception of tradition' cannot 'save its champions from wallowing' – even though, unlike Woolf, he distinguishes between the 'serious critical organ' and 'the Press':

> when we consider, for instance, the processes of mass-production and standardization in the form represented by the Press, it becomes obviously of sinister significance that they should be accompanied by a process of levelling-down.[15]

And just as Leavis is clearly the inheritor of Matthew Arnold's social and cultural views, in which the newspaper is the epitome of the 'provincial spirit' while the 'exercise of a creative power' (in 'the production of great works of literature or art') is 'the highest function of man', much of Woolf's distrust of the pale world of journalism, where the bug is 'malodorous glistening/but only semi transparent' (31–2), has its roots in the Victorian legacy that journalism was not 'hard work', not legitimate literary or artistic activity.[16] Her father, Sir Leslie Stephen, for instance, always felt journalism to be 'not a very exalted profession'.[17] As Noel Annan recounts, Sir Leslie once told his wife to 'tell some young man that "it would be more virtuous to starve or take a public house" than earn a living by journalism'.[18] And Caroline Emelia Stephen, Sir Leslie's sister, frowned upon the young Virginia Stephen's means of entrée to the literary world through the practice of journalism. In response, Virginia Stephen grumbled that

> I got sat upon as usual by the Quaker [Caroline Stephen] – (who thinks it right to criticise her relations, and *never* to praise them) for 'journalism' – She thinks I am going to sell my soul for gold, which I should willingly do for gold enough, and wants me to write a solid historical work!! People do take themselves so seriously: she sits and twiddles her fingers all day long, but she exhorts me to realise the 'beauty of hard work' as she says profoundly. (*L*1, 166)

A year later, by which time Virginia Stephen had been published in the *Guardian*, the *Times Literary Supplement*, the *Academy & Literature* and the prestigious *National Review*, Aunt Stephen was still questioning her niece's status as a writer: 'The Quaker writes "When I asked what you were doing I meant writing." Do you see the excessively subtle point of that sentence? Somehow she drew a distinction between reviewing and other kinds of literature,' (*L*1, 212). The intellectual status of many of the journals for which Virginia Stephen was reviewing was high and the effort she devoted to her reviewing was considerable, but it appears that Aunt Stephen's faculties of judgement were influenced by the rhetoric surrounding the perception of journalism in the late nineteenth and early twentieth century.[19] Her opinion that reviewing did not awaken Virginia Stephen to the beauties of hard, or appropriate intellectual, work when, for example, in the space of one week (Saturday 11 to Saturday 18 March

1905)[20] her niece did not let one day pass in which she was not involved with reviewing, is similar in attitude to Matthew Arnold's view that the 'new journalism', though it is 'full of ability, novelty, variety, sensation, sympathy, generous instincts', in short, energy and industry, is still *'feather-brained'*.[21] Writing three reviews and one essay, plus notes, reading three set books and others for background information will always be considered less than adequate employment if journalism itself is seen as occupying an immovable place at 'the bottom of a hierarchy of cultural forms'.[22]

The implication that journalism was not 'hard work', not legitimate literary or artistic activity, was one with which Virginia Woolf struggled throughout her career. While she acknowledged the pleasure of writing and being published, she often derogated the quality of her work and dismissed the quantity as having no relevance to worth – either to her worth as a literary reviewer and essayist, or the objective worth of the pieces she published.[23] While she recorded faithfully one aunt's criticism she omitted even to mention another's praise. Aunt Annie Thackeray Ritchie, herself a late nineteenth-century journalist of distinction, 'highly praised' part of Virginia Stephen's review 'Literary Geography'; Virginia Stephen did not mention it.[24] Any praise that was acknowledged provoked a kind of shame rather than pride. As if expiating a sin, praise for her journalism led Virginia Woolf to '[promise] to translate a bit of tough Greek, as a penance'.[25] Despite her admission of pleasure in reviewing and her continued practice as a reviewer, to 'struggle with my novel' was worth while; 'my reviews dont count at all' (*L*1; 375). They, like the blood/prose emitted by J.B., 'pale' by comparison with the depth of fiction or legitimate history.

Pitted against this idea that journalism was not 'real' work was the actuality of the time and effort Virginia Woolf put into each piece. Leonard Woolf, in his introduction to *The Death of the Moth and Other Essays* noted that 'I do not think that Virginia Woolf ever contributed any article to any paper which she did not write and rewrite several times' and cites the example of an unspecified review with an original draft and 'no fewer than eight or nine complete revisions of it which she had herself typed out'.[26] The industry that characterised Woolf's work in 1905 was consistent throughout her career: a leader slightly in excess of three columns on Conrad, for instance, commissioned by the *Times Literary Supplement* after his death in August 1924, went through twenty-three pages of drafts in manuscript.[27] Similarly, for her late essay on Ellen Terry, offered to *Harper's Bazaar* in 1940, Virginia Woolf read Terry's *Memoirs*, Edward Gordon Craig's *Ellen Terry and Her Secret Self* and *Ellen Terry and Bernard Shaw: A Correspondence* and wrote in excess of fifty pages of draft.[28] This industry, however, while it contradicted the criticism of journalism as an inconsequential pastime, indulged in in order to make a little cash, was converted into a burden of drudgery. For Woolf, journalism became something that ate up time, time that could be spent on more respectable ventures. Hence, in reading through her voluminous correspondence and diaries one comes across incessant references to the desire to escape from the crushing weight of journalistic demands. In 1917 Woolf wrote to Clive Bell that 'you don't waste your time on reviews', a freedom from toil which would enable him to try 'a few experiments' in prose; journalism, once again, is seen as antithetical to modernist 'experiment' (L2, 167). Her own time spent in a 'horrid burst of journalism' (L4, 187) was 'such hard labour in the doing that one cant read them [the articles] without remembering the drudgery' (L4, 195). In 1910, therefore, she vowed 'never shall I write a review again' (L1, 440). This desire she reinvoked in 1920, when she reasserted that 'my private aim is to drop my reviewing' (D2, 34), and again finally, in 1937, when she decided she would not write articles 'at all except for the Lit Sup' (D5, 91). At no point did Woolf withdraw from reviewing; nor did she limit herself to a particular journal like the *Times Literary Supplement*. After the 1937 declaration, articles appeared in the *New Statesman and Nation*, the *Yale Review*, the *Atlantic Monthly*, the *Listener* and the *New Republic* and by early 1938 she had decided to sever her connection with the *Times Literary Supplement*, rather than restrict herself to writing for it. The anomaly, continuing long past the time when financial considerations governed her actions, of spending apparently inordinate amounts of time perfecting a product to which she apparently attributed no value, was a permanent feature of Woolf's professional writing life.

This fact alone should indicate the need for critical attention to be directed towards the non-fiction corpus, but criticism has tended to follow the lead Woolf herself laid down, in which she condemns journalism as an impediment to creativity and health. Like the hideous bug J.B., sucking the life blood from his host, the onerous activity of writing articles and reviewing, she declared, consumed Virginia Woolf's time, drained her of energy and imagination and left her railing against its invasion of her life and its detrimental effect on her fiction. 'I have had to scribble all day to finish an article and this leaves one very much out of language' (L2, 583), she lamented, especially as 'after a dose of criticism I feel that I'm writing sideways, using only an angle of my mind' (D2, 248–9). And not only did Woolf blame journalism for its effects on her creative abilities, she even went so far as to attribute her emotional difficulties to it, suggesting once again that threats to the writing self are experienced as threats to the physical body. She recognised that

I'd been depressed since Jan. 3rd. We ran it to earth, I think, by discovering that I
began journalism on that day. Last Thursday, I think, I returned to fiction, to the
instant nourishment & well being of my entire day. (*D2*, 234)

Journalism was an ultimate scapegoat, starving her of the nourishment
necessary for every type of health – a sustenance only the writing of fiction
could provide. Just as the journalist J.B. is a parasite on the body of the
lady, so journalism is a parasite on the body of fiction, eating away the
mental and physical energy the writer needs to create 'art'.

The art, as 'Fantasy' suggests, is the 'high' art of the 'private lady',
what later twentieth-century critics have come to call high modernism.
Having J.B., the representative of the newspaper, and 'monarch' of a
whole 'drab world', pitted against the lady therefore describes both a
personal scenario and a larger critical paradigm. J.B. becomes a metonym
for mass culture, the lady for high art; the former is a parasite on the body
of a more pristine capitalised Culture, leaching away its life-blood. This
figures one of the contemporary and posthumous constructions of
modernism.[29] John Carey, for example, defines modernism as a literature
of 'hostile reaction' and 'exclusion', generated through the almost patho-
logical antagonism between the modernist high culture of the intellectuals
and 'the masses'.[30] Andreas Huyssen also poses the same opposition as
fundamental to the definition and self-constitution of modernism, but
maintains a more balanced attitude to the movement and its practitioners.
According to Huyssen,

> ever since the mid-19th century, the culture of modernity has been characterized by
> a volatile relationship between high art and mass culture [. . .] Modernism
> constituted itself through a conscious strategy of exclusion, an anxiety of con-
> tamination by its other: an increasingly consuming and engulfing mass culture.[31]

And even though 'there has been a plethora of strategic moves tending to
destabilize the high/low opposition from within [. . .] these attempts have
never had lasting effects'.[32] Carey and Huyssen's vision of mass culture as
modernism's 'Other' fits neatly with the high/low oppositions worked out
through the language of class distinction and the graphic descriptions of
contamination and consumption in 'Fantasy'. In 'Fantasy', however, the
gendering and the connotations of the parasite/host binary opposition
present problems which illustrate the internal destabilisation of the
opposition that Huyssen mentions, but also indicate that the effects of
this destabilisation are more influential than he suggests. In particular,
ambiguities of gender and the conjunction of host and parasite in 'Fantasy'
imply a more ambivalent relationship between mass and high culture.
They point to the need for a more complex paradigm for the reading of
movements like modernism than a binary opposition, however volatile.

The issue of gender is already implicated in the question of opposition for, as Hélène Cixous argues, wherever there is a binary opposition, there is a hierarchy and that hierarchy is gendered. According to Cixous, the 'two-term system' is 'related to the couple man/woman' – 'hierarchization subjects the entire conceptual organization to man'.[33] According to Huyssen, the modernism/mass culture dichotomy is no exception. As modernism's 'Other', mass culture is also inescapably 'female', that being the side, as Cixous outlines it, of 'Low', 'slave', 'subordination'.[34] Huyssen concurs with this process of gendering, declaring that mass culture, since the mid- to late nineteenth century, has consistently been gendered feminine: 'the political, psychological, and aesthetic discourse around the turn of the century consistently and obsessively genders mass culture as feminine'.[35] But J.B., Woolf's representative of mass culture, is male; he is, ironically, considering his lodging house origins, the 'Gentleman who converted his impressions of a private house into cash'. In the interests of historical accuracy, both in terms of the actual intruder who arrived in the Daimler, and in terms of Woolf's experience of the proportion of women involved in 1930s' journalism, J.B. had to be a 'he'; in terms of his opposition to Woolf as woman writer the inversion of gender is equally understandable. Through the poet/bug opposition, Woolf establishes a binary apparently only to undermine it in terms of gender and class.

Despite J.B.'s obvious masculinity, certain of his habits do mark him as female; when read through his behaviour rather than his appearance, J.B.'s gender becomes less well defined. He sips blood, for instance, and his body bleeds into print, both images that have particularly strong resonances for feminist literary critics. According to Susan Gubar,

> one of the primary and most resonant metaphors provided by the female body is blood, and cultural forms of creativity are often experienced as a painful wounding [. . .] for the woman artist who experiences herself as killed into art may also experience herself as bleeding into print.[36]

The perceived feminine associations of blood are paralleled by the gendering of food and consumption. In Woolf's fiction and in the majority of critical assessments of the relationship between food and gender, consumers are almost always women and the association between food and femininity is always negative. In *Mrs Dalloway*, for example, the voracious Miss Kilman greedily consumes her eclair in a pang of barely suppressed desire; and in the sketch 'Portrait 5', an unnamed woman luxuriates over sugared pastry while affirming her own self-satisfaction; even the central and celebratory dinner in *To the Lighthouse* has its ominous side, as Mrs Ramsay serves up Paul and Minta to a future of restrictive married life just as she serves up the Bœuf en Daube.[37] And such imagery is not limited only to Woolf's fiction. One of the last observations she made in her diary was of women eating in a Brighton tea shop, ironically named 'Fullers'. There sat

> a fat, smart woman, in red hunting cap, pearls, check skirt, consuming rich cakes. Her shabby dependant also stuffing [. . .] They ate & ate [. . .] Something scented, shoddy, parasitic about them [. . .] Where does the money come to feed these fat white slugs? (D5, 357)

Scenes of physical consumption lead naturally to questions of material and economic consumption, with the consumer usually a woman, and frequently both bestial and malevolent. The Brighton women in the tea shop are likened to slugs, Doris Kilman to a monster, and the lady in Portrait 5 carries a 'gland in her cheek' from which scent drops, like a cat intent on marking its territory.

In terms of his literary companions in Woolf's works and his bodily functions, then, the sucking, bleeding J.B. attracts all the negative connotations of debased femininity. His feminine aspects are therefore entirely in keeping with the gendering of the culture he represents and which Virginia Woolf, in her less generous moments, derided. But for all his feminine attributes, J.B. is still seen in his masculine garb of 'rubbed grease stained tweeds' (21). The greasiness of his appearance, however, in combination with his lodging-house origins destabilises his pretensions to 'gentleman' status: he is the ironically misnamed 'gentleman' to the poet's 'lady'. So the division between masculinity and femininity is neither easy nor simple, and is complicated and inflected by distinctions of class, which are themselves unstable. Factoring these ambivalences into the opposition of high and low art and the subsequent construction of an oppositional and exclusionary literary modernism therefore renders these models, and many readings of Woolf as modernist and radical feminist, highly problematic.[38] In her writing, and as the fact of her writing both journalism and modernist novels indicates, the notion of exactly what constituted high and low culture was not fixed immutably for Virginia Woolf, either in her imagination or in practice; strict divisions between art and journalism, high and low, break down. In her fiction lower-class figures, singing a kind of demotic babble, are often shown to be the bearers of messages of cultural significance, yet have their meanings 'read' by people from elite social and cultural backgrounds; so too in her characterisation of the journalism/art binary Woolf establishes an opposition only to question its absolute polarity.[39] In the poem on J.B., inflexible hierarchies of host and parasite crumble, as the poet refuses to kill the beast who afflicts her. She contemplates his destruction, but decides against it because 'if you kill bugs they leave marks|on the wall' (38–9). By letting the bug live she suffers the intermingling of her blood and his to continue; she permits the transgression of boundaries. Once on the skin of his host their separate identities merge, her blood mingles with his, and his body, like Donne's flea, 'swells with one blood made of two'; J.B. is now 'you *and* I':[40]

> he
> sipped blood. my blood; anybodies blood to make a
> bugs body blue black.
>
> (32–4)

The physical conjunction of the bug and the poet, effected through the transfer of blood, of prose, for 'the bug's body bleeds in pale|ink' (39–40), reveals the living presence of journalism, Woolf's writing 'Other', in her literary output and its presence in her construction of herself as a writer. By dismantling the borders between the journalist and the poet, the poem therefore encodes the ambivalence Virginia Woolf felt towards journalism as a profession and herself as a practitioner. The particular construction of the bug|poet binary, in which two apparently distinct entities are joined and yet separate, indicates the need to rethink those models of modernism which rely on a clearly demarcated oppositional construction. An examination of the dynamics of the bug/poet relationship, especially the vocabulary and form in which that relationship is depicted, suggests a theoretical model which may elucidate the role of journalism in Woolf's life and those versions of modernism which exclude it by maintaining a strict high/low antithesis.

'Fantasy', which relies on animal, food and body imagery, and which describes a state of revulsion and horror, displaying the results in fractured poetic prose, echoes the language Julia Kristeva outlines in her exposition of abjection. The abject, to quote Toril Moi, 'represents the first effort of the future subject to separate itself from the pre-Oedipal mother'; it is caused by 'what disturbs identity, system, order. What does not respect borders, positions, rules. The in-between, the ambiguous, the composite'.[41] In terms of narrative, according to Kristeva

> linearity is shattered, it proceeds by flashes, enigmas, short cuts, incompletion, tangles, and cuts. At a later stage, the unbearable identity of the narrator and of the surroundings that are supposed to sustain him can no longer be *narrated* but *cries out* or is *descried* with maximal stylistic intensity (the language of violence, of obscenity, or of a rhetoric that relates the text to poetry). (141)

And, echoing the reliance on metaphors of food and digestion that was particular to Woolf's own language of disgust and horror,[42] Kristeva points to the centrality of images of debased consumption to the phenomenon she terms abjection: 'food loathing is perhaps the most elementary and most archaic form of abjection' (2), and the abject 'confronts us [. . .] with those fragile states where man strays on the territory of *animal*' (12). Not only does the 'first dietary trespass', the taboo at the base of abjection, involve an 'animal temptation', but a 'feminine' one too; the animal, the feminine and food are all linked at the point of abjection (96). In the extremity of the poet's reaction to J.B. we see the horror of the bestial, but we also see the power he exerts over her imagination, a power which prevents her from killing him. In the poet's decision not to kill the bug and in Woolf's decision to continue journalism we may see something of the 'fascination of the abomination' that Conrad notes in *Heart of Darkness* and Kristeva sees as typical of the phenomenon of abjection, in which 'so many victims of the abject are its fascinated victims' (9).[43] In its depiction of an opposition between a self and an 'Other', which is also a conjunction of self and 'Other' in such a way that the distinction becomes lost, 'Fantasy' also reflects the pre-mirror-state realm of subject formation that is described by the process of abjection. The abject is not a 'correlative' of the nascent subject which 'allow[s it] to be more or less detached and autonomous', but a revulsion from, without a rejection of, an opposition without separation, of an object, or 'a "something"' that helps to create the 'I' (1–2). Woolf's language of abjection, which emerges so clearly in relation to journalism, illuminates the positive as well as the negative role of journalism in her career, and points towards a method of reading modernism which acknowledges the significance of the journalism of modernist writers like T. S. Eliot, W. B. Yeats, Ezra Pound, Dorothy Richardson and May Sinclair, *within* the construction of modernism as a high art movement. Reading journalism as something that is opposed to the writing of the literature that is characterised as modernist, while recognising that it cannot be separated from it; perceiving journalism as being antithetical to literature while not being entirely rejected by the writers in question; reading journalism as analogous to the ambiguous construction of abjection: all allow for a higher priority to be given to non-fiction, and journalism in particular, within critical readings of the modernist period.

Reading 'Fantasy' and Woolf's journalism through the matrix of abjection helps to explain journalism's continued presence and significance in Woolf's writing life. Obviously Woolf did recognise the power as well as the horror of journalism as she did not kill her own particular bug and spent nearly forty years recording her own impressions of books, people, pictures and houses in newspapers for cash. Part of the fascination of journalism for Woolf was its potential to expose her to a new literary world, and to guarantee a degree of fame in this new environment. Being monarch of a drab world by definition lacks glamour, but it does not necessarily deprive one of the excitement of the new. The position of eminence has its own advantages, not the least of which is the satisfaction of personal vanity. The antics of the fictional J.B. provoked Virginia Woolf to ask

> Why did he want to be 'seen.' What corkscrew
> urge from the surge of his stew, his gobbets and
> gibbets forced him out of the here, to this chair,
> to be seen? when the spring was there?
> to be seen sitting there, sprawling, self conscious.
>
> (22–6)

In these lines of poetry, Woolf repeats the phrase 'to be seen' three times, reinforcing the element of public prominence and exposure to an audience involved in journalism. In her more private personal writing, her letters and her diaries, she records with some pride the popularity she achieved through journalism, acknowledging that 'this social side is very genuine in me' (*D2*, 250) and that the sense of 'writing for an audience always stirs me' (*D3*, 135). In 1919 she wrote that 'I've got to write articles without end. I'm very highly thought of – as a reviewer' (*L2*, 391); in 1923 she recorded privately that 'I can't help thinking myself about as successful journalistically as any woman of my day', then added the proviso 'but that is not saying much' (*D2*, 251). Yet she recorded with evident delight that Lytton Strachey 'thinks me the best reviewer alive, & the inventor of a new prose style, & the creator of a new version of the sentence' (*D1*, 277). Journalism gave Woolf popularity amongst the public and amongst her friends, and also a sense of her own worth as a writer within the public sphere. In 1918 she noted that 'when I have to review at command of a telegram [. . .] I feel pressed & important & even excited a little' (*D1*, 197); in 1932 she recalled 'how proud I was to be asked to do the T.L.S. article! [on Thomas Hardy]' (*D4*, 119); and in 1938 she remembered 'how pleased I used to be when L[eonard Woolf] called me "You're wanted by the Major Journal!"' (*D5*, 144–5).

Journalism therefore gave Woolf fame and prestige and situated her within the commercial world of work as well as the private world of fiction writing. Recognising this helps to free her from the charge of being a coterie writer who had no experience of 'the real world', and who wrote solely for a restricted audience. Acknowledging the presence of the bug of journalism on the wall of the house of fiction highlights Woolf's connections with a multitude of diverse organs, from the *Times Literary Supplement* to *Good Housekeeping* to the *Daily Worker*, and alerts readers to the fact that the pronouncements lifted from these articles and used to support various critical constructions of both Virginia Woolf and modernism were conditioned as much by the journalistic exigencies of space available for copy, editorial policy and audience expectations, as by Woolf's particular modernist sensibility.

Recognising the presence of journalism in Woolf's life also means recognising its importance to that private modernist sensibility. To kill the offensive bug, to sever the links with the world of journalism would, in a double sense, be 'selfe murder'.[44] Woolf would be killing off that portion of her writing self that found expression through journalism and also injuring, perhaps fatally, the more privileged self who wrote fiction, but who wrote it bolstered by the knowledge that relief was at hand in the form of journalism and that one sense of the value of that work was generated by its opposition to journalism. Both Virginia and Leonard Woolf remark on the fact that Virginia needed a less demanding activity to afford her relief from the mental strain of writing fiction. For many years writing reviews was that relief. It allowed Woolf to express a part of her intelligence and imagination that could not necessarily find an outlet in her fiction; for Leonard Woolf 'it gave her the relief which some thinkers find in chess or crossword puzzles'.[45] Accustomed as she was to express herself in binary oppositions, contrasting fiction with fact and novels to criticism and privileging one pole of the pair (a privilege later critics have been eager to maintain), Woolf also recognised that to express herself adequately she needed to write in both modes. Even when the excuse of financial necessity had passed, therefore, she continued to write reviews. Every resolution to abandon journalism was followed by a return to it: 'Yes I've been slipping into the frying pan of journalism – letting myself in for a monthly article, making, or attempting to make, £15.15 terms. All this is very frittering, exciting, degrading' (*D*5, 240).

This pull between excitement and degradation, explored and depicted in 'Fantasy', allows us to glimpse a modernist and a modernism defined less through opposition than through oscillation, doubleness and ambiguity. Just as the relationship between the lady and the bug, which shadows the patterns of the process of abjection, is parasitic and symbiotic, so it points to the way in which modernism can be read through a critical framework sensitive to interdependencies as well as oppositions. Acknowledging these interdependencies results in recognising the presence of so-called minor forms, like journalism, and the significance of gender and class complications, within definitions and constructions of modernism. Focusing on the horror of the bug of journalism as a figure of abjection reveals its power to disrupt narratives: the actual narrative of the poem, the literary critical narrative of 'Virginia Woolf' writer of modernist fiction not journalism, and the narratives of some of the constructions of modernism itself.

NOTES

1. These lines are taken from the 'poem' 'FANTASY UPON A GENTLE-MAN WHO CONVERTED HIS IMPRESSIONS OF A PRIVATE HOUSE INTO CASH', reproduced in Appendix B of Quentin Bell, Virginia *Woolf: A Biography*, (Hogarth: London, 1972), Vol. 2, 253–4; original typescript version in Monk's House Papers, University of Sussex (hereafter MHP), A. 19. Further quotations from the poem (hereafter in the text referred to as 'Fantasy') are indicated by line numbers in parentheses in the text; this excerpt, ll. 12–16. All quotations retain Woolf's idiosyncrasies of spelling and punctuation.

2. John Butt (ed.), 'The Dunciad,' Book IV, *The Poems of Alexander Pope*, (Methuen: London, 1968), 799–800; ll. 640, 654–6.

3. Anne Olivier Bell and Andrew McNeillie (eds), *The Diary of Virginia Woolf*, 15 vols (Penguin: Harmondsworth, 1979–85), Vol. 5, 72–3 (further quotations in parentheses in text, volume and page numbers following the initial *D*).

4. Very few critics consider Woolf as a journalist, the major exceptions being: John Mepham, *Virginia Woolf: A Literary Life* (Macmillan: London, 1991); S. P. Rosenbaum, *Edwardian Bloomsbury: The Early Literary History of the Bloomsbury Group*, Vol. 2 (Macmillan: London, 1994); and Rachel Bowlby in her introductions to Woolf's *Selected Essays*, *A Woman's Essays* and *The Crowded Dance of Modern Life* (Virago: London, 1992 and 1993 respectively). On lack of academic interest in journalism see Laurel Brake, *Subjugated Knowledges: Journalism, Gender and Literature* (Macmillan: London, 1994).

5. On Richardson and Sinclair, see Bonnie Kime Scott (ed.), *The Gender of Modernism: A Critical Anthology* (Indiana UP: Bloomington and Indianapolis, 1990). In *Dorothy Richardson* (Harvester: Hemel Hempstead, 1991), Jean Radford notes Richardson's recognition of journalism's importance to her writing life (7), but then concentrates almost exclusively on assessing her fiction.

6. On Woolf's essays in relation to modernism see: N. Takei da Silva, *Modernism and Virginia Woolf* (Windsor Publications: Windsor Park, 1990); Mark Goldman, *The Reader's Art: Virginia Woolf as Literary Critic* (Mouton: The Hague, 1976); Jean Guiguet, *Virginia Woolf and Her Works*, tr. Jean Stewart (Hogarth: London, 1965). On her essays in relation to feminism see Michele Barrett (ed.), *Virginia Woolf: Women and Writing* (Women's Press: London, 1979) and Jane Marcus, *Art and Anger: Reading*

Like a Woman (Ohio State UP: Columbus, 1988); in relation to the essay see Graham Good, *The Observing Self: Rediscovering the Essay* (Routledge: London, 1988).

7. Brenda R. Silver, 'What's Woolf Got to Do with It? or, The Perils of Popularity', *Modern Fiction Studies*, 38 (1992) 22.

8. John Carey, *The Intellectuals and the Masses: Pride and Prejudice among the Literary Intelligentsia 1880–1939* (Faber & Faber: London, 1992), 9. The *TLS*, however, is a different matter: in 1924, for instance, the average net sale for July was 26,675 copies weekly (*TLS*, 14 August 1924).

9. See Woolf's dismissal of journalism in Nigel Nicolson and Joanne Trautmann (eds), *The Letters of Virginia Woolf*, 6 vols (Chatto & Windus: London, 1980–3), Vol. 2, 599 (further quotations from the letters in parentheses in text, volume and page numbers following the initial *L*.).

10. Silver, 'What's Woolf Got to Do with It?', 22–3.

11. See 'Reviewing', in Virginia Woolf, *The Captain's Death Bed* (Hogarth: London, 1950) for Dickens and reviewers, and D1, 156, n. 8 for the Underworld.

12. Virginia Woolf, *A Room of One's Own* (Penguin Books: London, 1945 [1928]), 99.

13. Bloom as editor appears in MHP, B. 3. f.

14. 'Salutation the Third', from *Blast* in Ezra Pound, *Collected Shorter Poems* (Faber: London, 1973), 165.

15. F. R. Leavis, 'What's Wrong with Criticism?', *Scrutiny*, 1 (Sept. 1932), 140; and F. R. Leavis, 'Mass Civilization and Minority Culture', in his *Education and the University: A Sketch for an 'English School'* (Chatto & Windus: London, 1948 [1943]), 158, 147.

16. Matthew Arnold, 'The Function of Criticism at the Present Time', in Miriam Allott (ed.), *Selected Poems and Prose* (Dent: London, 1978), 191. For Virginia Woolf's Victorian heritage see Gillian Beer, 'The Victorians in Virginia Woolf: 1832–1941', in her *Arguing with the Past: Essays in Narrative from Woolf to Sidney* (Routledge: London, 1989), 138–58.

17. Sir Leslie Stephen, *Mausoleum Book* (Clarendon Press: Oxford, 1977), 85 and 87.

18. Noel Annan, *Leslie Stephen: The Godless Victorian* (Random House: New York, 1984), 112.

19. See Joel H. Wiener (ed.), *Papers for the Millions: The New Journalism in Britain, 1850s to 1914* (Greenwood Press: New York, 1988).

20. See Mitchell A. Leaska (ed.), *A Passionate Apprentice: The Early Journals of Virginia Woolf* (Hogarth: London, 1990) for details of the reviewing (here, 250–5) and also the notebooks with quotes and ideas from her reading: MHP, B. 1. a).

21. Matthew Arnold, 'Up to Easter', in Fraser Neiman (ed.), *Essays, Letters, and Reviews* (Harvard UP: Cambridge, MA, 1960), 347.

22. Laurel Brake, 'The Old Journalism and the New', in Wiener, *Papers for the Millions*, 2.
23. See Leaska, *Early Journals*, 219, on pleasure in being published.
24. Rosenbaum, *Edwardian Bloomsbury*, 157.
25. Woolf, *Early Journals*, 229.
26. Virginia Woolf, *The Death of the Moth and Other Essays* (Hogarth: London, 1942), 7.
27. See the drafts on the verso pages of the manuscript of *Mrs Dalloway*: British Library, ADD MS 51046.
28. MHP, B. 5. a) & c).
29. On relations between mass culture and high art see Walter Benjamin, 'The Work of Art in the Age of Mechanical Reproduction', in Hannah Arendt (ed.), *Illuminations*, tr. Harry Zohn (Fontana: London, 1992).
30. Carey, *Intellectuals*, vii and 21. See also Theodor Adorno and Max Horkheimer, *Dialectic of Enlightenment*, tr. John Cumming (Allen Lane: London, 1972).
31. A. Huyssen, *After the Great Divide: Modernism, Mass Culture, Postmodernism* (Macmillan: London, 1986).
32. Ibid.
33. Hélène Cixous, 'Sorties', in Elaine Marks and Isabelle de Courtivron (eds), *New French Feminisms: An Anthology* (Harvester Wheatsheaf: Hemel Hempstead, 1981), 90 and 91.
34. Ibid., 90, 91 and 92.
35. Huyssen, *After the Great Divide*, 46.
36. Susan Gubar, ' "The Blank Page" and Issues of Female Creativity', in Elizabeth Abel (ed.), *Writing and Sexual Difference* (Harvester: Sussex, 1982), 78.
37. Virginia Woolf, *Mrs Dalloway* (Penguin: London, 1992 [1925]), 141–5; Virginia Woolf, 'Portraits', in Susan Dick (ed.), *The Complete Shorter Fiction of Virginia Woolf*, revised edn (Hogarth: London, 1989 [1985]), 242–6; and Virginia Woolf, *To the Lighthouse* (Penguin: London, 1992 [1927]), 110.
38. This complicates the equation of gender and class position in 'Thinking back through Our Mothers', in Jane Marcus (ed.), *New Feminist Essays on Virginia Woolf* (Macmillan: London, 1981).
39. Virginia Woolf, *Jacob's Room* (Penguin: London, 1992 [1922]), ch. v; *Mrs Dalloway*, 88; *The Years* (Penguin: London, 1992 [1937]), 'Present Day'.
40. 'The Flea', in John Donne, *Poetical Works*, ed. Herbert J. C. Grierson (Oxford UP: 1971 [1929]), 36–7, ll. 8 and 12.
41. Toril Moi (ed.), *The Kristeva Reader* (Blackwell: Oxford, 1986), 238. Julia Kristeva, *Powers of Horror: An Essay on Abjection*, tr. Leon S. Roudiez (Columbia UP: New York, 1982), 4; further quotations from Kristeva in parentheses in the text.
42. See Stephen Trombley, *All that Summer She Was Mad: Virginia Woolf and Her Doctors* (Junction Books: London, 1981).

43. Joseph Conrad, *Heart of Darkness* (Penguin: Harmondsworth, 1985 [1902]), 31.

44. Donne, *Poetical Works*, 37, l. 17.

45. See Leonard Woolf, *Downhill all the Way* (Hogarth: London, 1967), 62–3.

10

THE LAW OF CRITICISM: LAURA RIDING'S EDITORSHIP OF *EPILOGUE*

RACHEL POTTER

Laura Riding's writing constitutes one of the most concerted attempts to defend the cultural authority of poetic knowledge during the 1920s and 1930s. Her defence depends on shifting foundational claims: her work of the 1920s and 1930s locates linguistic authority in the different subject positions of the poet-prophet, the critic as judge and 'woman'. However, when she abandoned poetry after 1941 in order to work on the project that was published as *Rational Meaning* in 1997 the idea that language is intrinsically rational replaced what she came to see as the linguistic limits of poetry.[1] This chapter analyses the way that the idea of linguistic authority is defined by the journalistic language it is seen to supersede. It analyses the interplay between conceptions of journalistic language and poetic language in Riding's writing of the 1930s by concentrating attention on *Epilogue*, a literary journal Riding edited and largely wrote during 1935–8.[2] For the purposes of this chapter, *Epilogue* includes *Epilogue* 4, which became the large volume entitled *The World and Ourselves*, published in 1938.[3]

In 1932 Riding and Robert Graves wrote a novel called *No Decency Left* under the pseudonym 'Barbara Rich'.[4] The novel fictionalises Riding's construal of the gendered nature of authority and the agonistic relationship between ethics and journalism. Set in the fictional state of Lyonesse, it tells the story of a day in the life of a shop-assistant called Barbara Rich. When Barbara's desires begin to come true she gets engaged to the Prince of Lyonesse and becomes a millionairess. Then there is a Communist revolution. Barbara and the Prince fly into the city-centre and Barbara organises the workers in order to feed the people. She finds herself in front of a huge crowd, which includes all the journalists of Lyonesse. She explains why the Monarchy has failed, why Communism cannot function effectively, why democratic government is cumbersome and slow, and why Lyonesse needs the direction of one leader. To shouts of 'We Want You' Barbara becomes the autocratic leader of the State. The novel ends with Barbara musing on the ethical connotations of her assumption of supreme State power: she asks herself whether the destruction of one system of law and the imposition of another means that there 'is no decency left?'

Initially intended to be a best-seller after Graves's success with *Good-Bye to All That* in 1929, *No Decency Left* flopped and failed to produce the large sales or the film deal that Riding and Graves had hoped for. The novel manipulates and stretches the component parts both of the revolutionary situation and of the romantic novel: the replacement of a decadent monarchy with the authority of a single strong individual via a Communist revolution represents a narrative of fascist overthrow but undercuts this narrative by putting a woman rather than a man in the position of supreme State power; and the romantic novel's teleology of marriage is frustrated by the more pressing event of Barbara's assumption of State leadership.

The novel thus manipulates two generic narrative scenes and undercuts both by frustrating expectations about gender and authority. Riding's writing consistently lays bare the way in which authority, whether political, poetic or critical, relies on an undisclosed understanding of gender. *No Decency Left* depicts a modern revolutionary scene in which the existing law is destroyed and replaced by Barbara. The representation of an unmediated relationship between a working woman, law and authority constitutes a bizarre image of skewed modernity. The aims of women's liberation movements, in the 1910s and 1920s in Britain and America, cohere around the objective of legal representation. *No Decency Left* offers a fictional recognition of these aims whilst breaking apart their presuppositions. Barbara's seizure of the legal apparatus founds an authoritarian regime at odds with the democratic principles of feminist objectives, yet in the name of woman. Riding's use of the category of 'woman' to destabilise the sexed genealogy of authority serves to replace man by woman in a hierarchy of authority rather than to destabilise the structure of this hierarchy.

In *No Decency Left* revolution is dependent on journalism to represent and produce the signs of authority. Journalists come to imagistic life in the figure of a bloated ex-Communist called 'Scandals', who is driven by purely monetary desires. Barbara asks Scandals: 'You admit that you write very utter bilge?' and Scandals replies:

'I do. We journalists are the most abject prostitutes of the pen.'
'That's stolen from Dostoevsky.'
'Probably. I steal everything.'

(115)

Later in the scene, the journalist's prostitution is linked to a sensual symbiotic relationship between journalism and 'public' opinion:

> I flourish a mighty nib. I have ease, bonhomie, information. I can make the public laugh or weep, can tickle the public's curious palate, rouse the public's indignant conscience, move the public's great, hungry, thumping human heart – in a word, I can *write*. (119)

The image of the bloated Scandals brings to life Riding's caustic references to journalism, and captures the mixture of sensual knowledge and monetary drives that she associates with journalistic language. Scandals' writing is a prostitution in both the monetary and the sexual sense: his 'mighty nib' that 'makes', 'tickles', 'rouses' and 'moves' the public foregrounds linguistic sensuality and obscures the ethical properties of writing. Barbara's assumption of political authority fills the ethical vacuum that is symbolised by Scandals' prostitution of the pen.

Whilst Barbara's assumption of power is dependent on journalists to produce the signs of authority, the content-matter of cultural 'decency' or ethics resides in the fictional figure of authority rather than in these journalistic signs. The disjunction of ethics and journalistic language grounds Riding's writing: her work attempts to realign ethical and poetic knowledge within the wider context of a severance of language from its ethical components. When the realities of political totalitarianism began to impinge on Riding's own life, she attempted to fuse her linguistic project with an ethical response to politics. Other modernist writers who attempted to align poetry with authority or politics engaged, in the context of totalitarian political realities, with similar questions. Peter Nicholls has discussed the work of Ezra Pound and George Oppen in the light of these questions, and suggests that whilst Pound produced increasingly dogmatic assertions of poetic meaning in the later Cantos, Oppen formulated a poetics of ethical recognition which 'hovers on the brink of intelligibility' rather than asserting fixed meanings.[5] This chapter suggests that Riding's criticism in *Epilogue* in the period 1935–8 poses similar questions, but that neither poetic dogmatism nor an 'undecidable' poetics solved the questions that she wanted to answer through writing.

Laura Riding's sixteen-year career as a poet in effect ended on the publication of her *Collected Poems* in 1938.[6] Other events surrounded the publication of this collection: the Spanish Civil War had forced Riding and Robert Graves to flee their Mallorca home in 1936; and brief sojourns in London, Switzerland, Surrey and France during 1936–9 had proved unsatisfactory refuges from the stultifying atmosphere of British society, on the one hand, and the threat of Nazi Germany on the other. Riding and Graves travelled to America in April of 1939: by the Spring of 1941 she had severed her ties with Graves, married Schuyler Jackson, stopped writing poetry and stopped publishing criticism.

Before this abrupt end to Riding's European and poetic existence she had been a vocal and prolific figure on the margins of British culture. During her association with Robert Graves, whose prose works such as *Good-Bye to All That* and *I Claudius* commanded large sales, publishers were persuaded to publish her books of poetry, critical works, short stories and novels.[7] None of these texts sold well, most of them were criticised aggressively by the literary press, and most of these criticisms were belligerently 'answered' by letters from Riding or Graves. Riding's reply, in 1932, to a review criticising the difficulty of her poem 'Laura and Francisca' is typical:

> If I have an experience of undisputed authenticity and importance to communicate, then the burden of understanding it is on the reader, to whom I have fulfilled my responsibility by setting it down . . . An authentic and important experience cannot be the slave of readers of unknown capacities for response.[8]

Riding's six-year relationship with Geoffrey Grigson's magazine *New Verse* ended on a curter note. When she responded to a hostile review of her *Collected Poems* in a letter to the editor, rather than once more seeking to defend the diction, style and matter of her texts, she wrote simply: 'Sir, I observe with pleasure that you have at last recognized that praise from yourself or anyone associated with you would not be acceptable to me. Yours faithfully, Laura Riding.'[9]

Yet this critical belligerence is part of a commitment to poetry that produces what many have considered some of the best poetry of the period. In 1939 Robert Fitzgerald hailed the *Collected Poems* as 'a kind of Principia' for truth telling in poetry, while Graves's retrospective judgement, written in 1966, that 'She can now be seen as . . . the most original poet of the Twenties and Thirties', is one that has been reiterated by a range of writers and critics.[10] This poetic originality is tied to her uncompromising stance on the accuracy of her poetic language and the terms of its production. Her refusal to 'be the slave of readers' is based on her conviction of the authority of the poem rather than the critical authority of the reader.

Riding's writing can be seen to respond to three distinct kinds of readerships: she published work in privately funded little magazines and set up her own journal in 1935; she conducted heated battles with the British literary establishment, which reviewed with hostility most of her books of criticism and poetry; and her writing consistently has recourse to the idea of a mass popular, or journalistic, readership.

Whilst Graves and Riding relied financially on the saleability of

Graves's 'journalistic pot-boilers', they both regarded 'value' as residing in the profitless language of poetry. The nature of this non-monetary value is elusive: Riding's first critical essay, 'A Prophecy or a Plea', published in 1925, and the two critical books, *Anarchism Is not Enough* and *Contemporaries and Snobs*, both published in 1928, assign value to language that transcends the two readerships of the literary establishment and the journalistic. *Contemporaries and Snobs* opens with a description of poetry as a 'sense of something more real than life', 'which can in its origin be only a personal one'.[11] 'Unfortunately', this sense 'is easily profession-alised' and thereby subsumed under the influence of two ideologies of language: first, individuality and poetry must assert themselves against the idea of the contemporary, summarised as the 'Zeitgeist', 'journalism', history and 'a temporary aggregate of ideas'; second, individuality and poetry must assert themselves against the literary snobbism, or 'criticism', that prevails as a response to the *Zeitgeist*. The book opens by describing two kinds of authority that can be appealed to in writing: the literary sense 'comes to be the authority-to-write which the poet is supposed to receive, through criticism, from the age that he lives in'. This produces a situation in which 'Less and less is the poet permitted to rely on personal authority' (10).

During the 1920s and 1930s most reviews of Riding's poetry and prose, in both literary journals with small circulations and literary papers with larger circulations, criticised it for being unsuccessfully metaphysical, abstract or 'difficult'. Arnold Bennett, for instance, reviewing *Contemporaries and Snobs* for the *Evening Standard* declares that it is 'meta-physics' and that he 'would not read (the book) again for £100'.[12] Yet the abstract or difficult nature of Riding's writing is consistent with her understanding of poetic language as 'more real than life', as an abstraction from the events and knowledge her writing seeks to judge and unify. *Contemporaries and Snobs* and *Anarchism Is not Enough* insist, in both style and propositional statement, that poetry and criticism are precisely an abstraction, a supersession of the particularities of history, the market and the journalistic. In the introduction to the 1980 edition of her poems, Riding retrospectively describes this faith:

> *If* poetry could not comprise transcendence from immediacies of predictive eloquence to realities of immediate truth of word in which it surpassed its historical identity as a literary area of utterance, its value would prove itself inevitably to be – *to have been no more than* – a course of utterance in which what was said was said in isolation from the influences of common, prevailing modes of verbal expression.[13]

Riding retrospectively suggests that poetry which appears to transcend immediacy and history may merely be language which takes place in

isolation from dominant 'modes of verbal expression'. Whilst she retrospectively describes the fine line between transcendence and isolationism,
in the 1930s her writing confidently asserts the transcendent authority of
poetry.

Riding and Graves attempted to avoid both contemporary journalism
and literary 'snobbism' by founding their own publishing press in 1928.
During the 1920s and 1930s the modernist journal and private press
offered forums for the publication of avant-garde writing, which defined
itself against the cultural values of the literary reviews. The availability
of private money from patrons such as Harriet Shaw Weaver and Nancy
Cunard, who also ran her own Hours Press, offered a space for a culture
of writing which could disregard the judgement of the market. It also
offered room for energetic publicists such as Pound to create for
themselves the literary authority of the new culture. Yet the relationship
between literary value, the market and judgement remained fraught.
Many writers claimed the rights to the money and advertising of
established publishing houses and newspapers, whilst insisting on their
indifference to the market as an adjudicator of literary value. This
contradictory position prompts an attempt, central to Riding's writing,
to demarcate and define the nature of cultural value against the values of
the market. This defence opposes the market criteria of 'popularity',
accessibility and anthology readerships, and instead defends literature on
the grounds of its ethical content. In the process, poetry is made to
function as ethical knowledge, akin to law and authority rather than to
linguistic play.

Riding and Graves established their own publishing venture in 1928 in
order to have full control over the content and production of their writing.
The name, 'The Seizin Press', reflected the aims of the press: 'Seizin',
usually spelt 'Seisin', is a legal term that denotes 'possession as of a
freehold', but which also suggests possession of objects 'with quiet
enjoyment'. The dual meaning of possession suggestively defines the
aims of the press: they tried to craft books which were beautiful
possessions and to publish works that would embody the linguistic value
of poetry against market criteria.

The idea of possession also describes Riding's understanding of her
relation to her spoken and written words: she attempts to align her
personal authority to her words by retaining possession of the meaning
of her language. The 'possessive' nature of Riding's relation to her own
work is suggested by her 1920s' and 1930s' letters to the press explaining
her works. This possessiveness extends beyond the point when she
stopped publishing poetry after 1938. During the 1960s and especially
after Schuyler's death in 1968 she began again to write letters of

response to journals, particularly those that had published articles treating her automatically as in Robert Graves's shadow, concentrating on her full part in the collaborative work she did with him. This insistence on intellectual possession is understandable given the fact that William Empson, in his claim that *Seven Types of Ambiguity* was indebted to the close reading of Sonnet 129 in *A Survey of Modernist Poetry*, excised Laura Riding's authorship of the book and attributed it solely to Robert Graves.[14] This excision repeats the omission of her name in many initial reviews of the book. James Jensen's article on *Seven Types of Ambiguity* in 1966, which includes comments from I. A. Richards and Robert Graves, prompted Riding to respond in two letters of 1971 and 1975:

> I learned only in recent times of an epistolary performance of Mr. Robert Graves in your pages . . . in which he added to his progressive and extensive snappings-up from the thought-substance, speech-substance, work-substance, of mine, the trove of 'most of the detailed examination of poems in *A Survey of Modernist Poetry*.'[15]

Riding's sustained claim of 'possession' of her written words makes sense given the sustained attempt by critics and collaborators to take them away from her and attribute them to someone else. The excision of her name is often explicitly gendered. Yet this does not alter the fact that Riding's understanding of the relation between poet and poem, writer and text is fundamentally possessive. Her writing pre-empts the attempt to snap up her thought, speech and work by forcing the writer's authority into the language. With the launch of *Epilogue* in 1935, with her as editor and Graves as assistant editor, this linguistic possessiveness, and its attendant understanding of authority, becomes the critical principle of the journal.

Riding had considered some kind of editorial role since their move to Mallorca in 1929 and in 1930 she writes to Alan Steele, 'I am thinking of a newspaper. I have always wanted a newspaper. How would you like to distribute a newspaper?'[16] Five years later she succeeded in founding, editing and largely writing a hard-backed journal rather than a newspaper, but the idea of 'newspaper-like' knowledge defines the critical judgements of the journal. The name of the journal *Epilogue* again suggests its aims: it styles itself as a final statement, or 'epilogue' on everything from film to bull-fighting. This broad critical subject-matter suggests something of the claims made for the journal, that *Epilogue* resembles a court of law in which right and wrong, truth and falsity are judicially weighed and judged, a kind of 'epilogue' or final judgement on the world.

In setting out the aims of the journal, Riding explains why *Epilogue* resembles a court of law, and why it is 'interested in everything . . . like a newspaper':

> We do not mean to create or anticipate particular kinds of reactions to our findings; and in this we imitate the mood of a court of justice rather than of a newspaper. A court has an extensive patience with all the minutiae of evidence and argument, and assumes in those present no different mood from its own. The mood of a court is a coherent attention to the case before it. We mean to maintain the mood of a court, in the matter of style; and a newspaper-like energy in the matter of content.[17]

The journal's organising principle of justice and judgement is imagined as a court of law. The 'energy' of journalism is here embraced as content-matter that is styled by the legislative judgement of the journal. Justice and judgement are separated out from this 'newspaper-like' content-matter and judgement is understood as permanent *vis-à-vis* the shifting nature of historical events.

In the next paragraph, Riding suggests that the image of the law also provides a way of revealing the elusive nature of value: 'we have a judicial compulsion to identify and define the missing factor of value, and a corollary compulsion to reveal truth as a compound of completeness and order – a universe of values' (3). As with the description of the journal's principles, judgement, or 'the judicial compulsion', is separated out from the content-matter of 'value'. Again, judgement is external to the subjects and objects it surveys: in this instance, the identifying and defining sense discovers that value is 'missing' from the newspaper-like topics that it judges.

Riding's editorial vision, then, establishes a boundary between judgement and 'newspaper-like energy' whilst also engaging directly with contemporary news events. Rather than developing a theory of the relationship between economics, value and writing, *Epilogue* authorises its own critical judgements by legislating value. If value is 'missing' from writing, individuals and society, then *Epilogue* will provide a set of values to fill this gap. It is judgement itself that will provide this missing value: by imposing the permanent values of Riding's critical court of law on the news ephemera, the disparate elements of society will be unified. Judgement provides the 'completeness and order' that unifies the fragments of newspaper events and knowledge. An advertisement for the journal reflects these critical aims: 'The object of *Epilogue* is to unify modern critical attitudes into a coherent view of life and thought.'[18]

The image of the law, or a 'governing standard', continues to serve as the defining metaphor for the functioning of the journal's critical claims:

> Our central theme is a time-surviving truth, and a final unity of values in this truth. We welcome contributors who will take pleasure in thus adjusting their interests, which is to say their work, to a governing standard: who feel the need of stabilizing their work in accordance with a standard whose finality is verified by its applicability to other work, other interests, other subjects as well. (4)

The journal vacillates between locating this 'governing standard' in Riding herself and locating it in words: 'And we are not "literary" except in that we regard words as the most authoritative indexes of value, since they are at once the most specific and the most sensitive instruments of thought' (5). In all these attempts to define value, Riding describes a stable and permanent language outside of history and the journalistic subject-matter of the journal. During her editorship of *Epilogue*, Riding began consistently to locate this standard in 'woman'.

In the unfinished works written in the same period as *Epilogue* and later published under the name *The Word 'Woman'* Riding identifies this 'final unity' with woman:

> We cannot get truth because his [man's] consciousness records only difference; he is an egocentric, not universal-minded, being. We can get truth – how things are as a whole – only from woman: man operates through the sense of difference, woman through the sense of unity.[19]

A familiar conceptual pattern appears in this description: difference, particularity, history are opposed to unity, the universal, truth. Here the opposition is constructed through the frame of gender and gender difference is made to conform to the opposition. Gender categories are construed as agonistic conceptual spaces and the 'nature' that is woman's referent is posited as permanent to the transitory nature of masculinity.

Riding's attempt to produce a stable language from which to judge, then, becomes entangled with a developing theory of gender difference. This assumption of a position of authority demotes the defining importance of poetry, and instead construes authority as the ability to judge 'truly' on 'everything'. *Epilogue* reflects this set of aims. It published articles on a variety of subjects: notes on 'Film-Making' by Len Lye, the Australian film-maker, and Laura Riding; 'Homiletic Studies: Laziness' by Ward Hutchinson; 'The Bull Fight' by Laura Riding; 'Advertising' by Karl Goldschmidt, Robert Graves, Laura Riding and Norman Cameron.[20]

Inevitably, then, when Riding and Graves were forced to leave Mallorca in 1936, the political events behind their emigration became a significant subject-matter of the journal. *Epilogue* 3 was organised whilst they were in London and the articles reflect an attempt to address the issue of the Spanish Civil War and the impending European conflict: the several articles 'The End of the World, and After' and 'Politics and Poetry' discuss the relationship between poets and the 'Next Great War'.[21] As with the 'Preliminaries' section of *Epilogue* 1, Riding attempts to demarcate a conceptual space of permanent poetic value amidst the difference of history: 'poets are those among us who have "always" existed' (1). The permanence of poetic language is aligned to linguistic possession: 'by poets we mean those of us who are fully, constantly awake, in free possession of our existence, of existence' (1–2). Yet the little group of forcibly expatriated writers working in temporary residences found the construction of such linguistic stability increasingly at odds with their own existence.

Epilogue 4 responds to this contradiction by explicitly 'abandoning . . . our manner of seeming indifference to time' and instead engages directly with the forced expatriation, the Spanish Civil War and the impending European conflict (14). Riding summarises *Epilogue* 4 as heralding a shift from 'general criticism' to 'the state of the world to-day'. This shift from criticism to 'the world' inverts the subject–object relation that defines the previous editions of the journal. Rather than applying judgement to the newspaper-like energy of events, the war in Spain and the impending conflict with Germany thrust themselves into the language of the journal, and the invasion of the journal's interior by the external world becomes part of the theory of the journal.

Violent events in Spain from 1936 onwards, and German and Italian support for Franco's troops, had forced writers and artists to respond, or 'take sides'. The British government were reluctant, and militarily unprepared, to get involved in another European war. The *Left Review* pamphlet, *Authors Take Sides*, organised by Aragon, Auden, Cunard, Spender and Tzara amongst others, and published in 1937, asked 'the Writers and Poets of England, Scotland, Ireland and Wales' to 'take sides' on 'the struggle in Spain'. The pamphlet stated that 'The equivocal attitude, the Ivory Tower, the paradoxical, the ironic detachment, will no longer do' and asked 'Are you for, or against, the legal Government and the People of Republican Spain? Are you for, or against, Franco and Fascism?'[22]

Riding was critical of Communism and of political poetry. She was consistently engaged with Marxist and revolutionary writing, particularly on the relationship between politics and poetry. During Riding's child-hood, her father had been involved in the New York Socialist Movement, and had entertained hopes that his daughter would become 'America's Rosa Luxemburg'.[23] Whilst she maintained a political understanding, she was critical of the attempt to align politics and poetry. In the *Epilogue*-related book, for example, that she wrote with Harry Kemp in 1939, *The*

Left Heresy in Literature and Life, she claimed that writers such as Auden and Spender subsume poetry under political objectives.[24] This resistance to writing poetry that is designed to fulfil objectives that are outside poetry itself is central to the ethos of *The World and Ourselves*. Nonetheless she shared the attempt by the *Left Review* project to demand from writers a response to the political situation, to abandon the 'equivocal' and 'ironic' attitude.

Like the *Left Review* Riding began by sending 'A Personal Letter, With a Request for a Reply' to individuals whom she felt were qualified to respond to the political situation. Riding's criteria for qualification were somewhat different from those of the *Left Review* pamphlet, however. In addition to sending the letter to writers, artists and poets, she sent it to 'private' women as representatives of individuals who embody what she terms 'the inside sense'. A theory of gender cuts right across the project: letters from American housewives are printed alongside letters from prominent feminists and writers. The result is a 529-page book eventually entitled *The World and Ourselves* with a copy of Riding's letter, copies of the replies, Riding's specific response to specific letters, her fourteen-point conclusion and a final section of twenty-seven 'Resolutions'.

The idea of the 'inside sense' depends on an opposition between the inside and the outside, or between the private and the public sphere. Her letter states that it is specifically interested in the response of people 'who have been able to treat the outer mechanism of life as subsidiary to its inner realities'.[25] The 'quality of the inside world – the world inside the houses and the minds – is, in the wide use of the word, female', while

> the world of political and diplomatic traffic – grows more and more harshly male, more and more inimical to the inner happiness which men and women have together formulated. The terms 'male' and 'female' must be understood as representing no mere primitive opposition of sex to sex; but as defining two worlds of differing quality, in either of which men and women may jointly move and live. (16)

This sharp distinction between the public and private spheres reasserts Riding's dualistic frame of understanding and insists that the State is a distinct sphere of political activity that has no impact on the morality of the domestic sphere. Notwithstanding Riding's attempt to dislocate the terms 'male' and 'female' from any sexed referent, the alignment of women with privacy flouted feminist assertions of women's democratically 'public' legal rights. Her letter unsurprisingly provoked criticism from feminist respondents. Christina Stead and Naomi Mitchison both question the dualistic structure of Riding's thinking and her association of 'woman' with the domestic sphere. As Stead suggests,

> The dichotomy – 'inside', 'outside' – seems to be quite inexact. At least half of all great painters, poets, writers, have been social rebels, politicians, strong partisans, men of action . . . women artists of all kinds are almost invariably social rebels, since they have to break upwards from an economically inferior class (that of the domestic woman or underpaid working-woman) to the dominant class. (69)

Riding defends the dichotomy by asking why writers are forced to be social rebels:

> That painters, poets and writers were moved to violent protest against social conditions would confirm, rather, the justice of my distinction: of the existence of an outside of such harsh difference from their inner world that they felt they must in some way make the two more consistent with each other. (71)

Whilst *Epilogue* 1 and 2 create an ethical law to fill the 'missing factor of value', the 'inner world' as it is identified in *The World and Ourselves* struggles to produce a coherence out of this 'harsh difference'. This defence clings to the dualisms of inside and outside, female and male, poetry and journalism, morality and history. Poets and artists protest against the difference of public and private and attempt to synthesise the two through poetry. This is an accurate description of what Riding claims for *The World and Ourselves*. It is precisely a 'protest' that prints the voices of the 'inner world' in order to produce a coherent statement, or 'resolution' out of difference: 'all these outside affairs are the less important ones; they are subsidiary to what goes on inside the houses' (15).

In accordance with the collaborative aims of *The World and Ourselves*, Riding calls for a more general publication of the voices of the 'inside' sphere by demanding a new kind of newspaper: she asks for 'a reform of newspaper technique – by presenting news from the point of view of the woman reader' (437). This critique of the 'public' or 'male' nature of newspapers is accompanied by the assertion of a 'new moral law' which will generate a private moral coherence. Number eleven of the concluding points is entitled 'Indications for a New Moral Law', and it states that 'The moral stability of the world depends on the framing of a new moral Law from the point of view of women' (478). The new moral Law depends on a difference between female and male time: 'female time has a rhythmic constancy with a significance of final repose, while the rhythmic impulse of male time is toward variety in infinite progression' (479). Repeating the gendered distinction in *The Word 'Woman'*, the male is aligned with difference and particularity: 'male time . . . its [male time] original rhythmic impulse was toward differentiation and its rhythmic

energy is a will to be at variance' (479). She continues to link differentiation with history: the difference between female and male 'is an accurate
definition of the relation between time as an ever-immediate moment and
time as a historical series' (480). The new moral law depends on these
distinctions: 'The new moral Law that now needs to be given to the world
by its inside voices must no longer appeal to physical fear or imaginative
courage, but be a Law of *reassurance*' (480). Riding's law of reassurance is
a law of justification and recognition:

> some of us, the watchful part of existence, must assume this charge of justifying the
> final whole of existence: only so can the variegated part be moved to recognize what
> is unjustifiably different from the whole – too different to exist. (483)

The 'dreadful eventualities that are being enacted on the world stage' are
those things that are 'too different to exist'. In this description, history
and difference are resolved, 'reassured' and 'justified' by an ethics of
reassurance and recognition which replaces the legislative authority of
Riding's earlier critical pronouncements. The writing of these inside
people will legislate a new moral code to solve and resolve the problems of
history and violence.

An ethics of reassurance, then, emerges out of the ethical legislations of
the earlier volumes of *Epilogue*. The *Times Literary Supplement* greeted
The World and Ourselves with one of its few positive endorsements of her
writing, asking:

> How were reasonable people to make head or tail of this new situation? Miss Riding
> had the excellent idea of asking them . . . . Reasonable people are not such a few – let
> them cooperate, if only by recognizing each other's existence. They may go so far as
> to act together, but their action will, of course, not be violent, because then it would
> defeat its own object – they would cease to be reasonable people.[26]

The review reiterates Riding's emphasis on recognition, reason and non-
violence, and highlights the way in which *The World and Ourselves*
performs as well as represents its theory of collaborative ethics.

The theory of collaboration and recognition that emerges from *The
World and Ourselves* is also retrospectively cited by Riding as one of the
reasons why poetry fails to perform the ethical task that it sets out for
itself. In the new introduction to the 1980 edition of the *Collected Poems*
she describes why:

> Poetry bears in itself the message that it is the destiny of human beings to speak the
> meaning of being, but it nurses it in itself as in a sacred apartness, not to be
> translated into the language of common meanings in its delivery . . . My kind of
> seriousness, in my looking to poetry for the rescue of human life from the
> indignities it was capable of visiting upon itself, led me to an eventual turning
> away from it as failing my kind of seriousness. (9)

According to her later understanding, then, Riding still believed in 1938 that poetry carried within it a 'quality of linguistic universalness', but she was in the process of realising the fundamental privacy, or 'apartness' of poetic language: 'I did not know when I put the final touches to *Collected Poems* for the 1938 edition that I had reached a limit in the possibility of holding these commitments within one frame of endeavour' (8). By 1941 Riding had turned away from the beliefs represented in the two texts published in 1938: the privacy of poetry, Riding's editorial role and the engagement with politics are all abandoned for the language project that largely occupied her until the early 1980s.

The first volumes of *Epilogue* describe the boundary between a judicial language and the events that it judges. The judicial boundary is dependent on conceptual dualisms between poetry and journalism, law and history, unity and difference, woman and man, privacy and 'the world': the former term is privileged at the expense of the latter in these dualisms. If the history that accompanies the publication of *Epilogue* signals a turning point for Riding's understanding of the cultural, political or ethical function of poetry, her turn away from both the privacy of poetry and the public nature of political engagement consolidates rather than shifts her attempt to offer a linguistic transcendence of journalistic language. The linguistic effects of the 'mighty nib' of the 'prostitutes of the pen' continue to haunt Riding's writing. As she states in the opening to *Rational Meaning*:

> In the early thirties I began to feel a practical sense of urgency about something that had long troubled me. This was, that the use of words was in a bad way . . . I committed myself to trying to make a new opening into the area of word-knowledge – the knowledge, that is, of what words mean. (7)

Later in the book, she ascribes the disintegration of word-knowledge to journalists amongst others:

> And all the while the literary users of words multiply – and the journalistic users of words, too, who have come to vie with them in the promotion of special vocabularistic and usage trends; and the users of words, all, more and more confound one another, using their words with an easy freedom, looking to this quarter or that as possibly a seat of authority for their use of them, but possibly not, utterly unhesitant, and utterly unsure. (91–2)

As in Riding's fictional and critical writing of the late 1920s and 1930s *Rational Meaning* continues to define linguistic authority by demarcating ethics from journalism. Her creation of coherence out of the 'newspaper-like energy' of contemporary events depends on different kinds of authority: *Epilogue* asserts a legislative criticism; and *The World and Ourselves* suggests that a 'female' ethical language will resolve the harsh differences of contemporary journalistic values. After 1941, Riding exchanged what she considered to be the privacy of these projects for an engagement with the 'universal' and rational nature of language itself.

NOTES

1. After 1941 (Riding) Jackson and her second husband Schuyler B. Jackson devoted themselves to the project that was published as *Rational Meaning: A New Foundation for the Definition of Words and Supplementary Essays*, ed. William Harmon (University of Virginia Press: Charlottesville and London, 1997); subsequent references in text. This chapter refers to Laura (Riding) Jackson as Laura Riding, the name under which she wrote during the period analysed here. Quotations from her work are by permission of her Board of Literary Management and, for works published by them, of Carcanet Press, Manchester, and Persea Books, New York. I would also like to thank Alan J. Clark for his very generous comments on this chapter.

2. Many of the articles in *Epilogue* are signed by Riding, she wrote footnotes to most of the other articles and she also wrote for the journal under the pseudonym 'Madeleine Vara'.

3. To retain the close focus on Riding's criticism of the 1930s, this chapter does not cite her poems and short stories.

4. Barbara Rich, *No Decency Left* (Jonathan Cape: London, 1932) – subsequent references in text.

5. Peter Nicholls, 'Of Being Ethical: Reflections on George Oppen', *Journal of American Studies*, 31:2 (1997), 153–170 (169).

6. Laura Riding's first published poem 'Dimensions' appeared in *The Fugitive*, 2:7 (June–July, 1923), 124. Her last poems appeared in *Collected Poems* (Arthur Barker: London, 1938).

7. Robert Graves, *Good-Bye to All That* (Jonathan Cape: London, 1929) and *I Claudius* (Barker: London, 1934). In 1955 the proceeds from *Claudius* allowed him to 'hold his head up': see Martin Seymour-Smith, *Robert Graves: His Life and Work* (Bloomsbury: London, 1995), 229.

8. Laura Riding, 'The Matter of Communication', *Times Literary Supplement*, 3 Mar. 1932, 155.

9. Laura Riding, 'Sour Puss': letter from Laura Riding, *New Verse*, N.S. 1.1 (Jan. 1939), 30.

10. Robert Fitzgerald, 'Laura Riding', *Kenyon Review*, 1 (Summer 1939), 341–5; Robert Graves, 'Comments', *Modern Language Quarterly*, 27:3 (Sept. 1966), 255–6 (256).

11. Laura Riding, *Contemporaries and Snobs* (London: Jonathan Cape, 1928), 9 – subsequent references in text.

12. Arnold Bennett, 'The "Monstrous Conceit" of Some Modernists', the *Evening Standard*, 1 Mar., 1928; William Troy criticises the 'esthetic idealism of *A Survey of Modernist Poetry*', 'Poetry in Vacuo', *New Republic*,

6 Feb. 1929, 328; Louis Macneice describes her poetry as 'appallingly bleak and jejune', 'Miss Riding's "Death" ', *New Verse*, 6 (Dec. 1933), 18–20 (19).

13. Laura Riding, 'Introduction', *Collected Poems* (Manchester: Carcanet, 1980), 1–13 (3) – subsequent references in text.

14. Laura Riding and Robert Graves, *A Survey of Modernist Poetry* (Heinemann: London, 1927). For a discussion of the history of Riding, Graves and Empson see K. K. Ruthven, 'How to Avoid Being Canonized: Laura Riding', *Textual Practice*, 2:5 (Summer 1991), 242–60 (250–1).

15. Laura Riding, 'Correspondence', *M.L.A.*, 32 (Dec. 1971), 447–8.

16. Letter to Alan Steele, dated February, (probably 1930), Cambridge University Library, ADD MS 8698/R37.

17. Laura Riding, 'Preliminaries', *Epilogue*, 1 (Autumn 1935), 1–5 (2).

18. 'An Advertisement for *Epilogue*', *The Spectator*, 4 June, 1937, 1063.

19. Laura Riding, *The Word 'Woman': and Other Related Writings*, ed. Elizabeth Friedmann and Alan J. Clark (Carcanet Press: Manchester, 1994), 40–1.

20. Len Lye and Laura Riding, 'Film-Making', *Epilogue*, 1 (1935), 231–5; Ward Hutchinson, 'Homiletic Studies: Laziness', *Epilogue*, 2 (1936), 76–83; Laura Riding, 'Marginal Themes: The Bull Fight', *Epilogue*, 2 (1936), 193–207; Karl Goldschmidt, Robert Graves, Laura Riding and Norman Cameron, 'Advertising', *Epilogue*, 3 (1937), 230–58.

21. Laura Riding, 'The End of the World, and After', *Epilogue*, 3 (1937), 1–5 – subsequent references in text.

22. *Authors Take Sides on the Spanish Civil War* (Left Review: London, 1937).

23. Deborah Baker, *In Extremis: The Life of Laura Riding* (Hamish Hamilton: London, 1993), 28.

24. Harry Kemp and Laura Riding, *The Left Heresy in Literature and Life* (Methuen Publishers: London, 1939). This is Riding's only collaborative work in which her name does not appear first, suggesting that the writing is predominantly Harry Kemp's.

25. Laura Riding, 'A Personal Letter, with a Request for a Reply', in her *The World and Ourselves* (Chatto & Windus: London, 1938), 15–19 (16).

26. 'Light and Leading': review of *The World and Ourselves*, by Laura Riding, *Times Literary Supplement*, 26 Nov. 1938, 751 and 755.

INDEX